D1104895

REPRINTS OF ECONOMIC CLASSICS

A PLAN OF THE ENGLISH COMMERCE

[DANIEL DEFOE]

A

P L A N

of the

ENGLISH COMMERCE

Being A

COMPLEAT PROSPECT

of the

TRADE of this NATION,

as well the HOME TRADE as the FOREIGN

SECOND EDITION

[1730]

REPRINTS OF ECONOMIC CLASSICS

AUGUSTUS M. KELLEY · PUBLISHERS
NEW YORK · 1967

First Edition 1728

(London: Charles Rivington, *at The Bible & Crown,
St. Paul's Churchyard*, 1728)

Second Edition 1730

Reprinted 1967 by
AUGUSTUS M. KELLEY · PUBLISHERS

LIBRARY OF CONGRESS CATALOGUE CARD NUMBER
67 - 26365

PRINTED IN THE UNITED STATES OF AMERICA
by SENTRY PRESS, NEW YORK, N. Y. 10019

PLAN of the *English* Commerce.

BEING A

COMPLETE PROSPECT

OF THE

TRADE of this Nation, as well Home as Foreign.

In THREE PARTS.

Containing, among many Others, the following Curious Particulars;

VIZ.

Of the *Rife, Growth,* and *Encreafe* of the *Englifh Commerce,* together with its *Prefent State,* more efpecially of that Part which relates to the *Woollen Manufacture.*

A View of the *Englifh Trade,* as it refpects *The Exportation, The Importation, The Re-Exportation,* and *Home Confumption.*

A folid Enquiry into the Queftion, Whether our *Trade* is decreafed or not?

Of the *Englifh Improvements* in Trade upon the *Inventions* of other *Nations,* and the *Increafe* of our *Commerce* on thefe *Improvements;* and of the *Improvements* likewife made upon our own *Product.*

A Propofal for exterminating the Pyrates of *Tunis, Tripoli, Algier* and *Sallec.* With a Scheme for reftoring tha ancient *Commerce* on the North and North-weft Coaft of *Africa.*

A Propofal for the *Encreafe* of *Commerce* upon the Weftern Coaft of *Africa,* the Coaft of *Guiney* from *Siera Leon* to the Coaft and Gulph of *Benin.*

And Another for the *Encreafe* of *Commerce* on the Eaft Coaft of *Africa.*

A Propofal for turning the *Whole Trade* for *Naval Stores* from the Eaft Country, and *Norway* and *Sweden,* to our own COLONIES, without putting the Government to the dead Charge of Bounty-Money on that *Importation.*

Humbly offer'd to the Confideration of KING *and* PARLIAMENT.

By the late Ingenious Mr. DANIEL DE FOE.

Here is an undifcover'd Ocean *of* COMMERCE *laid open to us, and fome* Specimens *are offer'd; which, if enter'd upon with the* Authority, Power *and* Vigor *of the* Publick, *would, open fuch* New Channels *of* TRADE *among us, as it would be very hard for our Manufacturers to over-flock the Market, and fuch as no petty Prohibition in* Europe *could flop the Current of.* See PREFACE.

The SECOND EDITION.

LONDON.

Printed for C. RIVINGTON, at the *Bible* and *Crown,* in St. *Paul's* Church-yard. M.DCC.XXXVII.

THE

PREFACE.

N a Nation rais'd as we are by Trade, fam'd for carrying on the moſt extended Commerce in the World, and particularly proſperous in the greateſt Undertakings, whether for Improvement at Home, or Adventure Abroad, nothing is more wonderful, than to ſee how ignorant the Generality of our People are about it; how weakly they talk of it, and how little has been made publick for their better Information.

Every Man knows his own Affairs, moves in his own Circle, purſues the Mechaniſm of his own particular Buſineſs; but take him out of his Road, he knows nothing of the Reaſon, or the End of what he is about: The Clothier ſorts his Wool, dyes and mixes the Colours; the Comb, the Card, the Wheel, the Loom, are all ſet on Work by his Direction, and he is call'd a Maſter of his Art, and he is ſo; but ask him where

his

*his Cloths are fold, by whom bought, to what
Part of the World they are fhipt, and who are
the laft Confumers of them, he knows nothing
of the Matter ; he fends them up to* London
to the Factor that fells them, whether at
Blackwell-Hall, *or in his private Ware-
houfe, and when fold, he draws Bills for the
Money ; there his Circle meets ; the Money
buys more Wool to be forted, and comb'd, and
fpun ; and fo on, he ends juft where he begins, and he begins juft where he ended.
To talk to him of Trade, Ships, Exportation, Markets Abroad, and Returns
in Specie, or in Merchants Goods, tis
as much out of his Way, as the Race
and the Paddock is to a Carryer's Pack-
horfe.
The Merchant on the other Hand
moves in another Sphere ; and he being
a Man of Correfpondence, befides his
own Adventure, receives Commiffions from
Abroad to buy fuch and fuch Goods, and
good Remittances by Bills to pay for them,
then he fhips them according to Order,
fends his Invoyces and Bills of Loading by
the Poft ; and there's his Circle finifh'd. As
to the Wool which is the Principal of the
Manufacture ; as to the many Hands it goes
thro' ; how many Thoufand Families are
employed by it ; how the Poor are fubfifted,
the Provifions confum'd, the landed Intereft rais'd, the Nobility and Gentry
enrich'd, and the whole Nation fupported*
by

by the very Goods he buys; he neither knows or concerns himself about it.

The Captains, Masters, Owners, and Navigators of Ships, they move in another Orb, but still act in the same Round of Business; the Ship is built, and fitted out for a Voyage; Thousands of Tradesmen and Workmen subsist upon the petty Demands of the Captain or other Persons who direct the Voyage; the Timber, the Plank, the Iron-Work, the Masts, the Rigging, the Tar and Hemp, the Flax and Oyl, all pass thro' different and numberless Hands, till they center in the Builder's Yard; there the Frame of a Vessel is set on the Stocks. What Hands are then employ'd to creat the beautiful useful Form of a Ship! and what Art to perfect and launch her into the Water!

The Carpenters, Caulkers, Mastmakers, Joyners, Carvers, Painters, Smiths, &c. finish the Hull; the Tradesmen are employ'd to furnish and fit her out; the Sail-Makers, the Rope-Makers, Anchor-Smiths, Block-Makers, Gun-Founders, Coopers, and (for a Thousand small Things too trifling to mention, tho' absolutely needful) the Ship Chandler, and at last the Brewer, Butcher, Baker, &c. for Provision to victual her, all help on the Voyage.

All these supported by that glorious Head of Commerce, called the Merchant, are employed in the Outset of the Ship, but know nothing

nothing how to manage the Ship in the Ocean, how to cause her to find her Way on the wild and pathless Surface of the Water; they fit her out, and deliver all to the Commander, &c. *But as to the sailing Part, that belongs to another Class of People, called the Sailers or Navigators; and when the Tradesmen have put the Ship into their Hands, their Work is done, till the Ship returns, and then they begin all again: So the Circle is continued, for ever the same.*

Again, the Navigator or Commander, he puts up his Ship on the Exchange for such a Voyage, Lisbon, *or* Cadiz, *or* Hamburg, *or* Leghorn; *he takes in the Merchants Goods, carries them safe to the delivering Port; he reloads there, and brings back his Cargoe; he knows no more; even his* Bills of Loading *are sign'd, under a needful Profession of his Ignorance, naming the Bulk of what he receives on Board (so many Hogsheads, or Butts, or Bales) but adds* the Contents unknown, *&c.*

When he brings home the Ship, he makes his Report at the Custom-house, and unlivers his Cargo, as they call it; then he receives his Freight, pays his Men, and lays the Ship up, and there's his Circle finish'd; his Sphere of Action, however important, reaches no farther; as to Trade or Commerce, whether general or particular, he knows no more of it than just lies before him.

I

*I might run thro' almoſt all the Branches
of Buſineſs, and all the Claſſes of the Men
of Buſineſs, and give Examples of the like ;
but 'tis enough, the Concluſion is ſhort :
Hence then a general or univerſal* Plan of
Commerce *is certainly much wanted in
the World.*

*When we ſpeak of ſome Men, who are
the moſt acquainted in the World of Buſineſs, we ſay they are Men of a general
Knowledge ; and ſuch a Man is an univerſal Merchant ; I have indeed heard ſuch
Language talked among the trading Part of
Mankind, but I cannot ſay that I ever ſaw
the Man.*

*The Commerce of the World, eſpecially
as it is now carried on, is an unbounded
Ocean of Buſineſs ; Trackleſs and unknown,
like the Seas it is managed upon ; the Merchant is no more to be follow'd in his Adventures, than a Maze or Labyrinth is to be
trac'd out without a Clue.*

*The Author of this Work is not quite
ſo arrogant, after a Complaint of this Nature, as to tell you he ſhall preſent you with
this univerſal Plan, for the whole Trade
of the World : It is enough, if he is able to
offer a Plan for the Trade of our own
Country, in which it is but too true, there
are many that talk of the general Commerce to one that underſtands it.*

*Nor even in this Plan of our Commerce,
does he direct what the Trade of* Europe,

in general is with us; but what and how great our particular Commerce is ; how it is arriv'd to its prefent Magnitude ; how to be maintained and fupported in its full Extent ; (and which is, or ought to be, the true End of all fuch Attempts :) How it may yet be improv'd and enlarg'd.

We have loud Complaints among us of the Decay of our Trade, the declining of our Manufactures, and efpecially of our woollen Manufacture ; the contrary of which is, I think, evidently prov'd in this Tract, and the Reafons given for it, will not be eafily refuted. It is not any little Negative put upon our Manufactures, as to their Confumption in this or that petty Province or Country in Germany, or elfe where : Our Manufacture, like a flowing Tide, if 'tis bank't out in one Place, it fpreads by other Channels at the fame Time into fo many different Parts of the World, and finds every Day fo many new Outlets, that the Obftruction is not felt ; but like the Land to the Sea, what it lofes in one Place, it gains in another.

It is plain, the Manufacture cannot be declin'd, if the Quantity of Wool is wrought up, and the Goods are confum'd ; on the other Hand 'tis evident, the Confumption of our Manufactures, both abroad and at home, is exceedingly encreas'd ; the firft by the Encreafe of our Correfpondencies, and the laft by the Encreafe of our People ; and that to fuch

a

a Degree, as infinitely out-weighs all that can be pretended of the Prohibitions of them in Germany, or the Imitations of them in France; nor are those things able to wound us so deep as our phlegmatick Complainers would insinuate.

But that a full Answer may be given to all they can say of what Loss we yet suffer, and to all they can suggest of what we may suffer hereafter; this Work is calculated, to shew how we may counteract it all at once: Namely, by improving and encreasing our Trade in other Places where those Prohibitions and Imitations cannot reach, and where, if half Europe should drop our Manufacture, which yet 'tis apparent can never happen, we shall raise an equivalent Vent for our Goods, and make Markets of our own; in which the whole World could not supplant us, unless they could subdue us.

This is the Substance of this Tract; 'tis the original Thought which gave Birth to the whole Work; if our Trade is the Envy of the World, and they are conspiring to break in upon it, either to anticipate it, or block it out, we are the more engaged to look out for its Support; and we have Room enough: The World is wide: There are new Countries, and new Nations, who may be so planted, so improv'd, and the People so manag'd, as to create a new Commerce; and Millions of People

shall

shall call for our Manufacture, who never call'd for it before.

Nothing is to me more evident, than that the civilizing the Nations where we and other Europeans *are already settled; bringing the naked Savages to Clothe, and instructing barbarous Nations how to live, has had a visible Effect already, in this very Article. Those Nations call upon us every Year for more Goods, than they did the Year before, as well woollen Manufactures, as others. The* Portuguese *Colonies in the* Brazils, *and on the East Coasts of* Africa, *are an unanswerable Proof of this. The* European *Manufactures now sent to those Colonies, are above five Times as many as were sent to the same Places, about* 30 *to* 40 *Years ago; and yet the* European *Inhabitants in those Colonies are not encreased in Proportion. We might give Instances of the like in other Places abroad, and that not a few.*

New planting Colonies then, and farther improving those already settled, will effectually encrease this Improvement; for like Causes, will have like Effects; Clothing new Nations cannot fail of encreasing the Demand of Goods, because it encreases the Consumption, and that encreased Demand is the Prosperity of our Trade.

Here then is an undiscover'd Ocean of Commerce laid open to us, and some Specimens are offer'd, which if entred upon,

with

*with the Authority, Power, and Vigor of
the Publick, would open such new Channels of Trade among us, as it would be
very hard for our Manufacturers to over-
stock the Market, and as no petty Prohibitions in Europe could stop the Current of.*

*It is surprizing that in a Nation where
such Encouragements are given for planting
and improving, where Colonies have been
settled, and Plantations made with such
Succefs ; where we may truly be said to
have filled the World with the Wonders of
our growing Poffeffions, and where we have
added not Provinces only, but Kingdoms to
the* Britifh *Dominion, and have launched
out even to an Ocean of Commerce. That
now, I say, We should, as it were, put a
full Stop at once to all our great Defigns;
check the Humour of Encreafing, and from
a kind of a myfterious unaccountable Stupidity turn indolent on a fuddain. Not as if
we found no more Room to launch out, for
the Contrary to that is apparent ; but as
if we had enough, and fought no more
Worlds in Trade to conquer.*

*In all other Cafes, and among all other
Nations Succefs encourages Men to go on;
encreafing, they endeavour to encreafe,* Cref-
cit amor nummi, &c. — *So in Trade, the
growing and enlarging the Bounds of a Plantation, the fwelling and thriving of · Commerce, and the Advantages to the Merchant and Planter in all thofe Things, cer-*
                                                    tainly

*tainly encreafes the Defire of planting, en-
larges the Commerce and fires the Merchant with the Defires of enlarging his Adventures, fearching out new Colonies, forming new Adventures, and pufhing at new
Difcoveries for the Encreafe of his Trading Advantages.*

*It is fo in other Nations, and it feems
wonderful it fhould not be fo here; the*
Spaniards *tho' an indolent Nation, whofe
Colonies were really fo rich, fo great,
and fo far extended, as were enough even
to glut their utmoft Avarice; yet gave not
over, till, as it were, they fat ftill, becaufe
they had no more Worlds to look for; or till
at leaft, there were no more* Gold *or* Silver *Mines to difcover*

The Portuguefe, *tho' an effeminate, haugh-
ty, and as it were, a decay'd Nation in
Trade; yet how do they go on Daily encreafing their Colonies in the* Brazils, *in* Africa,
*as well on the Eaft Side, as the Weft? And
how do they encreafe their Commerce in all
thofe Countries, by reducing the numerous
Nations in* Melinda, *in* Zanguebar, *in* Con-
go, *in* Angola, *in the* Brazils, *as well North
as South, and every where elfe, to the
Chriftian Oeconomy, and to the Government
of Commerce! by which they fubdue whole
Nations of Savages to a regular Life, and
by that Means bring them to be fubfervient
to Trade as well as to Government.*

But

*But how little have we done of this kind?
How little have we gain'd upon the Natives of* America *in all our Colonies? How
few of them are brought to live among us,
how few to be subject to us? How little
Progress of that kind can we boast of? All
our Colonies seem to be carried on upon the
meer Strength of our own People. Nor can
we say we have any one considerable Nation
reduced to entire Obedience and brought to
live under the Regularity and Direction of a
Civil Government, in all our Plantations;
a few (very few) in* New England *only
excepted.*

*As for new Colonies and Conquests, how
do we seem entirely to give over, even the
Thoughts of them, tho' the Scene is so large,
tho' the Variety is so great, and the Advantages so many? On the Contrary, we
seem to forget the glorious Improvements of
our Ancestors, such as the great* Drake, Ca-
vendish, Smith, Greenfield, Somers, *and a-
bove all, the yet greater Sir* Walter Raleigh,
upon the Foot of whose Genius almost all the
English *Discoveries were made, and all the
Colonies and Plantations, which now form
what they call the* English Empire *in* America *were settled and established. These I
say we seem to sit down with, as if we
had done our utmost, were fully satisfied
with what we have, that the enterpri-
sing Genius was buried with the old Dis-
coverers, and there was neither Room in the
World*

World or Inclination in our People to look any farther.

Whereas on the Contrary, the World pre-sents us with large Scenes of Trade, new Platforms for Bufinefs, enough to prompt our Ambition, and even to glut our Ava-rice; yet we feem to have no Heart for the Adventure.

Nor is there any want of People among us ; on the contrary, here are Thoufands of Families who want Bufinefs, want Employ-ment, want Encouragement, and many that want no Stocks to carry with them, and are ready to go abroad, were the adventuring Spirit reviv'd, and fome Men fired with Warmth for the Undertaking, and but vi-gorous enough to make the Beginning.

This is the Way to raife new Worlds of Commerce, to enlarge and extend new Funds of Trade, to open Doors for an Encreafe of Shipping and Manufacture ; the Places are fo many and the Advantages fo great for the making fuch Attempts ; that I fay nothing is more wonderful of its kind, than to fee how backward we are to pufh on our own Advantages, and to plant in the moft agreeable Climates in the World, in a manner fo advantageous as never to be fupplanted, and fuch as fhould make the Englifh *Poffeffions abroad five Times as Great, as Opulent and as Profitable to Old* England, *as they have been yet.*

The

The Defcription of thefe Places, fo pro-
per for Planting, fo fuited to Commerce,
and fo qualified to enrich and aggran-
dize the Britifh *Nation, is a Work not only*
too large for this Tract, but feems not fuited
to our prefent Taft ; it muft lye till the
Trading Genius revives and the adventur-
ing Temper is reftored among us : Then it
will appear, there will neither want En-
couragment to fuch Undertakings or Under-
takers to embrace the Encouragements which
offer.

As thefe are Things of the utmoft Im-
portance to our Trade in general, and in
that to the Profperity of all his Majefty's
Dominions in particular, the Author hum-
bly hopes it fhall not be thought affuming,
that as we fay in our Title, they are hum-
bly referr'd to the Confideration of the
King and Parliament ; they are Things
worthy of a King, and worthy of a power-
ful Legiflature to confider of ; no Power
lefs than that of King, Lords and Com-
mons, can put thefe Wheels of Improvement
into due Motion : And I conclude with
an inexpreffible Satisfaction, in faying, that
as we know his Majefty has the Profpe-
rity of all his Kingdoms at Heart, and will
be always ready to liften to reafonable and
practicable Propofals for that Purpofe ;
and that the Parliament has always fhewn
their Readinefs to concur in the fame juft
Endea-

Endeavour ; and which is yet more, that the Proposals here offered, and others yet behind, are apparently practicable and rational ; it cannot be doubted, but that the Time will come, and is near at Hand, when the Improvement of the Britifh *Commerce fhall no more appear in Project and Theory, but fhew it felf in a due and daily Progreffion, till it compleats the Glory and Profperity of the whole Nation.*

THE

THE
CONTENTS.

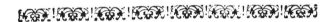

PART I.

CHAP. I.

CHAP.

The CONTENTS:

CHAP. IV.

CHAP. V.

CHAP. VI.

CHAP. VII.

The CONTENTS.

PART II.

CHAP. I.

CHAP. II.

PART

The CONTENTS.

PART III.

Chap. I.

Chap. II.

The CONTENTS.

The CONTENTS.

CHAP. V.

PAGE 312, *for* Cap. XI. *read* Chap. II.

Books Printed for CHARLES RIVINGTON, *at the* Bible *and* Crown *in* St. Paul's *Church-Yard.*

I. THE *Compleat English Tradesman*, in familiar Letters; directing him in all the several Parts and Progressions of Trade, *viz.* 1. Of acquainting himself with Business during his Apprenticeship. 2. Of writing to Correspondents in a Trading Style. 3. Of Diligence and Application, as the Life of Business. 4. Cautions against Over-Trading. 5. Of the ordinary Occasions of a Tradesman's Ruin ; such as expensive Living — Too early marrying ⊷ Innocent Diversions — Too much Credit — Being above Business ⊷ Dangerous Partnerships, *&c.* 6. Directions in the several Distresses of a Tradesman when he comes to fail. 7. Of Tradesmen Compounding with other Tradesmen, and why they are so particularly severe to one another. 8. Of Tradesmen ruining one another by Rumour and Scandal. 9. Of the Customary Frauds of Trade, and particularly of Trading Lies. 10. Of *Credit*, and how it is only to be supported by *Honesty*. 11. Of punctual paying Bills, and thereby maintaining Credit. 12. Of the Dignity and Honour of *Trade* in *England*, more than in other Countries.

To which is added, a SUPPLEMENT; *containing,*

1. A Warning against Tradesmens borrowing Money upon Interest. 2. A Caution against that destructive Practice of drawing and remitting, as also of discounting Promissory Bills, meerly for a Supply of Cash. 3. Direction for the Tradesman's Accounts, with brief, but plain Examples, and Specimens for Book-Keeping. 4. Of keeping a Duplicate, or Pocket-Ledger, in Case of Fire. The Second Edition. Price 5 s. 6 d.

II. The

II. The *Compleat Englijh Tradefman.* Vol. II. In Two P A R T S.

P A R T I. Directed chiefly to the more *Experienced Tradefmen*; with Cautions and Advices to them after they are *thriven,* and fuppofed to be *grown rich,*

V I Z.

1. Againft running out of their Bufinefs into *needlefs Projects* and *dangerous Adventures,* no Tradefman being above *Difafter.*

2. Againft oppreffing one another by *Engroffing, Underfelling, Combinations* in Trade, *&c.*

3. *Advices,* that when he *leaves off* his Bufinefs, he fhould *part Friends* with the World; the great *Advantages* of it; with a Word of the fcandalous Character of a *Purfe-proud Tradefman.*

4. Againft being *litigious* and *vexatious,* and *apt to go to Law* for Trifles; with fome Reafons why Tradefmens Differences fhould, if poffible, be all ended by *Arbitration.*

P A R T II. Being ufeful *Generals* in Trade, defcribing the Principles and Foundation of the *Home Trade* of *Great Britain*; with large T A B L E S of our *Manufactures, Calculations of the Product, Shipping, Carriage of Goods by Land, Importation from Abroad, Confumption at Home,* &c. by all which the infinite Number of our *Tradefmen* are employ'd, and the *General Wealth* of the Nation raifed and increafed.

The Whole calculated for the *Ufe* of all our *Inland Tradefmen,* as well in the City as in the Country,

O F

OF

TRADE

IN

GENERAL.

CHAP. I.

RADE, like Religion, is what every Body talks of, but few underſtand : The very Term is dubious, and in its ordinary Acceptation, not ſufficiently explain'd.

WHEN 'tis particular to a Place, 'tis *Trade ;* when general, 'tis *Commerce ;* when we ſpeak of it as the Effect of Nature, 'tis *Product* or Produce ; when as the Effect of Labour, 'tis *Manufacture :* In its Management 'tis the ſame, for when we

ſpeak

fpeak of it in the grofs, 'tis *wholefale ;* when of the particulars, 'tis *retale ;* when we fpeak of Nations, 'tis call'd *Correfponding ;* when of foreign Import only, 'tis called *Merchandizing ;* 'Tis the fame alfo in the Manner, when we exchange Goods 'tis call'd *Barter ;* when we exchange Coin, 'tis call'd *Banking, Negoce* and *Negotiating ;* Hence, our Money - Goldfmiths were formerly called *Bankers,* and our great national Treafury of Commerce is at this Day called the *Bank.*

THE general heads of Home-Trade are beft contain'd in the *two* plain and homely Terms *Labouring,* and *Dealing.* 1ft. *The labouring Part,* this confifts of Arts, Handicrafts, and all Kinds of Manufactures ; and thofe who are employ'd in thefe Works, are properly called *Mechanicks ;* they are employ'd, generally fpeaking, about the firft Principles of Trade, *(viz.)* the Product of the *Land* or of the *Sea,* or of the Animals living on both : In a Word, the ordinary Produce of the *vegetative* and *fenfative Life ;* fuch as Metals, Minerals and Plants, the immediate Produce of *Vegetation,* or fuch as Flefh, Skins, Hair, Wool, Silk, *&c.* grown with, and produc'd by the Animals, as the Effect of *fenfitive Life.*

2. *The Dealing Part ;* this confifts of handing about all the feveral Productions of Art and Labour, when finifh'd by the Hand of the induftrious Mechanick, and made
uſeful

ufeful to Mankind ; conveying them from
Place to Place, and from one Country to
another, as the Neceffity and the Convenience of the People call for them ; and
that upon fuch Terms and Conditions of
Delivery, as they can beft agree about a-
mong themfelves, and this is Trade ; whether it be carry'd on by the general Medium
of all Exchangings call'd Coin, or by fomething fubftituted as Coin, and in the room
of it, which we call Money.

   N. B. ANY Thing that is by the Autho-
    rity of a Nation eftablifh'd as the Me-
    dium of their Exchanges, is properly
    the MONEY of the Nation, tho' feldom
    any Thing but Gold, Silver, or other
    Metals is call'd COIN.

THUS Dealing and Manufacturing com-
prehends all Trade ; that is to fay, in its
meer natural and original Situation ; and
all the fubfequent Divifions and Diftinctions of Terms, by which we are taught to
exprefs the particular Parts of Trade, are
but modern Names introduc'd by Cuftom,
and legitimated by length of Time, and
general Ufage of the Men of Art, to diftinguifh Things, as accident and the Variety of the feveral Productions in Mechanifm required.

So the Word GOODS is a general Term,
comprehending all the feveral Kinds and
Sorts, whether of Manufactures or Product, that the greateft Dealer in the World
                      can

can be fuppofed to Trade in ; it is a ufual Thing to exprefs it fo to this Day, in
the Language of Trade ; *for Example*, in
retailing, we fay, fuch a Shop is well furnifh'd with all Sorts of GOODS : In *wholefale* Trade, fuch a Dealer has his Ware-
houfe well fill'd with GOODS : In *Houfekeeping*, all the Furniture of a Houfe are
called the GOODS, or the *Houfhold-goods :* In
Merchandizing, fuch a Ship was Loaden
with BALE GOODS ; and in the *Eaft India*
Ships, after the *bulky Goods*, (fo they call
the Pepper, Salt-petre, Red-earth, Tea,
and fuch like) are taken out, it is faid the
reft of the Loading was made up with
PIECE GOODS.

AS the Terms in Trade are various, fo
the People concern'd in Trade bear differing
Titles, and are ordinarily known by differing Denominations.

THOSE concern'd in the meaner and firft
Employments, are called in common, Working Men or Labourers, and the *labouring
Poor* ; fuch as the meer Husbandmen, Mi-
ners, Diggers, Fifhers, and in fhort, all
the Drudges and Labourers in the feveral
Productions of Nature or of Art : *Next
to them*, are thofe who, tho' labouring perhaps equally with the other, have yet fome
Art mingled with their Induftry, and are
to be particularly inftructed and taught
how to perform their Part, and thofe are
called Workmen or Handicrafts.

SUPERIOR

SUPERIOR to thefe, are the Guides or Mafters in fuch Works or Employments, and
thefe are call'd Artifts, Mechanicks or Crafts-
men ; and in general, all are underftood in
this one Word Mechanicks ; fuch are Clothiers, Weavers, &c. Handicrafts in Hard-
ware, Brafs, Iron, Steel, Copper, &c.

SUPERIOR to thefe are the Dealers who
only buy and fell, either by wholefale or
retale as above ; thefe are the Factor, the
Pedlar, and the Merchant.

ALL thefe come under the general Denomination of Trading Men, and they are the
principal Kinds or Profeffions which *juft
now* carry on the Trade of the World.

HAVING thus, once for all, accounted for
thefe feveral Diftinctions, and for the trading People in their refpective Denominations as above, we fhall have no more Occafion to explain the Terms as we go a-
long, or trouble the Reader with running
out to enquire our Meaning, when we
fpeak of the feveral Branches of *Commerce*
in their proper and particular Diftinctions
or Terms of Art.

WE muft alfo remove fome Scandal out
of the Way as we go on, and this is another Difficulty. This Scandal relates to the
Dignity, Antiquity, and other Honours
due to Trade, and claim'd in its Behalf;
concerning which we meet with much
weak headed Strife in the World ; and
which, as I take it, belongs properly to
this

this Place, at leaſt I ſhall diſcharge my ſelf of it here, and by doing ſo, ſhall have no more Occaſion to trouble you with it in the reſt of our Debate, however, the impertinent Cavils of the Times may importune me upon that Head.

PRIDE, in Conjunction with abundance of Ignorance, is frequently in Arms againſt the peaceable trading World about Precedence, and in a Plea of Antiquity: They would divide the World into two Parts only, *(viz.)* the Gentry and the Commonalty ; among the Gentry they rank the Nobility, the ancient Families of Gentlemen, (as they call them) Barons, *&c.* and thoſe who were formerly called Barons ; and with ſome Difficulty they admit the Men of Learning, and the Men of Arms, *(viz.)* the Soldiery and the Clergy, and all the Families, who by the Heraldry of their Houſes claim to have been Gentlemen unmix'd with plebeian Blood for immemorial Ages.

THIS Family Jargon, *for it is no more,* they oppoſe to the trading Part of the whole World, whom they diveſt of all Dignity, as well as of Degree ; and blend together under one general, or rather common Denomination of *Mechanicks;* tho' by the Accidents of Time, and Circumſtances of Things, ſome of them *are,* and for many Ages *have been* true Members of the Gentry by collateral Branches ; nay ſometimes by
the

the chief Lines of the beft and moft ancient Families in the Nation.

 N.B. Observe, here I fpeak of our own
Country chiefly, and of the Miftake,
as it is particularly efpoufed in *England,*
and nowhere elfe.

 First, as to Antiquity; and *even in
this,* I think the Tradefmen and the Gentry
fhould never cap Pedigrees, fince the moft
noble Defcendants of *Adam's* Family, and
in whom the Primogeniture remained, were
really *Mechanicks ;* for honeft Jubal and
Tubal were the firft *Fidle-*makers and
Tinkers in the World: The firft invented
and made mufical Inftruments, *Fidles,*
&c. and the fecond was the firft *Hard-ware
Manufacturer,* that is in *Englifh,* a *Tinker,*
and no better ; *N.B.* for long, (many long
Ages) after them, the Sons and Grandfons
of thefe Mechanicks were Kings and Princes,
Dukes and Lords.

 After the fecond Peopling of the
World, before there were any Diftinctions
of Nobility, or Mechanicks, they feem
to have been all Labourers ; as at the
erecting that ftupendous Work called *Ba-
bel* for Example; to be fure, the Free-
Mafons and their Brother Bricklayers, who
were the Mafter-Builders there, were fome
of the top of their Gentry at that Time.

 As the World encreafed, Sidon, *Noah's* Grandfon, built a City, which remains
in

in the fame Place, and bears the fame Name to this Day.

Here Navigation began, and as *Noah* was the firft Shipwright, or according to us, the firft *Ship-Carpenter*, (a true Mechanick) his Pofterity built the firft Boats, and afterwards Ships at this Place ; with thefe they traded to and with the neighbouring Nations upon the Coaft, as Nature, Reafon and Neceffity guided them. In the Infancy of their navigating Skill, they Row'd along in thefe Boats, (for at firft they had no Sails) from Place to Place Northward, to the Gulph of *Alexandria* now *Scandaroon*, and fo on to the Coaft of *Cilicia* where they built *Tarfhifh*, the firft *grand Arfenal* or Place for Ship-building in the World ; whence great Ships were afterwards called *Ships of Tarfhifh* for many Ages, no Ships of Burthen being built any where elfe.

Also South they coafted to *Joppa*, now *Jaffa*, thence to *Damiata* and *Egypt*, where their great Grandfather Cham reigned Emperor of all *Africa* for many Ages. See Sir *Walter Rawleigh*'s Hiftory of the World.

Encreasing thus in People, and in Wealth (by Trade) and growing too great for the Compafs of one City, or the Commerce of one Port, they fpread themfelves by way of Colony, and fettled firft at *Tyre*, a convenient Situation alfo for Shiping and for Merchandizing. Here

HERE they encreafed again to fuch a Prodigy of Bufinefs, as I have good Reafon to believe, was never equall'd in the World, except juft now, *(viz.)* by the great Trade carry'd on at this Time in *England*; of which in its Place.

AND here to prove to you beyond the Power of Cavil, that the Antients thought it not below their Quality to be Tradef-men ; the Prophet *Ezekiel* fays, *Thy wife Men were thy Pilots, and thy Merchants are Princes ;* or as fome read it, *Thy Princes are Merchants,* as it is exprefly in another Place, *Ezekiel* xxvii. 21. *The Princes of* Kedar *were thy Merchants.*

THUS much is fufficient for the Antiquity of Trade and Navigation ; as to the Antiquity of trading Families, I fay with a late low born Poet, but a Man of Wit,

Let Cæfar *or* Naffau *go higher.*

And why then are we to defpife Commerce as a Mechanifm, and the Trading World as mean, when the Wealth of the World is deem'd to rife from Trade ? as the fame Text faid of *Tyre, v.* 33. of the fame Chapter, *Thou didft enrich the Kings of the Earth with thy Merchandife.*

BUT to bring this down to our felves ; Are we a rich, a populous, a powerful Nation, and in fome Refpects the greateft in all thofe particulars in the World, and do

we

we not boaſt of being ſo ? 'Tis evident it
was all deriv'd from Trade. *Our Merchants
are Princes,* greater and richer, and more
powerful than ſome ſovereign Princes ; and
in a Word, as is ſaid of *Tyre,* we have
*made the Kings of the Earth rich with our
Merchandiſe,* that is, with our Trade.

I F Uſefulneſs gives an Addition to the
Character, either of Men or Things, as
without doubt it does; Trading-men will
have the Preference in almoſt all the Diſputes
you can bring : There is not a Nation in
the known World, but have taſted the Benefit, and owe their Proſperity to the uſeful Improvements of Commerce : Even the
ſelf-vain Gentry, that would decry Trade
as a univerſal Mechaniſm, are they not every where depending ˊupon it for their moſt
neceſſary Supplies ? If they do not all *ſell,*
they are all forc'd to *buy,* and ſo are a kind of
Traders themſelves, at leaſt they recognize
the Uſefulneſs of Commerce, as what they
are not able to live comfortably without.

N A Y, in many Parts of *Britain,* they
are really Traders, both Buyers and Sellers ;
for Example, where the Landlords are
obliged to take their Rents in kind, as the
Clergy do their Tithes ; here they are (in
a word) general Traders ; they ſell their
Barley to the Malt-makers, their Wheat to
the Millers and Bakers, their Oates to the
Corn-factors, their Sheep and Bullocks are
ſold at the Markets to the Butchers,   or
                                          at

at Fairs to the Graziers ; they are Sheep-
Shearers, and fell their Wool to the Stapler
or Clothier; and when they kill a Bullock,
or a Calf, or a Sheep, for their Family-
Ufe, they are beholding to the Felmonger,
and the Tanner, to buy the raw Hides
and Skins; when they fell their Timber,
they are oblig'd to turn Mechanicks, and
fell the Bark to the Tanners, the Timber
to the Ship-wright and the Carpenters, the
Brufhwood and Bavins to the Baker and
the Brick-maker.

IN a Word, ufeful Trade fupports the
Gentleman; and without thefe Mechanicks
he could not difpofe the Produce of his
Eftate, or make any Rent of his Land ; and
rather than not difpofe of it, fuch is his Neceffity, that we fee he will ftoop to buy and
fell for himfelf, and trade and deal like a
meer Mechanick.

BUT this is not all, if they would look a
little nearer, they would fee themfelves not
by Practice only degenerated into Trading Men, but even their Fortunes, nay,
their very Blood mingled with the Mechanicks, *as they call them;* the Neceffity of
their Circumftances frequently reconciles the
beft of the Nobility to thefe Mixtures; and
then the fame Neceffity opens their Eyes
to the Abfurdity of the Diftinctions which
they had been fo wedded to before.

IT is with the utmoft Difgrace to their
Underftanding, that thofe People would diftinguifh

ftinguifh themfelves in the Manner they
do, when they may certainly fee every Day
profperous Circumftances advance thofe
Mechanicks, *as they will have them called*, into the Arms, and into the Rank
of the Gentry: and declining Fortunes reduce the beft Families to a Level with the
Mechanick.

T H E rifing Tradefman fwells into the
Gentry, and the declining Gentry finks into
Trade. A Merchant, or perhaps a Man of
a meaner Employ thrives by his honeft Induftry, Frugality, and a long feries of diligent Application to Bufinefs, and being
grown immenfely rich, he marries his
Daughters to Gentlemen of the firft Quality,
perhaps a Coronet; then he leaves the Bulk
of his Eftate to his Heir, and he gets into
the Rank of the Peerage; does the next Age
make any Scruple of their Blood, being thus
mix'd with the antient Race? Do we not
juft now fee two Dukes defcended by the
Female Side, from the late Sir *Jofiah
Child*, and the immediate Heir a Peer of
Ireland? Many Examples of the like Kind
might be given.

O N the other Hand, the declining Gentry, in the Ebb of their Fortunes, frequently pufh their Sons into Trade, and they a-
gain, by their Application, often reftore the
Fortunes of their Families: Thus Tradefmen become Gentlemen, by Gentlemen becoming Tradefmen. I could give Exam-
                                          ples

ples of this too, but they are too recent for our naming.

THEY that learn thus to defpife Trading People as fuch, muft either be intirely ignorant of the World, or perfectly uncapable of the juft Impreffions of thefe Things; they muft forget fure, that the Gentry are always willing to fubmit to the raifing their Families, by what they call *City Fortunes*; and how ufeful Trade has always been, and ftill is in the World on that Account; while others who call themfelves Gentlemen, by Way of Diftinction, became unworthy, by the Scandal of their Morals, to match with the meaneft Citizen, if fhe be a Woman of Modefty and Virtue.

BUT to go on in generals, which is proper to the Head I am talking of; Trade is the univerfal Fund of Wealth throughout the World; the Gold of *Africa* and *Brazil*, the Silver of *Mexico* and *Peru* had but for Trade remained undifturbed in the Mines, and in the Sands of the Rivers of *Guinea* and *Chili* : The Diamonds of *Golconda*, and of *Borneo* had been glittering in the Dirt, and remain'd unpolifh'd to this Day, if Diligence had not found them out; if Navigation had not affifted the Difcovery, and if Trade had not fpread and difpers'd them over the whole Globe.

EVEN *Solomon* had wanted Gold to adorn the Temple, unlefs he had been fup-

piy'd

ply'd by Miracles; if he had not turn'd Merchant-Adventurer, and fent his Fleets to fetch it from the *Eaft Indies*, that is to fay, from *Achin*, on the Ifland of *Sumatra*, which is fuppofed to be the *Ophir* which his Factors procur'd it at.

So effectually has Trade rais'd the Wealth of the World, that 'tis remarkable, and worth the moft curious Obfervation, that throughout the known World, Nations, and Kingdoms, and Governments are rich or poor, as they have, or have not, a Share of the whole Commerce of the World, or more or lefs, fome Concern in it.

The *Turks*, who are Enemies to Trade, and who difcourage Induftry and Improvement, 'tis plain they difpeople the World, rather than improve and cultivate it: View their Condition; they are miferably poor! diftreffedly poor! they are idle, indolent and ftarving, their Governments have fome Wealth, becaufe they are tyrannical, and take what they pleafe from the poor People, throughout a vaft Extent of Dominion; fo that if it be but a little in a Place, it a- mounts to a very great Sum in the whole, the People and Nations which are tributary to them, being fo many; but thofe People and Nations are poor and wretched to the laft Degree, and all for Want of Trade.

As to Trade, excepting what the *Europeans* and the *Jews* drive among them, it is
fo

fo little, that it hardly deferves the Name
of Commerce; they have neither Produce of
the Land, or Labour of the People; neither
Merchandife or Art, nothing is encouraged
among them; Ignorance boafts indeed of
the rich Return we bring from them, fuch
as Drugs, Hair, Silk, &c. But we know it
is not of *Turky*, or the Growth of *Turky*,
but is either the Product of *Armenia* and
Georgia, the Provinces of *Guilan* and *In-
doftan*, Part of *Perfia* on the Shoar of the
Cafpian Sea, quite out of the *Turk*'s Dominions, and even there they are the Product of the old Chriftians Labour, the original Inhabitants of thofe Provinces ; the
Mahometans, have little or no Hand in it;
they abhor Bufinefs and Labour, and defpife
Induftry, and they ftarve accordingly; or
thofe Goods are the Produce of the Iflands
in the *Levant* and the *Archipelague*, where
the *Cotton-yarn*, the *Grogram* or *Goats-
Hair* Yarn, the white or *Beladine Silks*, &c.
are the Manufacture of the poor *Greeks* Inhabitants of thofe Iflands, and who by their
Labour in Cultivation, caufe the Earth to
produce the Silk and the Wool, and by their
Labours in Manufacturing, fpin and make it
up into Yarn, and into Form, as we have
it from them. Now, *fee the Confequence* ;
as the *Mahometans* I fay have little Trade,
fo they have little Wealth, the Produce of
their Lands yields little, and that little fells
for fuch a little Value, that one would pity

fo vaft a Body of People labouring, as it
were, for nothing : All the fruitful rich
Countries of *Natolia* and the *Leffer Afia,*
from the *Ægean* to the *Euxine Sea,* once
the moft rich, populous, and fertile Provinces of the World, with all the *Morea,*
the *Achaia,* (the *Peloponnefus* of the Antients) and the fruitful Plains of *Thef-*
faly, Macedonia, and *Thrace,* from the
Ionian Sea, to the Banks of the *Danube ;*
what do they now produce? The great City of *Conftantinople* is fupplied with Corn
indeed, but how? (*N. B.* This is the Reafon of mentioning it) when produc'd, fold
to the Merchant, fhipt on Board the Veffels
which carry it by Sea, the Freight paid, and
all Charges of loading and unloading ; yet
their Barley has been bought in the Market
at *Conftantinople* for 3 *d. per* Bufhel.

I f this were fome Ages ago, if it were
not known to be fo very frequently, and
if there were not fome Merchants now living in *London,* who are Perfons of undoubted Credit, who affure me they have
bought it fo : I fay if it were only, that it
had been fo fome Ages ago, it had been
nothing extraordinary, for all know it has
been thus in *England* ; but this has been
fo at *Conftantinople* within thefe Ten or
Twelve Years, and I doubt not it might be
prov'd is often fo ftill in the fame Place,
when plentiful Years of Corn happen ;
what the poor Husband-man muft have for
his

his plowing, fowing, harvefting, threfhing, and carrying it out, is hard to imagine; or what the Landlord has for the Land: But I fuppofe the Grand-Seignior is general Landlord, and has his Tax from the whole Country, inftead of Rent.

Now, whence is all this Poverty of a Country? 'tis evident 'tis Want of Trade, and nothing elfe: And we may go back for an Example of it to our own Country, when the Product of the Land, and the Labour of the People were as low here, when good Wheat was worth about 4 *d.* *per* Bufhel, a fat Sheep about 3 *s.* 4 *d.* and a fat Ox about 18 to 24 *s.* and when was this? But when we had no Trade, and becaufe we had no Trade; neither is the prefent Difference owing to any Thing elfe, but to the Increafe of Commerce, as well here as in other Parts of the World; and 'tis evident the Rate of Provifions, and the Value of Lands in all Parts of the World are high or low, great or fmall, as the People have or have not Trade to fupport it.

TRADE encourages Manufacture, prompts Invention, employs People, increafes Labour, and pays Wages: As the People are employ'd, they are paid, and by that Pay are fed, cloathed, kept in Heart, and kept together; that is, kept at Home, kept from wandering into Foreign Countries

to

to feek Bufinefs, for where the Employment is, the People will be.

THIS keeping the People together, is indeed the Sum of the whole Matter, for as they are kept together, they multiply together; and the Numbers, which by the Way is the Wealth and Strength of the Nation, increafe.

As the Numbers of People increafe, the Confumption of Provifions increafes; as the Confumption increafes, the Rate or Value will rife at Market; and as the Rate of Provifions rifes, the Rents of Land rife: So the Gentlemen are with the firft to feel the Benefit of Trade, by the Addition to their Eftates.

AND here it would not have been improper to have made a Tranfition to our *Englifh* Hiftory, and to have enquir'd how punctually the Courfe of Things have obey'd the Laws of Nature in this very particular; how as Trade has increafed; fo by equal Advances, Provifions have been confum'd, Lands cultivated, Rents raifed, and the Eftates of the Gentry and Nobility been improv'd: I mean as to Periods of Time, as well as to the Proportion of Value; which Enquiry would have been an unanfwerable Proof of the Fact; but I am confin'd here to Generals, and muft only lay it down as a Propofition.

As the Confumption of Provifions increafe, more Lands are cultivated; wafte

Grounds

Grounds are inclofed, Woods are grubb'd up, Forrefts and common Lands are till'd, and improv'd ; by this more Farmers are brought together, more Farm-houfes and Cottages are built, and more Trades are called upon to fupply the neceffary Demands of Husbandry : In a Word, as Land is employ'd, the People increafe of Courfe, and thus Trade fets all the Wheels of Improvement in Motion ; for from the Original of Bufinefs to this Day it appears, that the Profperity of a Nation rifes and falls, juft as Trade is fupported or decay'd.

As Trade profpers, Manufactures increafe ; as the Demand is greater or fmaller, fo alfo is the Quantity made ; and fo the Wages of the Poor, the Rate of Provifions, and the Rents and Value of the Lands rife or fall, as I faid before.

And here the very Power and Strength of the Nation is concern'd alfo, for as the Value of the Lands rifes or falls, the Taxes rife and fall in Proportion ; all our Taxes upon Land are a Kind of Pound Rate; and bring in more or lefs, as the ftated Rents of the Land are more or lefs in Value ; and let any one calculate, by the Rate of Lands in *England,* as they went in the Times of *Edward* IV. or even in King *Henry* VII. Time, when Trade began, as it were, juft to live in *England* ; and tell us how much they think

a

a Land Tax would then have brought in :
For Example,

I f a Tax of Four Shillings in the
Pound now brings in above Two Millions, I fuppofe it would have been thought
very well then, if it had brought in Three
hundred thoufand Pound, all the reft is an
Increafe occafion'd by Trade, and by nothing elfe ; Trade has increas'd the People,
and People have increas'd Trade ; for Multitudes of People, if they can be put in a
Condition to maintain themfelves, muft increafe Trade ; they muft have Food, that
employs Land ; they muft have Clothes,
that employs the Manufacture ; they muft
have Houfes, that employs Handicrafts ; they
muft have Houfhold Stuff, that employs a
long Variety of Trades ; fo that in a Word
Trade employs People, and People employ
Trade.

I once faw a Calculation of Trade for
the planting a new Town in the South
Parts of *England,* where, for the Encouragement of People to come and fettle, the
Lords of the Manors, (for the Place lay in
three Manors,) agreed to give a certain
Quantity of Lands to Fifty Farmers, who
would undertake to bring each two hundred
Pound Stock with them, and fettle there.

T o every fuch Farmer, they allotted
two hundred Acres of good Land, Rent-
free for Twenty Years ; and if the Farmer
brought three hundred Pound Stock, he
had

had three hundred Acres; befides the Land, the faid Lords agreed to find Timber, and all other Materials for the Building, to every Farmer a Houfe, and out of their own Pockets to build to each Houfe a Barn and Stables; and thus, with other Encouragements, Fifty Families of fubftantial Farmers were brought to live in a Kind of Circle within themfelves, with every one a good Farm to manage, and fufficient Quantity of Land Rent-free; the Land was good in it felf, tho' never cultivated before, fo that being clear'd and inclos'd, and gradually plow'd or improv'd, it foon return'd them a profitable Increafe.

THE Land was fo laid out in a large Circle, that all the Farm-houfes being built at the Extremities of the refpective Farms, toward the Center, left a handfome large Square Piece of Land which the Lords referv'd for the building a Town; and as the Farm-houfes were fo regularly plac'd, as to front all inwards, they left Ten Spaces like Streets before their Doors, of which Five of the Farm-houfes, with their Out-Houfes, made one Side, and the other remained to build into a Street as Occafion fhould prefent.

AT the fame Time they publifh'd, That whoever would come and build on that vacant Ground, fhould have a certain proportion'd Meafure of Land allow'd him, according to the Size of the Houfe he would build,

build, fhould have Timber given him gra-
tis, out of the Woods belonging to the
Eftate, fufficient for his Building ; and to
every Houfe, Land alfo added for a Garden
and Orchard, no Rent to be paid for ten
Years, and then a moderate Rent for twenty
Years more ; and then a certain Rent (not
at laft immoderate) for the Time to come.

When the Farmers were fettled, for
there is the Subftance and Reafon of the
Thing, and in this it is exactly to my Purpofe ; immediately comes a Butcher, and he
runs up a little Shed for the prefent, till he
could build a Houfe, and fets up a Shop,
to kill and fell Meat for the Farmers.

> *N. B.* As thefe Farmers had every one
> two Hundred Pounds Stock to begin,
> fo they are fuppofed to be all Men of
> Families, that had Wives and Chil-
> dren, and every one had at leaft one or
> two, and fome three Servants.

Nor could one Butcher be fufficient to
furnifh Meat to fifty Families, but they
were oblig'd to fend to neighbouring
Towns for Provifion, till the firft Butcher
having Encouragement, two or three more
came afterwards, and fet up alfo.

After the Example of the Butcher, in
the next Place came a Baker, and he erects
an Oven to fupply them with Bread.

Fifty Families of Farmers muft neceffarily find Work for a Smith or Farrier to
Shoe their Horfes, and at leaft two Wheel-
wrights

wrights to make and repair their Carts, Waggons, Plows, Harrows, *&c.* and thefe with the neceffary Iron-work for fo much Building, called in a couple of Black-fmiths, whereof one being a Man of Subftance, made himfelf a kind of Iron-monger, laying in a Stock of all Sorts of wrought Iron and Brafs for Building and Furniture, which on fuch an Occafion they could not be without.

THIS Colleſtion of Tradefmen naturally requir'd a Shoe-maker or two to fet up, who foon found Trade enough to fupply the growing Numbers of People with Shoes and Boots ; and likewife a good honeft Country Cobler or two could not fail of Employment to repair them ; and (to add the other Trades working in Leather,) they could not be without a Collar-maker or two, for Harnefs, Pannels, Saddles, and all the neceffary Things relating to a Team.

ADD to thefe a Turner, an Earthen-ware Seller, a Glover, a Rope-maker, three or four Barbers, (perhaps a *Midwife*) and feveral fuch Trades as the Nature of things required.

BUT to go back to the building Part, three Mafter Carpenters would be the leaft that could be employ'd in building Houfes, and thefe would require at firft five or fix Pair of Sawyers at leaft, with Journeymen ; that is to fay, Workmen; two or three Bricklayers, with their Servants and

Labour-

Labourers, and perhaps hard by a Brick and Tile-maker.

To fupply thefe, one of the Carpenters, a Man of Subftance, builds himfelf a Wind-mil, and another builds a fecond, and they both find Work enough (as the Town en-creafed) to keep them conftantly employ'd.

The Town going thus forward, and ftanding in the great Poft Road, comes an honeft Victualler, and he fets up an Ale-houfe; and foon after, he is follow'd by five or fix more; as the firft encreafing in Stock, fees Room for it, he enlarges his Building, and makes his little Ale-houfe out into a good Inn, and a fecond follows him, and then a third, and in Procefs of Time, the Number of Public-Houfes encreafe to eleven or twelve in all; whereof as above, three are very handfome Inns, and per-haps fell Wine as well as ftrong Drink.

By this Time the Lords of the Manors begin to think it proper to build their new Tenants a Church, for which they lay out a handfome Piece of Ground in the Center of the Town, and a large Burying-Ground added to it; and obtaining Licence from the Bifhop, they confecrate the Building; and being joint Patrons, prefent in Turn, getting a Law to erect it into a Parifh, and to affertain the Tithe and Maintenance of the Incumbent, as in like Cafes.

Hitherto Nature acted it all, but this Part indeed, the Piety of the Patrons fupplies;

our

our Bufinefs is (in both) to obferve the ordinary Courfe of Things, the Concourfe of
Tradefmen follow the Concourfe of People,
as naturally as Warmth attends the Ap-
proach of the Sun ; the Settlement of the
Farmers gives a Summons to the Tradefmen
that fupply them with Neceffaries, and lets
them know, that there they may find Bufinefs and Employment : The neceffity of
Meat and Drink, brings the Butcher, Baker and Victualler to fettle with them, as
naturally as Sutlers follow an Army.

BUT to proceed; Fame fpreads the News
of a Town newly erected, and a Number
of Families brought together ; A Grocer
goes to fee if there is no Room for him,
and finding no Supplies of his Kind, he
takes a Piece of Ground in one of the
principal Streets, and marks himfelf out a
Place for his Houfe ; but firft, as before,
runs up a Booth or Shed, ftores it with
Goods, and opens a Shop, and two or
three Chandlers Shops do the fame in remoter Parts, buying their Goods perhaps of
him.

AN Apothecary does the like next Door
to him, and a Mercer next to him ; then a
Haberdafher of Hats, a Draper and a Mil-
lener ; and thus the Town is inhabited and
furnifh'd by Degrees with all Sorts of neceffary People and Things ; till after fome
Time, the Lords of the Manors, to carry
on the Improvement, get a Patent for a
Market

Market once a Week, and a Fair perhaps
twice a Year, or oftner, as there is Occafion.

In thefe advanc'd Circumftances, other
Trades fall in ; as 1*ft*, more Ale-houfes ;
2*d*, a common Brewer ; 3*d*, a Cooper for
Casks of all Sorts ; a Pewterer, two or
three Lawyers, (or Attorneys, rather) for
drawing Writings, making Bonds, Bargains
and Agreements between Man and Man,
and one of thefe in Time gets himfelf made
a Juftice of Peace, and fo there is an immediate Magiftrate among them.

In the mean Time other Trades fill up
the Streets ; a Malt-houfe, perhaps two or
three are erected, that the Inhabitants may
brew their own Beer if they pleafe ; a Sur-
geon in Cafe of Difafter, for by this Time
the Town begins to grow populous.

The good Women alfo being diligent,
and good Houfe-wives, they fpin, and in
Confequence of that, there muft be a Linen Weaver, and a Woollen-weaver, a Flax
and Hemp-dreffer, and in a word, whatever
depends upon their Thrift.

Thus far the Nature and Confequence
of Things agree with what is advanced a-
bove : Thus Towns and Families, nay Nations and Countries are planted and peopled, and made flourifhing and populous by
their Commerce.

Let us now caft up the Account,
and according to antient Cuftom Number
the

the People, the Lift by the Poll will ftand thus.

50 Farmers, with their Wives and Two Children each, one with a-nother, which I take to be the leaft that can be fuppofed. - - - } 200

Two Men Servants and one Maid to each Farmer, no Farmer with 200 Acres of Land could be fup-pofed to make Shift with lefs. } 150

The feveral Families of Tradefmen neceffarily brought together on fuch an Occafion, I caft up at 143 Families, at 5 to each Houfe. } 715

Add to thefe hired Servants which would fall in from other Coun-tries; Nurfes, Midwives, Hoft-lers, Apprentices, &c. In all } 335

———
1400

Here are fifty Farmers, who with their Servants make up but three hundred and fifty People in all; but neceffarily draw one thoufand one hundred People more to them. Thus People make Trade, Trade builds Towns and Cities, and produces every Thing that is good and great in a Nation; and wherever fifty Farmers were thus to fettle, I infift, that at leaft one thoufand People muft of courfe throng to them, and live about them.

THERE

THERE are Numbers of Examples to be given of it, the *Venetian* Republick began thus; a defpicable Croud of People flying from the Fury of the *Barbarians* which over-run the *Roman* Empire, took Shelter in a few inacceffible Iflands of the *Adriatic* Gulph.

HERE they had Safety indeed, and Life; but nothing elfe. But falling into Trade, applying themfelves to the Sea, to Navigation and Commerce; How foon did they raife themfelves in the World, fpreading themfelves into the *Archipelague,* and into the *Levant* ; conquering the great and rich Iflands of *Candia* and *Cyprus, Negropont* and *Scio,* poffefs'd the *Morea, Dalmatia* and *Epirus,* and gradually rais'd their Dominion to fuch a Degree, as was fuperior to many Kingdoms.

THEIR City we fee raifed to a prodigious Splendor and Magnificence, and their rich Merchants rank'd among the ancient Nobility, and all this by Trade : Their Fleets of Men of War have oftentimes engag'd and beaten the *Turkifh* Navy, driven them into Port, and dar'd them at the Mouth of the *Dardanelli ;* and all this Power is rais'd by Trade.

I might from this Example lead you to the *Hans,* the great Confederacy of Commerce, the greateft in the World ; who meerly by the acquir'd Greatnefs of their Trade, became fo rich, and fo powerful, that they

they were many Years the Terror of the
North; whoever hired their Men of War,
were fure to conquer their Enemies at Sea,
and feveral times they beat whole Fleets of
the *Danes*, and at laft brought the King of
Denmark to make a difhonourable Peace
with them; till the Kings of the neighbouring Countries grew juftly jealous of them,
and oblig'd all the Cities within their Jurif-
diction to withdraw from their Alliance,
and to renounce their Confederacy.

THE *Dutch*, I mean the States-General
of the united Provinces, when they broke
off from the Obedience of *Spain*, and as
it may be rightly faid, caft off the *Spanifh*
Yoke, were a poor, mean, frighted Generation, driven to the Refuge of the Water,
by the terrible Power of King *Philip*, and
reduc'd to fuch Diftrefs, that, but for the
Affiftance of Queen *Elizabeth*, they had
been ruin'd and deftroy'd; yet pufhing into Trade, and having Recourfe to the Sea,
they built themfelves upon their Marine
Power; and the Succefs of their Navigation
rais'd them to that Pitch of Naval Greatnefs
which we now fee them at, in which they
are fuperior to all the World, *Great Britain* excepted, of whom I fhall fpeak by
themfelves.

As it has been with Nations, fo it has
been with Cities and Towns; fuch has
been the Cafe of the Cities of *Hamburgh,
Dantzick, Lubec, Franckfort, Nurem-
berg,*

berg, *Rochelle,* *Marseilles,* *Genoa,* *Leg-horn,* *Geneva,* and many other Cities that might be nam'd, who have been rais'd to a Pitch of Opulence and Wealth, equal to some Principalities, by their meer Situation for, and Success in their *Commerce:* I on the other hand might name several Cities, which being depriv'd of their Trade, have sunk again in Proportion, as their Trade has been taken away; such as the City of *Antwerp,* the Towns of *Dunkirk,* *South-ampton,* *Ipswich,* and many more.

As their Trade has been cut off, their Merchants have removed, the Inhabitants decreased, and the Shells of the Towns remain without the Kernel, the Houses without the People, and the People without the Wealth.

When the *Dutch* cut off the free Navigation of the *Scheld* from the City of *Antwerp,* how did it decline? the *English* Staple remov'd to *Hamburgh,* the Fishing Trade to *Amsterdam,* and the Merchants followed; and what is that City now compar'd to what it formerly was?

When the King of *France* was oblig'd by the late War to demolish the Works, and ruin the Harbour of *Dunkirk,* so that the Navigation received a Blow; How did the Town sensibly decay? from eighteen thousand Families, which once inhabited that Place, 'tis said, not two Thirds remain; all the People depending upon the Naval
Affairs,

Affairs, are gone with the royal Arſenal; all the Magazines of Naval-Stores, either for the King or the Merchant, employ'd and carried off; and the Trade that attended that Part ſunk with it; few Ships now belong to it, few Merchants now reſide in it, and in a few Years more, the empty Houſes being unrepaired, may publiſh its Decay in a more viſible Manner, and ſhew the Wounds receiv'd by the Loſs of their Trade, as is the Caſe at *Southampton*, at *Ipſwich, &c.* in a viſible Manner.

I need not travel over the Globe, to give you Examples in remoter Places, where the great Emporiums, the greateſt trading Cities in the World, have ſunk into Ruin by the Stop of their Commerce, ſuch as *Tripoli, Sinope,* and *Trapezond* in the *Euxine* or *Black Sea,* whoſe Trade is cut off, by the *Turks* ſtopping the Navigation of the *Boſphorus*, and cutting off the Trade they carried on with *Europe;* or ſuch as *Suez,* and *Alexandria,* Ports antiently of prodigious Concourſe, both of Ships and Merchants; but emptied of both, by the *Europeans* finding the Way to the *Eaſt Indies* by the Cape of *Good-hope;* or ſuch as the famous Cities of *Tyre* and *Corinth*, who having been the Envy of the World for Wealth, and that Wealth obtain'd by their Commerce, were overturn'd; the firſt by the *Grecians,* the laſt by the *Romans,* purely for the avaritious Part; and
who

who, their Merchants being deftroy'd, and their Trade overthrown, never recover'd their Figure any more than their Fortunes in the World.

In a Word, it appears by innumerable Examples, that Trade is the Life of the World's Profperity, and all the Wealth that has been extraordinary, whether of Nations or Cities, has been raifed by it.

The Nature of the Thing indeed implies it; as the Induftry of Mankind is fet on Work, their Hopes and Views are rais'd, and their Ambition fir'd: The View and Profpect of Gain infpires the World with the keeneft Vigor, puts new Life into their Souls; and when they fee the Succefs and Profperity of trading Nations, it rouzes them up to the like Application.

Let us view the differing Face of the Nations, (and of the People who inhabit them) where they have no Trade; how miferable is the Scene of Life? The Countries look defolate, the People fad and dejected, poor and difconfolate, heavy and indolent; not for Want of Will to labour, but for Want of fomething to labour profitably at; the Rich are flothful, becaufe they are rich and proud, the Poor, becaufe they are poor and defpair; for it will ever be true

That Poverty makes Sloth, and Sloth
makes Poor.

We

We fay of fome Nations, the People are lazy, but we fhould fay only, they are poor ; Poverty is the Fountain of all Manner of Idlenefs; they have in fhort nothing to do, no Employment in which they can get their Bread by their Labour ; their Work gets no Wages for Want of Trade, and their Trade no Increafe for Want of Labour ; Diligence promotes Trade, and Trade encourages Diligence ; Labour feeds Trade, and Trade feeds the Labourer.

THERE is hardly that Country to be nam'd in the World, where there is no Room for Improvement by Induftry and Application ; nay, we find an induftrious People often thriving and wealthy, under the weighty Difcouragements of a barren Soil, an inhofpitable Climate, a tempeftuous Sea, a remote Situation, having yet fomething or other for Trade to work upon.

THE People of *Norway* and *Ruffia* having nothing but Mountains and Woods, and the moft barren inclement Air and Soil in the World ; yet, rather than not trade, and rather than not labour, they cut down their Trees, and fend them abroad to build Cities, and build Navies in other Countries, and have hardly any of their own.

IF their Woods grow remote from the Sea or Water Carriage, Induftry dictates to them to cut them down and burn them; and to trade, if it be but with the very

Sap

Sap and Juices of the Trees: Hence they send us Tar, Pitch, Rozin, Turpentine; and we fee as it were a whole Wood brought away in Cask; Ten, Twenty Thoufand Laft of Tar brought from *Ruffia* at a Time, every Laft being Ten to Twelve Barrels.

IF *Greenland* and *Spitsbergen* are unfufferably cold; if Nature, not being able to fupport the Violence of it, leaves thofe Places uninhabited; the diligent Trader not being to be difcouraged by Difficulties, flies directly thither; there among a Thoufand Dangers, furrounded with Mountains of Ice, terrible, and Horrors enough to chill the very Soul to defcribe them, *Hunts* the great *Leviathan* of the Seas, and loads his Ships with the fat (BLUBBER) of a Thoufand Whales.

I might inftance in the Severities of the torrid, as well as frigid Zone, and fhew the Hardfhips undergone in Places fcorch'd with the Violence of the Heat; and which are every Way as terrible in their Kind, as thofe of exceffive Cold; fuch are the Difeafes and Terrors of the long Calms, where the Sea ftagnates and corrupts for Want of Motion; and by the Strength of the Scorching Sun ftinks and poifons the diftreft Mariners, who are rendered unactive, and difabled by Scurvies, raging and mad with Calentures and Fevers, and drop into Death in fuch a Manner, that at laft
the

the Living are loft, for Want of the Dead,
that is, for want of Hands to work the Ship.

YET nothing difcourages the diligent
Seaman, or the adventrous Merchant in
Purfuit of Trade, and pufhing on Difcoveries, planting Colonies, and fettling Commerce, even to all Parts of the World.

Now as I faid before, that the Nations
who want Trade look dejected and fad, fo
on the contrary, let the curious Traveller
obferve, as he paffes thro' the World, the
trading manufacturing Nations have a quite
different Afpect ; their Labour, however
hard and heavy, is perform'd chearfully ;
a general Sprightlinefs and Vigour appears
among them ; their Countenances are blith,
and they are merrier at their Labour, than
others are at their Play ; their Hearts are
warm, as their Hands are quick ; they are
all Spirit and Life, and it may be feen in
their Faces ; or which is more, it is feen
in their Labour ; as they live better than
the Poor of the fame Clafs in other Countries, fo they work harder : And here the
fame *Antithefis* is obfervable as before, tho'
in its contrary Extreme ; for as I faid there,
that Poverty makes Sloth, and Sloth makes
Poor : So here,

*Labour makes Gain, and Gain gives
Strength to Labour.*

A 5

A s they labour harder, fo they get more for their Work than other Nations, and this gives them Spirit for their Labour. And this is the immediate Effect of Trade, for the Poor of the trading and manufacturing Countries are employ'd on better Terms, and have better Wages for their Work, than the Poor of thofe Countries where there is lefs Trade.

We are told, that in *Ruffia* and *Mufcovy*, when for want of Commerce, Labour was not affifted by Art ; they had no other Way to cut out a large Plank, but by felling a great Tree, and then with a multitude of Hands and Axes hew away all the Sides of the Timber, till they reduc'd the middle to one large Plank ; and that yet, when it was done, they would fell this Plank as cheap, as the *Swedes* or *Pruffians* did the like, who cut three or four, or more Planks of the like Size from one Tree by the Help of Saws and Saw-Mills : The Confequence muft be, that the miferable *Ruffian* labour'd ten times as much as the other did, for the fame Money.

We are told frequently, when fuch and fuch great Works or Buildings were finifhed, Men work'd for a Penny a Day here in *England ;* and perhaps they did fo ; but as I faid before, fpeaking of the Cheapnefs of Provifions, that it was before we had any Trade among us ; fo it muft be as to

Wages,

Wages, for as Trade raifes Wages, fo Wages raife Provifions ; and this is the Reafon, why, as all Foreigners grant that our
Poor in *England* work harder than they
do in any other Nation ; fo it muft be
own'd, they eat and drink better in Proportion ; and this is, becaufe they have better Wages.

I might examine this Article of Wages,
and carry it thro' almoft every Branch of
Bufinefs in *England ;* and it would appear, that the *Englifh* Poor earn more
Money than the fame Clafs of Men or
Women can do at the fame kind of Work,
in any other Nation.

NOR will it be deny'd, but that they do
more Work alfo : So then, if they do more
Work, and have better Wages too, they
muft needs live better, and fare better;
and it is true alfo, that they cannot fupport their Labour without it.

AND here I may grant, that a *French*
Man fhall do more Work than an *Englifh*
Man, if they fhall be oblig'd to live on the
fame Diet ; that is to fay, the Foreigner fhall
ftarve with the *Englifh* Man for a Wager,
and will be fure to win: He will live and
work, when the *Englifh* Man fhall fink
and dye ; but let them live both the fame
Way, the *Englifh* Man fhall beggar the
French Man, for tho' the *French* Man
were to fpend all his Wages, the *Englifh*
Man will out-work him.

IT

Iт is true again, the *French* Man's Diligence is the greateſt, he ſhall work more
Hours than the *Engliſh* Man; but the *Engliſh* Man ſhall do as much Buſineſs in the
fewer Hours, as the Foreigner who ſits
longer at it.

To conclude this Head, I would not
ſeem to be partial in Favour of our own
Country; but it muſt be added, that their
Work is better perform'd alſo; and I appeal for the Truth of it, to their ſeveral Performances, of which I could give Examples,
and which all the Markets in the World are
at this Time Witneſſes to; but this begins
to be particular, I ſhall ſpeak at large to
the ſeveral Examples of it in their proper
Places.

Iт is ſufficient to the Purpoſe here to
obſerve as above, that the diligent trading
manufacturing World work chearfully, live
comfortably; they ſing at their Labour,
work by their Choice, eat and drink well,
and their Work goes on pleaſantly, and with
Succeſs: Whereas the unemploy'd World
groan out their Souls in Anguiſh and Sor-
row, not by their Work, but for want of
it; and ſink, as I may juſtly ſay, under the
Weight of their Idleneſs and Sloth; what
little Work they do, is done with Reluct-
ance and Grief, becauſe the ſmall Wages
they have for it, gives them no Comfort
when it is done.

Tʀᴀᴠᴇʟ-

TRAVELLING in the North Part of *Britain*, I obferved, that, in the Time of their Harveſt, they had always an Overſeer to keep the Reapers to their Work, and a Bag-pipe to encourage them while they were at Work : And one of our Company obſerving that we had no ſuch merry Doings at our Harveſts in *England* ; another anſwer'd him, 'twas true, nor was there any need of it, for that the *Engliſh* work'd merrily enough without Muſick; adding, our Workmen have good Victuals and good Drink : Let's enquire how theſe poor People feed, ſaid he ; and ſo we did, when we found that the beſt of their Proviſion was a Cake of Oat Bread, which they call a Bannock, and a Draught of Water only ; and twice in the Day, the Farmer or Steward gave them every one a Dram of *Glaſgow* Brandy, as they call'd it ; that is to ſay, good Malt Spirits.

UPON the whole, it was evident, the poor Men had need enough of Muſic to encourage them at their Labour ; nor would the Muſic do neither, without the Overſeer or Steward being in the Field too, to ſee that they ſtood to their Work.

IN *England* we ſee the Farmers in Harveſt Time, providing good Beef and Mutton, Pyes, Puddings, and other Proviſions to a ſtrange Profuſion, feaſting their Workmen, rather than feeding them ; and giving them good Wages beſides : But let any

Man

Man fee the difference of the Work, thefe need no Mufic, the Feaft is better than the Fiddle, and the Pudding does more than the Bag-Pipe; *in fhort,* they work with a Vigor and Spirit, not to be feen in other Countries.

I could give like Examples among the Manufacturers; the Spirit and Courage of the Workmen, is feen in the Goodnefs and Subftance of their Manufacture; of which, this muft be faid, our Manufacture may not be fo cheap as the fame Kinds made in other Countries; but bring them to the Scale and try their Subftance, you will find the *Englifh* Man's Work, according to his Wages, out-weigh the other; as his Beer is ftrong, fo is his Work; and as he gives more Strength of Sinews to his Strokes in the Loom, his Work is firmer and fafter, and carries a greater Subftance with it, than the fame Kinds of Goods, and of the fame Denomination made in foreign Parts.

I remember in our former Contefts about Commerce, great Noife was made of the *French* imitating our woollen Manufacture, and making them to fuch Perfection, as to out-do us in foreign Markets; from whence it was inferr'd, that they would in Time fupplant our Trade, and carry away the Bufinefs from us : The Reafon that was given, was, that their Poor could work fo much cheaper than ours, that their Goods would be fold cheaper than
the

the *Englifh*, and confequently they would have the firft and beft of the Market always from us; and had this been fully and fairly made out; had they brought fufficient Evidence of the Facts fuggefted, the Inference had been good. Now to prove how finely the *French* perform'd, and how good their Cloths were; Patterns were fhew'd here of their feveral Cloths, as finifh'd for the *Turky* Trade, by the great Manufactory, as they call it, in *Languedoc*; for it was this Part that was brought for the Support of the Argument; and it is true, that the Patterns were extraordinary, the Cloth well drefs'd, the Colours well dy'd; nay, to Perfection; and to a fuperficial Eye, they rather went beyond the *Englifh*, than come fhort of them.

BUT when they came to be look'd well into by Clothiers and Workmen who underftood it, and whofe Bufinefs it was; the Deficiency foon difcover'd it felf; their Cloths appear'd to be flight, thin, without Subftance and Proportion, and unfit to do Service in wearing; in a word, they were no Way equal in Goodnefs to the *Englifh* Manufacture of the fame Kind. This was farther prov'd by the *Armenian* Merchants at *Aleppo*, at *Smyrna*, and other Places in *Turky*, where the faid Goods were ufually fold; where upon bringing the *Englifh* and *French* Cloths to the Scale, there was no Comparifon between them; but

but the *English* always out-weigh'd them
forty to fifty Pound *per* Bale, and sometimes much more ; the Confequence of
which was,

1. THAT thofe *Armenian* Merchants
would very feldom buy the *French Cloths*,
fo long as there were any of the *English
Cloths* left at the Market.

2. THAT when they did buy them,
they always had them at a much cheaper
Rate.

THIS is an evident Proof of the *English*
manner of performing ; and it will hold in
many other Cafes, perhaps in all Manufacturing Cafes : The ftrong Labour of the
English Workmen in all their manual Operations is very remarkable in the Works
themfelves : And I fay, it is evident in many
other Manufactures, befides that of Broad-
Cloths ; *in a word*, our Workmen, by the
meer Vigour and Strength of their Spirits,
fupported by their ftrong Feeding, and by
their better Wages than in any other Nation, are not ufed to work flight and fuper-
ficially, but ftrong and fubftantial in every
Thing they do ; and as they have better
Wages for it than other Nations give, and
perform their Work accordingly, fo their
Goods make it evident, for that they fetch
a better Price at Market, than any Goods
of the fame Species, made in any other
Country.

IT

IT is the fame Thing in their feveral Manufactures of Brafs and Iron, and other Hard-ware Works; but efpecially, in their building of Ships, in which it is evident, the *Dutch* and *French, Swedes* and *Danes,* build cheaper ; but the *Englifh* build ftronger and firmer ; and an *Englifh* Ship will always endure more feverity, load heavier, and reign *(as the Seamen call it)* longer, than any foreign built Ship whatever; the Examples are feen every Year, particularly in the Coal Trade, the Loading of which is very heavy, and the Ships fwim deep in the Water, by the Eagernefs of the Mafters, to carry large Burthens ; and yet it is frequently known, that a *New-Cafle* or *Ipfwich built Colier,* fhall reign, (as I fay the Seamen call it) forty to fifty Years, and come to a good End at laft ; that is, be broken up; not founder at Sea, or break her Back upon the Sands, as Ships weaker built, often, nay generally do.

THE firm Building, as well as beautiful Moulds of our Men of War confirm this alfo, in which they out-laft, as well as out-fhine, the ftrongeft and fineft built Ships of moft other Nations, if not of all Nations in *Europe,* except only thofe Caftle-built clumfy Things called *Galeons,* which are built fo ftrong, that is, fo thick, that they are fcarce fit for any thing.

THE Comparifon is ftill to my Purpofe in every Part, (*viz.*) that Trade invigorates
the

the World, gives Employment to the People, raifes Pay for their Labour, and encreafes that Pay as their Labour encreafes, and as their Performance excels; and it appears that what is faid of *England* is no Compliment to our own Country, but a real, hiftorical Truth; for that 'tis undeniable, that the Labour of the Poor is no where rated fo high as in *England*: There is no Nation in the World where the Poor have equal Wages for their Work as in *England*, in Proportion to the Rate of Money, and to the Rate of Provifions.

By this Means the labouring Poor are kept in Heart, kept ftrong, and made able for the Bufinefs they are employ'd in; and the contrary, is the Reafon why the *French*, the *Italians*, and moft other Nations, rather make their Manufacture (of any Kind) gay than good, fine than ftrong. I allow them to be as exquifite in Art, nay I may allow them to be more apt to invent and contrive, and perhaps finifh fome Things with more Ornament: But for Strength of Hand in their Works, where Strength is effential to the Value of the Work, there our People out-do them all.

I could carry this on thro' many Particulars, and it would lead me into fome very ufeful Speculations, but they would be remote from my Purpofe; I bring it back therefore to the fingle Point which I am upon; namely, the great Advantage of
Com-

Commerce to the World, and to particular Nations.

WHEN we had no Trade, we had no Ships, no populous Cities, no Numbers of People, no Wealth compar'd to what we fee now; Provifions bore no Price, Lands yielded no Rent; and why? The Reafon is plain and fhort; 'tis fum'd up in a Word, *Labour* brought in *no Wages*.

> *N. B.* OBSERVE by the Word, no, or none, is not meant litterally and ftrictly *none at all;* but comparatively none compar'd to what is feen now.

THE People were divided into Mafter and Servant; not Landlord and Tenant, but the Lord and the Vaffal; the Tenant paid no Rent, but held his Lands in Vaffallage; that is, for Services to be performed; fuch and fuch Tenants plow'd his Land; fuch and fuch fenc'd his Park; fuch and fuch Lands were let out to furnifh the Lord's Kitchen with Poultry, fuch with Eggs, fome with one Thing, fome with another; and thus the Lord liv'd, as the *Scots* call it, in the middle of his Geer.

THE under People to thefe Tenants held by Villenage; that is, the Labourers, thofe we now call Husbandmen and Cottagers, thefe did the Drudgery, were Grooms to look after his Horfes, drive his Teams, fell his Woods, Fence, Hedge, Ditch, Threfh, and in a Word, do all fervile Labours; and for this they had their Bread; that is,

they

they had a poor Cottage, fcarce fo good as a tolerable modern Hogftye to live in, they drank at the Pump, and eat at the Kitchen Door, Beggar-like : As for the reft, the Lord of the Manor was their King ; nay, if I had faid their God, I had not err'd, fo much as fome may think ; for they worfhip'd him with fuch a blind Subjection, that at his Command they would rebel againft their King, and take up the Bow and Arrow againft whomfoever he commanded them.

THIS was the Cafe, even in this flourifhing Nation of *England,* till Trade came in to make the Difference ; and give me leave to affume fo much, I infift upon it, that Trade alone made the Difference ; and the Climax is very remarkable.

BEFORE the People fell into Trade, what was the Cafe as to Wealth ? You fee how it ftood with the People ; but what was the Cafe of the Trade.

1. WE had no Manufacture ; we had Wool indeed, and Tin, and Lead, thofe were Funds, and brought in fome Subftance ; but who had it ? Truly, the Church and the Gentry ; the religious Houfes and the Barons had the Lands and the Sheep, and confequently the Wool : And we find that in King *Edward* III's Time, the Clergy and the religious Houfes gave the King a fifth Part of all their Wool for carrying on his Wars againft *France* : This

Wool

Wool was fent abroad to the *Flemings*, and this Money was the Wealth of the Nation.

2. THIS Money went all abroad again generally fpeaking, for thofe ruinous Wars, which for many Ages the Kings of *England* carried on, fometimes in *France*, fometimes in the *Holy Land*, fometimes in *Flanders*, fometimes in *Brittany*, and the like in o-ther Places ; fo that ftill the People were impoverifh'd, I mean the Gentry and Clergy ; for this Wealth was theirs, and they paid all the Taxes : As for the labouring Poor, they fcarcely knew what Money was.

3. As to Trade, it was carry'd on by the *Efterlings* ; that is to fay, the *Hans* Towns, and by the *Flemings* ; and they carry'd away your Wool, Lead, Tin, and whatever elfe you had, and fupply'd you a-gain with Cloths, Spice, (Wine there was none, or but little to be had) and in a word, with Hemp, Flax, Pitch, Tar, Iron, and whatever elfe was to be had from A-broad ; and thefe run away with all the little Wealth which the King and the Wars left among you ; they brought you Ships, they coin'd your Money, and they in fhort grew rich by you, and you look'd on and ftarv'd.

AT laft, by the Prudence of King *Henry* VII. you fell to Trade among yourfelves ; and gradually getting Ground of the World, you

you made yourfelves Mafters of your own
Manufactures, about the middle of Queen
Elizabeth's Reign; and what fhe did to encourage it, I fhall fhew in its Place. And
now what follow'd? The Confequences
were moft glorioufly feen in a few Years, as
follows.

1. Your People turn'd Merchants abroad,
as well as Manufacturers at home: They
tafted the Sweets of Commerce, and being
encourag'd by the Gain, foon fupplanted
their Supplanters, built their own Ships, fent
out their own Goods, brought Home their
own Returns, cafhier'd the *Efterlings*, for-
bid the Wool going Abroad, and thereby
ruin'd the *Flemings*; and thus they fet up
for themfelves.

2. As to the Country, the Revolution of
Trade, brought a Revolution in the very
Nature of Things; the Poor began to
work, not for Cottages and Liveries, but
for Money, and to live, as we fay, at their
own Hands: The Women and Children
learnt to fpin and get Money for it, a
Thing entirely new to them, and what they
had never feen before. The Men left the
Hedge and the Ditch, and were fet at Work
by the Manufacturers to be Wool-Comb-
ers, Weavers, Fullers, Clothworkers, Carriers, and innumerable happy Labours they
perform'd, which they knew nothing of before; nay the *Flemings* came over (for Money) and taught them how to perform thofe
Things

Things at firft, *I fay at firft,* for the People foon became able to fend Home their Mafters, and teach one another ; then the Villains and Vaffals were taken Apprentices to the Manufacturers, till coming to be Mafters, the Name, nay the very Things themfelves call'd Vaffalage and Villanage grew out of Ufe. The Vaffals got Money by Trade, and the Villains by Labour ; and the Lords found the Sweets of it too, for they foon buy off the Services, and bring the Lords to take Money. Thus the Cottagers growing rich, bought their little Cotts with right of Commonage for their Lives, renewable fo and fo, as they could agree, and this was called Coppy-hold. On the other hand, the Vaffals and Feuholders, as they are call'd to this Day in the *North,* growing rich, lump'd it with the Lords, and for a Sum of Money bought off their flavifh Tenures, and got their Leafes turn'd into Free-holds ; and to finifh the great Fabrick, the Farmers of Lands were now enabled to take them at a Rent certain, and the Gentry got a Revenue in Money, which they underftood nothing of before.

I might enlarge here upon the differing Effects of Luxury and Frugality, which became more than ordinarily vifible upon this Change of Affairs ; namely, that as the frugal Manufacturers, encourag'd by their Succefs, doubled their Induftry and
good

good Husbandry, they lay'd up Money, and
grew rich ; and the luxurious and Purſe
proud Gentry, tickl'd with the happy Encreaſe of their Revenues, and the riſing Value of their Rents, grew vain, gay, luxurious and expenſive : So the firſt encreas'd
daily, and the latter, with all their new encreas'd and advanc'd Revenues, yet grew
poor and neceſſitous, till the former began
to buy them out ; and have ſo bought them
out, that whereas in thoſe Days, the Lands
were all in the Hands of the *Barons;* that
is to ſay, the Nobility, and even the
Knights and Eſquires who had Lands, and
were call'd the Gentry, held them by ſer-
vile Tenures, as above : Now we ſee the
Nobility and the ancient Gentry have almoſt every where ſold their Eſtates, and the
Commonalty and Tradeſmen have bought
them : So that now the Gentry are richer
than the Nobility, and the Tradeſmen are
richer than them all.

I have given this Sketch of the growing
Wealth of the World by Trade, as in *England* ; that is, I have placed the Scene as in
England, becauſe being talking to the *Engliſh* Nation, it will be underſtood with the
more eaſe. But the Subject is general, and
the Thing is not of private Interpretation :
It will hold in its Degree, in all the
trading Nations of *Europe,* as well as here;
tho' perhaps in none more eminently, the
Trade here having made ſo viſible a Change
in

in the Face of the Nation, and in the Circumftances of the People, that the like is not to be fhewn of any other Nation, in fo very remarkable a Degree ; fo that if I had been Writing in any other Country or Language, I fhould certainly have fingled out *England* for an Example.

I may, however, refer to other Nations for Evidence in their Proportion, for in all the Manufacturing Countries in *Europe* the Cafe is the fame in Degree ; as Trade has encreas'd, the Miferies of the People have abated, the Poor being employ'd by Manufacture, by Navigation, and the ordinary Labours which Trade furnifhes for their Hands ; they have accordingly liv'd better, their Poverty has been lefs, and they have been able to feed, who before might be faid only to ftarve ; and in thofe Countries 'tis obfervable, that where Trade is moft effectually extended, and has the greateft Influence, there the Poor live beft, their Wages are higheft ; and where Wages are higheft, the Confumption of Provifions encreafes moft ; where the Confumption of Provifion is moft encreas'd, the Rate of Provifion is higheft ; and where Provifions are deareft, the Rents of Lands are advanc'd moft.

AGAIN, *for the Climax does not end here* ; where the Rents of Lands are advanc'd, the Taxes and Payments to the Governour are the larger ; and where the larger Taxes
are

are levy'd, the Revenue being encreafed, that Prince or Governour is the richer; and where Nations grow richer, they in Proportion grow more powerful.

THUS Trade is the Foundation of Wealth, and Wealth of Power: In former Days the Poverty of the northern Nations added to their Multitude, made them formidable; as the People encreas'd, the Country not being able to maintain them, the old ones drove the young ones out, as Bees caft their Swarms, to feek Place to dwell in, and by the force of their Arms, to make Room for themfelves in warmer Climates, and move in a more fruitful Soil. Thus the *Alani,* the *Gauls,* the *Hunns,* invaded *Italy;* the *Goths* overrun *Spain;* the *Vandals, Spain* and the Northern Parts of *Africa;* the *Thracians, Natolia* and *Macedonia,* and the like.

BUT in our Times, the Cafe alters univerfally, the Art of War is fo well ftudy'd, and fo equally known in all Places, that 'tis the longeft Purfe that conquers now, not the longeft Sword. If there is any Country whofe People are lefs martial, lefs enterprifing, and lefs able for the Field; yet, if they have but more Money than their Neighbours, they fhall foon be fuperior to them in Strength, for Money is Power, and they that have the *Gelt,* (as the *Dutch* call it) may have Armies of the beft Troops in *Europe,* and Generals of the greateft

Experi-

Exp.rience to fight for them at the fhort-
eft Warning imaginable; thus upon fudden
Quarrels, Princes and States do not now
go Home and raife Armies, and lift Men,
but they go Home and raife Money; and
that being done, they look abroad to hire
Armies, and hire Men, and even to entertain Generals; fo that they need never
bring any new raifed Troops into the Field,
but old *Veteran* experienc'd Soldiers, fuch
as *Swifs, Germans,* &c. well Officer'd,
and led on by the greateft Generals in the
World; fo that War is made in a trice, and
decifive Battles are fought now in fhorter
Time than Troops in former Times could
be brought into the Field.

THUS the *Venetians* have had their Generals *Shuylenbergh, Coningsmark, Baden,*
&c. to lead their Troops; the *Spaniards*
had their Marquis *de Lede*; the *Mufcovites*
their Duke of *Croy,* their Generals *Gordon,*
Konningfeck, &c. and Armies of *Danes,*
Pruffians, Lunenbergers, Saxons, Heffi-
ans, and *Bavarians,* and other *Germans,*
befides *Swifs* and *Grifons,* are to be hired
for Money, alternately to fight, for now
one Side, than another; I fay, *alternately,*
as the Perfons direct them whofe Money
they take; without Regard to Parties or
Interefts, either of Politicks or Religion,
tho' whether for or againft the Party or
Religion they profefs; to Day for Papift,

to

to Morrow for Proteſtant ; be it for God
or for *Baal*, as they're hired, they go

*And always fight according as they're
paid.*

THUS Money raiſes Armies, and Trade
raiſes Money ; and ſo it may be truly ſaid
of Trade, that it makes Princes powerful,
Nations valiant, and the moſt effeminate
People that can't fight for themſelves, if
they have but Money, and can hire other
People to fight for them, they become as
formidable as any of their Neighbours.

SEEING Trade then is the Fund of
Wealth and Power, we cannot wonder that
we ſee the wiſeſt Princes and States anxious and concerned for the Encreaſe of the
Commerce and Trade of their Subjects,
and of the Growth of the Country ; anxious to propagate the Sale of ſuch Goods
as are the Manufacture of their own Subjects, and that employs their own People ;
eſpecially, of ſuch as keep the Money of
their Dominions at Home, and on the contrary, for prohibiting the Importation from
Abroad, of ſuch Things as are the Product
of other Countries, and of the Labour of
other People, as which carry Money back
in Return, and not Merchandize in Exchange.

NOR can we wonder that we ſee ſuch
Princes and States endeavouring to ſet up
ſuch

such Manufactures in their own Countries, which they see are successfully and profitably carried on by their Neighbours, and to endeavour to procure the Materials proper for setting up those Manufactures by all just and possible Methods from other Countries.

HENCE we cannot blame the *French* or *Germans* for endeavouring to get over the *British* Wool into their Hands, by the help of which they may bring their People to imitate our Manufactures, which are so esteem'd in the World, as well as so gainfull at Home.

NOR can we blame any foreign Nation for prohibiting the Use and Wearing of our Manufacture, if they can either make them at Home, or make any which they can shift with in their stead.

THE Reason is plain ; 'tis the Interest of every Nation to encourage their own Trade, to encourage those Manufactures that will employ their own Subjects, consume their own Growth of Provisions, as well as Materials of Commerce, and such as will keep their Money or Species at Home.

'TIS from this just Principle, that the *French* prohibit the *English* Woollen Manufacture, and the *English* again prohibit or impose a Tax equal to a Prohibition, on the *French* Silks, Paper, Linen, and several others of their Manufactures. 'Tis from the same just Reason in Trade, that we prohibit the

wear-

wearing of *East India* wrought Silks, painted Callicoes, &c. that we prohibit the Importation of *French* Brandy, *Brasil* Sugars, and *Spanish* Tobacco ; and so of several other Things.

I remember a Story told me by a Gentleman who liv'd many Years in *Muscovy*, where as weak and sordid a Nation as the *Russians* were, and how gross soever in their Politicks ; yet this Principle prevailed with them, as the Result of meer Nature in Trade : The Case was thus ;

AN *English* Man who had lived long in the City of *Casan* upon the *Wolga*, and was it seems concern'd in the great Salt Mines there, had observ'd with Regret, the great vast Luggage Boats, as we might call them, and which he call'd *Ballatoons*, carrying Goods by the River from *Astracan*, and from the *Caspian* Sea, and perhaps from *Persia* to *Muscow* ; these Boats as the Relater told me, carry'd a prodigious Burthen, from 100 Ton, to near twice as much ; but were unwieldy, heavy, ungovern'd Things, and requir'd as they might well do, a great many Hands to guide, and perhaps to tow them up against the Stream of that mighty River, and the Distance being above 1800 Miles too, they were in Proportion a long Time on the Voyage.

THE *English* Man fancy'd with himself, that he could contrive a kind of Vessel, that tho' it should not carry quite so much

Bur-

Burthen, fhould yet carry near 100 Ton, and fhould, by the help of Sails and good Management, perform the Voyage in much fhorter Time, and with much fewer People.

> *N. B.* THOSE Ballatoons it feems had each 100 to 110 or 120 Men employ'd in them to drag them along; and the *English* Man propofed to do the fame Work with 18 or 20 Men, and perform the Voyage in about one third of the Time.

BIG with this Project, and expecting to be very well accepted at Court, and rewarded too, away goes the *English* Man to *Mofcow*, where after fome Attendance, and making known to fome of the Boyars and great Men, that he had a Propofal to make to the Great Duke, that would be very much to the Advantage of their Country, and for the Advantage of the capital City, and the like, he obtain'd Audience, and lay'd the whole Scheme before his Majefty.

THE Grand Duke, for they did not then call him Emperor, took the Thing very readily, and at the fecond and third Audience, called him to him, and began to queftion him about feveral Particulars, but chiefly this : How many Men were employed in thefe Boats before ? And the *English* Man anfwer'd, 120.

AND how many will you perform it with, fays the Grand Duke.

EIGHTEEN

Eighteen or twenty Men at moſt, ſays the Projeċtor.

And how long Time are my Subjeċts performing the Voyage now? Says his *Ruſſian* Majeſty.

About four or five Months, ſays the *Engliſh* Man.

And how long will you perform it in? Says his Majeſty.

In about two Months, ſays the *Engliſh* Man.

Upon this the Great Duke ſtop'd, and look'd angrily; but ſeem'd to be muſing, as if he was calculating the Thing; after ſome Pauſe, he turns to the *Engliſh* Man, And what Country Man are you? Says his Ducal Majeſty.

An *Engliſh* Man, ſays the Projeċtor.

Very well ſays his Majeſty, 'tis well for you, that you are not one of my Subjeċts; do you come hither to ſet up Projeċts, to ſtarve my People? Get you gone forthwith, and with the utmoſt Expedition out of my Dominions upon pain of Death: You perform that Work with eighteen Men, which now one hundred and twenty Men are employ'd, and get their Bread by! What muſt the hundred and two Men do, that are to be turn'd out of their Buſineſs! Muſt they periſh and be ſtarv'd for want of Employment! Get you gone, adds his Majeſty, and ſee my Court no more; and immediately gave Orders for having him carry'd

ry'd away directly to *Novogorod*, on the
Frontiers of *Muſcovy*, towards *Livonia* and
the *Swediſh* Dominions, left he ſhould propagate ſuch dangerous Inventions, as ſhould
leſſen the Employment and Labour of his
Subjects.

THE Folly of this Conduct makes a kind
of Jeſt upon the People of *Moſcow* ; but
the Moral of the Fable, be it ſo or not, is
good ; 'tis certainly the Wealth and Felicity
of a Nation, to have the People fully employ'd for Wages, let that Wages be what
it will.

BY the ſame Rule, thoſe Nations are the
richeſt and wealthieſt, as well in general
as in particular, where the Labour of the
People, without Injury to the Government,
brings the moſt Money for their Work.

IT is certainly a wrong Maxim which
ſome People dogmatize ſo very much upon,
viz. that it is the general Intereſt of this
Nation to reduce the Price of their Manufacture.

IT is true, there are ſome old Notions which chime in with this Piece of trading Policy, *viz.* that Cheapneſs cauſes
Conſumption ; and that by underſelling o-
ther Nations, we ſhall carry away the Trade
from them ; and there is ſomething popular
in the Notion too : But it will not hold
in all Caſes, and particularly not in our
Manufacture.

FIRST,

First, I infist, that if you would re-duce the Price of our Manufacture, by re-ducing the Wages of the Poor, who are the Workers or Manufacturers, it is not poffible but that you will reduce the Value and Goodnefs of the Manufacture.

If you expect the Poor fhould work cheaper, and not perform their Work flight-er and more overly, as we call it, and fuper-ficially, you expect what is not in the Na-ture of the Thing.

Again, if you lower the Wages of the Poor, you muft of Courfe fink the Rate of Provifions, and that of Courfe will fink the Value of Lands, and fo you wound the Capital at once ; for the Poor cannot earn little and fpend much, the End of that is, ftarving and mifery ; the Rate of Provifions will follow the Rate of Wages, there is no poffibility of its being otherwife ; it has ever been fo, and ever will be fo, the Na-ture of the Thing requires it.

This therefore is beginning at the wrong End of Trade; but the true Way is, keep up the Goodnefs of your Manufacture, fo as to make it excel in Quality, and its ex-ceeding in Price will be no Deficiency in Trade.

Things are not dear or cheap, accord-ing as they fell for more or lefs; but accord-ing as the Price they fell for, bears a Pro-portion to the goodnefs or meannefs of the Goods fold. A high priz'd Manufacture

may

may be as cheap, as a low priz'd Manufacture of the fame Kind, according to the well or ill performing and finifhing the Work; as a fine Piece of Painting may be cheaper than a coarfer Piece of the fame Dimenfions, in Proportion to the Goodnefs of its Workmanfhip ; tho' one fhould be fold for one hundred Guineas, and the other for one hundred Shillings.

LET your Manufacture gain the Credit of the beft in the World of its Kind, it fhall accordingly bear the beft Price of any in the World, and yet be cheap too ; that is, it fhall be cheap of the Price, tho' not under Price.

I fhall fpeak more of this in its Place ; 'tis only hinted fuperficially here, to argue the great Advantage to a Nation, of having fuch an Employment for their Poor, as may make them not live only, but live comfortably. The poor *Mufcovite* Wretches who mann'd the Ballatoon with one hundred and twenty Men, liv'd on that Employ ; that is to fay, they did not immediately perifh ; but the Truth is, they might be faid to ftarve at it, not live at it.

BUT our labouring Poor really live, keep Families, pay Taxes, Scot and Lot, as we call it, wear good Cloths, eat the Fat, and drink the Sweet ; and yet, labour hard too. And this is not only the Glory of Trade in general, but of our Manufacture in particular ; nay, and is the Support of the

Manu-

Manufacture too; for by this means, the
Manufacture is kept up to its Price at Market; the Goodness being kept up at Home,
the Credit of it is kept up Abroad, and one
reciprocally is the Life of the other; the
Wages support the Manufacture, and the
Manufacture supports the Wages; by the
good Pay, the Weaver and all his Dependent Tradesmen are encourag'd to make
the Wares good, by the Goodness their
Credit Abroad is kept up, by the Credit
the Price, and by that Price the Wages;
one Hand washes *t'other Hand*, and both
the *Hands* the *Face*.

HENCE I insist also, that our Manufacture is the cheapest in the World, because
it is the best; and our Poor work as cheap
as any Poor in *Europe,* because their Work
is best perform'd: And this I shall prove
more particularly as I go on.

LET us therefore cease those narrow Notions in Commerce, or at least lay less
Stress upon them; that Cheapness causes
Consumption, may be allow'd in many
Things; but 'tis not a Rule without Exception, nor a Foundation to build upon in
every Case; it is true, in the Consumption
of Trash, and in the Consumption of Eatables and Drinkables: If good Wine was
to be sold at six Pence a Quart, instead of
two Shillings, or at three Pence a Pot, as
strong Beer, there would be much more
Wine drank than is now; but in Things of
Substance,

Subftance, weighty and durable, the Cafe many times alters, and it is a true old Proverb, *the beft is beft cheap.*

NEITHER is it true in every Article, that the Confumption of Quantity is the Profperity of Trade, unlefs it be alfo true, that fome Gain is made by the Trade: For Example, when our Gold Coin in *England*, was with the greateft Infatuation imaginable, advanc'd from twenty one Shillings and fix Pence, to thirty Shillings each Guinea, the fame Price being not in Proportion raifed in foreign Countries, the *Dutch, Germans, French*, and *Portugueze*, hurry'd over their Gold hither, coin'd it at forty *per Cent*. Profit, and immediately vefted it in our Produce and Manufacture. Had they gone on thus, and bought all the Woollen Goods, Corn, Tin, Lead, wrought Iron and Brafs, Sugar and Tobacco in *England*, as they would foon ha' done with Gold at fix Pound an Ounce, that Confumption of Quantity would ha' ruin'd the whole Commerce; for they would have ftagnated all our Markets Abroad, being able to fell twenty or thirty *per Cent*. cheaper than the *Englifh* Merchants, they would in fhort have carried away all our Quantity, and left us full of Gold, at a third of Price more than it was worth.

BUT this is not all; neither may the carrying off the Quantity of our Goods be always a Benefit, if the Price fhould be reduc'd below
low

low the Standard of our Trade : By the Standard of our Trade, I mean, the ſtated ordinary Rate of the Poors Labour. What Benefit is a great Conſumption of your Goods,   at a Rate with which the Merchant cannot gain, and the Maker cannot live? There is no Queſtion, but you may fell all the woollen Manufaĉure at this Time in the Nation, in three Months Time, if you will give them at an Abatement of twenty to thirty *per Cent.* upon the Value ; and ſo the Cheapneſs will certainly cauſe the Conſumption.

BUT what Gain would this be to the Commerce,   and what Advantage to the Trade in general ? Since you cannot replace the Quantity at that Price, and you cannot hold the Trade upon that Foot without falling into Circumſtances as ruinous to Trade,   as want of a Market ; namely, the finking Wages, finking Proviſions, and finking Land ; which, in a word, is a *finking Fund* in the literal Senfe.

A much better Way to ſupport Trade, is to fink your Quantity at Home, proportioning the Quantity to the Conſumption, if you cannot proportion the Conſumption to the Quantity ; and you had much better have ſome of your People want Work, and ſeek Employment ſome other Way,   than to have all Hands at Work to no Profit : Of which alſo I ſhall ſpeak fully and at large in its Order.

UPON

Upon the whole, I infift, and doubt not to make it appear, (without any Impeachment of the old popular Notion, of Cheapnefs caufing Confumption;) That it is the true Intereft of any Trading People to keep up the Value, I mean the intrinfic Goodnefs of their Manufactures, to their juft Standard; and make them cheap by their real Worth, rather than by meer lowering the Price at the Expence of their Credit, and meerly to bring them to a low Rate at the Market.

I infift, that this keeping up the Credit of a Manufacture, by its intrinfic Worth, is the only Profperity of a national Production, by which the People that make it are enrich'd, and the Nation they live in made profperous and powerful.

It is apparent in the Manufactures of *China, India* and other Eaftern Countries, they have, it is true, the moft extended Manufacture, and the greateft Variety in the World; and their Manufactures pufh themfelves upon the World, by the meer Strefs of their Cheapnefs, which according to the Principle mentioned above, caufes their Confumption.

But then look back to the Country or Countries from whence they come, and there you fee the Confequence moft evident; the People who make all thefe fine Works are to the laft Degree miferable, their Labour of no Value, their Wages would fright us to talk of it, and their way of Living

ving raife a Horror in us to think of it:
Their Women draw the Plough inftead of
Horfes; their Men perifh and fink under the
Weight of their heavier Labour, becaufe the
Food they eat is not of fufficient Nourifh-
ment to fupport them, and the Wages they
get cannot provide better Food for them;
and yet their rigorous Task-mafters lafh them
forward as we (cruelly too) fometimes do
our Horfes.

MONS. *Niuenhoff* in his Defcription of
China gives fuch an Account of the Mifery of
the poor People dragging, or as we call it, tow-
ing the Boats up the Stream of the royal Canal
there, the greateft in the World; and how
their Drivers, like our Carters, whip them
on till the poor exhaufted Creatures drop
down and die under the Labour of it : I
fay, he gives fuch an Account as would
make the Heart of a merciful Man bleed to
think of it; and the utmoft of their Wages
for all this Labour does not, as I can calculate it, amount to fo much as 2 *d.* a Day
Sterling in *England;* and the like no doubt
is the Cafe in their Manufacture in Proportion.

IF then thefe Gentlemen, who are for
forcing the Confumption of our Manufacture in *England,* (or in any of thofe Countries in *Europe* where they work cheapeft,)
by their meer Cheapnefs, are content to reduce the Wages of the People that make
them, to the Rate of thofe in *China* or in
India,

India, there is no doubt they might encreafe the Confumption, and fell off the
Quantity ; but what would be the Advantage ? They would fell their Goods and ruin
their People ; the Benefit of which in the
Grofs, I confefs I do not underftand.

I fhall fpeak of all this again, as it more
particularly relates to our Commerce in
England; and therefore I only mention it
here, as this Notion of reducing the Price
of the Manufacture is received, for a general Principle in Commerce, and apply'd
by Miftake to particular Cafes.

THERE is an Exception in the Article of
Wages, which may be brought here againft
what I have advanc'd above as to *England*,
viz. that we give the higheft Wages to our
Poor, of any Nation in the World ; and
it may be thought I have either for-
got, or am ignorant of the high Wages
given in the *European* Colonies in *America*, as well *Englifh*, as *French, Spanifh,
&c.* where a Piece of Eight, or rather five
Shillings, and in *Jamaica*, fix to feven
Shillings *per* Day, is given to Handicrafts,
and labouring People for their Work ; and
where the Price of Slaves is rifen within
thefe few Years, from twenty Pound a
Head, to thirty and forty Pound, on the
meer Account of the Dearnefs of Wages.

BUT this is explain'd, and fully anfwered in few Words ; namely, that the Dearnefs of Wages there, is occafioned by two
things

Things, *viz.* the Dearnefs of Provifions, and the want of People; the Dearnefs of Provifions in the Iflands, and the want of People in the Colonies on the Continent ; and let any Man of Experience calculate the Proportion of thofe Things, and he will find that in a due Equality or Proportion to the Dearnefs of Living, the Wages are as cheap there as here, and in fome Articles rather cheaper ; the particular Examination of it, I refer to its proper Place.

Upon the whole, to fum it up in a few Words, Trade is the Wealth of the World; Trade makes the Difference as to Rich or Poor, between one Nation and another ; Trade nourifhes Induftry, and Induftry begets Trade ; Trade difperfes the natural Wealth of the World, and Trade raifes new Species of Wealth, which Nature knew nothing of : Trade has two Daughters, whofe fruitful Progeny in Arts may be faid to employ Mankind ; namely,

MANUFACTURE,
And
NAVIGATION.

See how they unite their Powers to do good to the World, and to teach Men how to live happy and comfortably ; let us fee, I fay, how thefe two join, and that in the only Means of living comfortably,

I mean

I mean Diligence, for a Life of Sloth and Idleneſs, is not Happineſs or Comfort; Employment is Life, Sloth and Indolence is Death ; to be buſy, is to be chearful, to be pleaſant ; to have nothing to do, is all Deje&tion, diſpiriting, and in a word, to be fit for nothing but Miſchief and the Devil.

MANUFACTURE ſupplies Merchandize.

NAVIGATION ſupplies Shipping.

MANUFACTURE is the Hoſpital which feeds the Poor.

NAVIGATION is the Nurſery which raiſes Seamen.

MANUFACTURE commands Money from Abroad.

NAVIGATION brings it Home.

MANUFACTURE loads the Ships out.

NAVIGATION loads them in.

MANUFACTURE is Wealth.

NAVIGATION is Strength.

To conclude, Manufa&ture for Employment at Home, and Navigation for Employment Abroad, both together, ſeem to ſet all the buſy World at Work ; they ſeem to joyn Hands to encourage the induſtrious Nations, and if well managed, infallibly make the World rich.

O F

OF THE

TRADE

OF

ENGLAND

In Particular.

Chap. II.

HEN I fpeak of the Trade of *England* in particular, as in the Title of this Chapter, I claim to to be underftood, not in too narrow and confin'd a Senfe, as if I meant it meerly of *England* abftracted; limited to its geographical Dimenfions, and that little Spot within the Lines of its Situation, as it appears on the Surface of the Globe, which is little indeed.

But I am to be underftood in the Language of Trade; and fo the Trade of *England* is the Trade of all the Places within the Dominions of *England*; or, as it is ufually

ally

ally exprefs'd, the Countries fubject to the *Englifh* Government.

I am not at all fond of that modern af-fum'd Stile, by which fome Authors think they do us an Honour, when they call the extended fcattered Colonies and Do-minions of the *Englifh* or *Britifh* Nation, *the Englifh Empire*: I don't think they do His Majefty or the *Englifh* Nation any Honour at all by it; 'tis enough the King of *Great Britain* has the Opulence of an Emperor, without affecting or at all valu-ing the Title.

Not but that as the Humour of the World goes, I believe in a few Ages more all Degrees of Men, or at leaft many of them, will advance their Plumes, and cock their Feathers, in proportion as their Pride increafes, in all the Nations about us, and that as the Counts and Princes are in-creafed in feveral Nations already, even to a Scandal; fo they will go on.

Thus in Time the Counts may be Dukes, the Dukes Princes, the Princes be Kings, and the Kings Emperors; in a Word, 'tis not improper, as we are talking of Trade, to obferve how Honour is become a Mer-chandize, Nobility grows cheap, and Dig-nities come to Market upon eafy Terms in the World; and what with the Church Politicks on one Hand, and State Politicks on the other, the World may in a few Years be overrun, not with real Honours, but

but with Titles. Honour blooms and runs to Seed; (I mean Abroad, not in *England*) and Titles without Merit are the Scandal of the World. But of this hereafter.

But I return, The Trade of *England*, *I say*, is the Trade of the *English* Dominions, the Commerce of the Countries subject to the *English* Government, particularly, 1*st*, The Trade of *Great Britain* and *Ireland*. And, 2*dly*, The Trade of the *English* Colonies and Factories in *America*, *Asia*, and *Africa*; These all put together, make the Trade of *England*.

When I come to speak of the general Commerce of the Subjects of *England*, in other Countries, where they are said to trade as Merchants, not to be possest of the Country in Sovereignty ; that is quite another Thing, and will be discoursed of in another Manner, for we must always distinguish between the Trade of a Country, and the Dealings of the People, by Correspondence in other Countries; and I shall take Care to preserve that Distinction, as Justice requires, on all Occasions as we go on.

The Trade of *England* is one Thing, the Trade of the *English People* is another ; the first is confin'd to the Place, the second is carried on by the Persons ; however, and wherever they may be scattered, removed, and by Industry settled, as Occasion directs,

rects, in any or every Part and Country of the known World.

IT is true the Greatnefs and Opulence of the *Englifh*, as a trading Nation, is very confpicuous on this very Account, *viz.* that not only the Merchandize, but the Merchants alfo of our Nation, are found in all the trading Parts and Ports of the known World; and which is ftill more, they are placed there, and fupported by the Strength of their own Stocks, and the Value of the Merchandizes they carry thither, more than of the Goods they buy there.

IN fome parts of the World, indeed, they feem to be fettled and employed rather *to buy*, than *to fell*; as in the feveral Factories and trading Ports of *India*, at *Mocha*, at *Suratte*, the Bay of *Bengale*, and all the Coafts of *India* and *China*; but in moft of the other Parts of the World, we rather *fell* than *buy*; at leaft we trade equally both Ways, to the great Advantage of the *Englifh* Commerce in general, and of the Merchants in particular; as in *Turky, Italy, Spain*, the Coaft of *Barbary*, and the Kingdom of *Portugal*; the *Dutch*, the *German*, and the *Danifh* Coafts, the *Baltick*, and *Northern* Seas, &c.

IN all thefe Countries, the Growth and Product of our Lands and Seas, as mentioned already, and the Labour and Manufacture of our People are the principal
Subject

Subject of our Merchants Bufinefs; and what *they buy* in thofe Countries is the Return only, or rather in Part of the Return for thofe Goods, which to our great Advantage they firft carried thither, and fold in thofe Markets; the Overplus or Ballance being made good, according to the Nature of Things, and of the Country, feveral Ways; fome by Exchanges, fome in Specie, fome directly, fome from one Country to another, as we fhall fee in its Place.

BUT the Trade of *England* in particular, as diftinguifh'd above, and as we are to fpeak of it under the Title *of the Englifh Commerce,* is contain'd in thefe Generals.

1. THE Product and Manufacture of the Country, for Exportation into foreign Parts only.

2. THE Shipping and Navigation.

3. THE Home Confumption of our own Goods, and foreign Importations.

4. THE Employment of the People in Confequence of all thefe, and in the particular Works for the Management of them.

UNDER thefe four Heads, what an immenfe Weight of Bufinefs is carried on, or, as it is ordinarily exprefs'd, is managed in this Kingdom? How many Millions of People are kept in conftant Motion, Men, Women, and Children employ'd, Infants (fo they may properly be called) of five, fix and feven Years of Age, made capable

of

of getting their own Bread, and fubfifting by the Labour of their own Hands, and a prodigious Wealth, accumulated among the common People ? infomuch, that it it were caft up together, the Poor, that is to fay, fuch as were formerly counted among the Poor, I mean the Tradefmen, the Shopkeeping, trading and labouring Part of the People, have more real movable Wealth among them, than all the Gentry and Nobility in the whole Kingdom, not reckoning the real Eftates in Lands, Tenements, &c. of which they poffefs a furprizing Share alfo.

AND here it is worth our making a Stop, and reflecting a little on a moft confiderable Incident, in the *Englifh* Trade, and which is to be parallel'd in no Place that I know of in the World; namely that the Fund of our Trade in *England* is raifed wholly within it felf; it is a Kind of Peculiar to us, that all our Commerce is deriv'd from our felves : It is not fo in other Nations; the Trade of the *Hollanders* is all exotick; it confifts in meer Buying and Selling, Fetching and Carrying, and they export little or nothing, but what they firft import; even the Linnen which they are faid to make, they import moft of the Yarn (for it) from *Silefia* and *Saxony*, and the Flax for the reft from *Ruffia* and *Poland*.

THE *Dutch* buy to fell, the *Englifh* plant, dig, fheer, and weave to fell; not
only

only our Manufactures are our own, but almoft all the Materials of them are our own; I fay almoft, becaufe there are fome Exceptions, but they are not many.

In our Manufacture of Wool, all the Materials are our own, but the Oyl, and fome dye Stuffs, fuch as the Galls, the Indigo, the Cocheneal, and a few others; as to *Spanifh* Wool, it is an Extra, 'tis a Step out of the ordinary Way; moft of our Manufactures are, *and might be,* made without it.

In our Manufacture of *Hard Ware,* the Tin, the Lead, is our own; the Copper, and Iron are our own, except a part of the Iron from *Sweden* and *Spain,* and but a part: For in the Grofs, and in all our Foundaries of Iron, the Metal is our own.

In our Manufacture of Silk, it is true, the grand and fundamental Materials are foreign. But then, 1. The Silk Manufactures are but of late called our own; it is an Improvement, and it is within the Reach of our Memory, that we bought all our wrought Silks, a few Ribbands excepted, from Abroad, to the Value of near two Millions a Year; and it may not be long before an improving Nation, as we are, may raife the Silk at Home too, or at leaft in our Colonies, as well as other Countries have done, which had none before, *viz. France, Italy* and *Spain:* For 'tis well known, that *Italy* at firft, and *France* but lately, had no Silk of their own, but

brought

brought it all from *Turky* and *India:* As to our Product for Exportation, 'tis all our own, or of our Colonies, which is the same thing, such as,

Corn,	Lead,	Alloms,	Cotton,
Coal,	Fish,	Sugar,	Melasses,
Salt,	Drugs,	Tobacco,	Ginger,
Malt,	Copperas,	Peltry (Furs,)	Indigo,
Tin,	Rice,	Flesh	&c.

THESE as Exportations, being all our own, and being in themselves so vastly great, are the Fund of our Wealth, and the Encrease of our Numbers.

A People numerous and rich, necessarily make a great Home Consumption, as well of their own Growth, as of foreign Importations: And this is the Sum of the *English* Trade.

IT is no Boast, much less is it assuming to say, that we consume at Home the greatest Quantity of Foreign Product, but the least of Foreign Manufacture of any trading Nation in the World; the only foreign Manufactures we may be said to import wholly, is Linen and Paper, and Tin Plates; and yet those not wholly neither, tho' 'tis acknowledged they are chiefly imported.

Spain imports the Manufactures of other Countries more than we, but very little of their Growth and Produce, except Fish; the like is said of *France*, tho' they have

now

now fo great a Share of Manufacture of their own.

We import Gold, Silver, Wine, Brandy, Hemp, Pitch, Tar, Flax, Wax, Oyl, Iron, Steel, Fruit, Wool, Silk, Hair, Drugs, Dye Suffs, Salt-Peter, Tea, Coffee, Timber, Spice: All thefe and many more. But thefe are all the *Growth* and *Produce* of the Lands, not the Manufacture and Workmanfhip of foreign Countries: And all thefe we confume at Home in fuch Quantities, as are not to be equalled in any other Country.

But of the Manufacture of other Countries, we import very little, Linen excepted, Paper and Tin-Plates ; and of all thefe, except Tin-Plates we make now great Quantities at Home alfo : The Confumption of Wine and Linen in *England* is prodigious, and we import more than any fingle Nation in the World, notwithftanding a very great Quantity of the firft made at Home efpecially in *Scotland* and *Ireland*; as for Eaft *India* Manufactures, the Quantity now confum'd in *England* is fmall, and thofe that are, (*viz.*) the *Callicoes* may be efteem'd as Linen, being of the fame Species as to their Ufe.

But to bring it back to the firft Head as a Trade, the Trade of *England* confifts then in fhort,

Of

Of the greateſt Inland Pro-⎫
  duction Exported, and the⎬ of any Na-
  greateſt foreign Production⎪ tion in *Eu-*
  imported⎭ *rope.*

THE Exportation lays in a Stock of Wealth from Abroad, multiplies and enriches our People, and our People in general being in good Circumſtances, I mean the middling, trading, and induſtrious People, living tolerably well, their well-faring gives Occaſion to the vaſt Conſumption of the foreign, as well as home Produce, the like of which is not to be equalled by any Nation in the World ; the Particulars we ſhall enquire into in their Order.

How far the Multitudes of our People are encreaſed by theſe very Articles, and that to ſuch a Degree as is ſcarce conceivable, is worth our Enquiry, were it not too tedious for this Place. What populous Towns are rais'd by our Manufactures, from within few Years! how are our Towns built into Cities, and ſmall Villages (hardly known in ancient Times) grown up into populous Towns ! Let any one that is curious in ſuch Obſervations, take notice of the manufacturing Counties and Towns, the Sea Ports, and the Coaſt Counties, and compare them with the Counties where there are no Manufactures carried on, and where there being no part of the Land bordering

on

on the Sea, the Encreafe of Trade could not have that immediate Influence on them; and let them but obferve the Difference between thefe in the Numbers of great and populous Towns, the Throngs and Multitudes of People, and the ftill encreafing Greatnefs of the Towns that were larger before.

L E T them fee how the People gather about the Manufacture, how they crowd into the clothing Countries, however barren and remote : And on the contrary, how thin of Inhabitants, compared to thofe populous Parts, tho' otherwife populous too, are the other Parts of the Country; fome of which are much more fruitful and fertile, the Soil richer, the Situation more agreeable, and the Air milder and wholfomer than thofe that are fo populous? But where the Trade is, there are the People, there the Wealth, there the great Markets, and the large Towns; and in a Word, there the ready Money : For it is the Trade that has made the common People rich, as Pride has made the Gentry poor.

W E L L might I fay, as in the foregoing Chapter, That it is a Scandal upon the Underftanding of the Gentry, to think contemptibly of the trading part of the Nation ; feeing however the Gentlemen may value themfelves upon their Birth and Blood, the Cafe begins to turn againft them fo evidently, as to Fortune and Eftate, that tho'
they

they fay, the Tradefmen cannot be made Gentlemen ; yet the Tradefmen are, at this Time, able to buy the Gentlemen almoft in every part of the Kingdom.

AND let me add, were it not for two Articles, by which the Numbers of the Families of Gentlemen are recruited when leffened by Fate and Folly, and reftored when funk and decayed, and both by Trade, this Nation would, in a few Years, have very few Families of Gentlemen left; or, at leaft, very few that had Eftates to fupport them.

1. THE ancient Families, who having wafted and exhaufted their Eftates, and being declin'd and decay'd in Fortune by Luxury and high Living, have reftor'd and rais'd themfelves again, by mixing Blood with the defpis'd Tradefmen, marrying the Daughters of fuch Tradefmen, as being overgrown in Wealth, have been oblig'd, for want of Sons, to leave their Eftates to their Female Iffue; we find innumerable Families not of Gentlemen only, but even of the Nobility of the higheft Rank, have reftor'd their Fortunes by fuch Heireffes, and by fuch Matches, to the Degree of 50, to 100 and 150 Thoufand Pounds at a Time.

2. AS thus the decay'd Eftates of the Nobility and Gentry have been reftored, and their Family Wounds heal'd by the Daughters of the richer Tradefmen ; fo on the

the other Hand, by the Tradefmen themfelves, or by their Sons, the Numbers of the Families of the Gentry have been recruited, when funk quite out of Rank, and loft in Poverty and Diftrefs:

Families are as effectually extinct, and loft, and as much forgotten, when the Heirs are left in Mifery and Poverty, and the Eftate fold from them, as if they were funk into the Grave. I could inftance at this Time, in a Family, who once flourifh'd within a few Miles of this City, the eldeft Son a Baronet without Bread, wears a red Coat without a Commiffion, and goes in a difguifed Name, that he may not have a SIR tack'd upon his Rags, and have his Honour be an Addition to his Mifery: The Children that are young, are kept upon Charity, and the grown Daughters go to Service, from a Coach and four Hories.

The Eftate (of one thoufand eight hundred Pound *per Annum*) is purchafed by a Citizen, who having got the Money by honeft Induftry, and perfuing a profperous Trade, has left his Books and his Warehoufes to his two younger Sons, is retir'd from the World, lives upon the Eftate, is a Juftice of Peace, and makes a compleat Gentleman: His eldeft Son bred at the Univerfity, and thoroughly accomplifh'd, is as well receiv'd among the Gentry in the County, and upon the valuable Fund

of

of his true Merit, as if he had been a Gentleman by Blood for a hundred Generations before the Conqueft.

I might add here, that it would be worth the while for thofe Gentlemen, who talk fo much of their antient Family Merit, and look fo little at preferving the Stock, by encreafing their own : I fay, it would be worth their while to look into the Roll of our Gentry, and enquire what is become of the Eftates of thofe prodigious Numbers of loft and extinct Families, which now even the Heralds themfelves can hardly find ; let them tell us if thofe Eftates are not now purchafed by Tradefmen and Citizens, or the Pofterity of fuch ; and whether thofe Tradefmens Pofterity do not now fill up the Vacancies, the Gaps, and Chafmes in the great Roll or Lift of Families, as well of the Gentry, as of the Nobility themfelves ; and whether there are many Families left, who have not been either reftored *as in our firft Head,* or fupply'd, *as in the fecond,* by a Succeffion of Wealth, and new Branches from the growing Greatnefs of Trade.

TRADE, in a word, raifes antient Families when funk and decay'd : And plants new Families, where the old ones are loft and extinct.

I dare oblige my felf to name five hundred great Eftates, within one hundred Miles of *London,* which within eighty

eighty Years paſt, were the Poſſeſſions of the antient *Engliſh* Gentry, which are now bought up, and in the Poſſeſſion of Citizens and Tradeſmen, purchaſed fairly by Money raiſed in Trade; ſome by Merchandizing, ſome by Shop-keeping, and ſome by meer Manufacturing; ſuch as Clothing in particular, of which Sort, notwithſtanding all that is, or has been ſaid of the Decay of our Manufacture, it is not difficult to find in the clothing and manufacturing Countries of *Wiltſhire* and *Glouceſterſhire*, many, (very many) Clothiers, worth forty to fifty thouſand Pounds a Man, and ſome of them worth from five hundred to one thouſand Pound *per Annum*, Eſtates in Land, beſides their Stock in Buſineſs; whoſe Poſterity will never be reproach'd with their being upſtart Gentlemen, or be thought Mechanick, for being of the Blood of a Clothier.

But to return to the populous Towns rais'd by theſe Manufactures, let the curious examine the great Towns of

Mancheſter,	*Leeds,*	*Froom,*
Warrington,	*Wakefield,*	*Taunton,*
Maccclesfield,	*Sheffield,*	*Tiverton,*
Hallifax,	*Birmingham,*	

and many others.

Some of theſe are meer Villages; the higheſt Magiſtrate in them is a Conſtable, and

and few or no Families of Gentry among them; yet they are full of Wealth, and full of People, and daily encreafing in both; all which is occafion'd by the meer Strength of Trade, and the growing Manufactures eftablifh'd in them; and of every one of them it may be faid, they have feverally more People in them, than the City of *York*; befides that, (as I have faid above) they are all vifibly and daily encreafing, which *York* is not.

From thefe which are all Inland Towns, let the fame curious Enquirer caft his Eye upon fome of our Sea-Port Towns, where Trade flourifhes, as well foreign Trade, as home Trade, and where Navigation, Manufacturing, and Merchandize feem to affift one another, and go Hand in Hand to encreafe both the Wealth and the People: Few Cities in *England*, *London* and *Briftol* excepted, can equal them; and in Time, fome of them bid fair to be fuperior to even *Briftol* it felf; fuch as

Yarmouth,	*Hull*,	*Plymouth*,
Leverpool,	*New-caftle*,	*Whitehaven*,
Colchefter,	*Lyn*,	*Biddeford*,
Deal,		and feveral others.

How are all thefe Towns raifed by Trade, and the Numbers of their Inhabitants drawn to them by the Employment, and confequently the Money which Trade
fpreads

ſpreads and diffuſes ſo liberally among the People.

But this is not all ; let the curious Enquirer travel a little farther, and look into the Countries adjacent to theſe Towns, and there they will ſee a manifeſt Difference in the very Face of Things, where the Manufactures are ſettled and carry'd on ; they ſhall ſee the Villages ſtand thick, the Market Towns not only more in Number, but larger, and fuller of Inhabitants ; and in ſhort, the whole Country full of little End-ſhips or Hamlets, and ſcattered Houſes, that it looks all like a planted Colony, every where full of People, and the People every where full of Buſineſs.

Let them view the County of *Devon,* and for 20 Miles every Way round the City of *Exceſter,* where the Trade of Serges is carry'd on.

The County of *Norfolk,* and for as many Miles every Way about the City of *Norwich,* where the Stuff-weaving is carry'd on.

The County of *Eſſex,* for near 40 Miles every Way, where the Bay-making Trade is carry'd on.

The County of *Wilts,* thro' that whole flouriſhing Vale, from *Warminſter* South, to *Malmsbury* North incluſive, and all the great Towns of *Bradford, Troubridge, Weſtbury, Tedbury, Froom,* and the *Devizes,* &c. where the Manufacture of fine
Spaniſh,

Spanish, and Medley-Clothing, and Drug-get-making is carry'd on.

The Counties of *Gloucester* and *Worcester*, from *Cirencester* and *Stroudwater*, to the City of *Worcester*, where the White-Clothing Trade, for the *Turkey* Merchants is carry'd on.

The Counties of *Warwick* and *Stafford*, every Way round the Town of *Birmingham*, where the Hard-Ware Manufacture and Cuttlery Trade is carry'd on; as also about *Coventry*.

The Counties of *Yorkshire* and *Lancashire*, round about, and every Way adjacent to the great Manufacturing Towns of *Manchester*, *Sheffield*, *Leeds* and *Hallifax*, where the known Manufactures of Cotton-ware, Iron-ware, *Yorkshire*-Cloths, Kersies, &c. are carry'd on.

In all these, and many others which might be mention'd, how infinitely populous is the Country? *not to say how rich*; how thick the Towns, how full the Markets, how stor'd with People are the Villages, and even the open Country! in so much, that in the Parish or *Vicaridge* of *Hallifax* alone, they reckon up sixteen Chapels of Ease, and an hundred thousand Communicants, besides fourteen or fifteen Meeting-houses, the People of all which live at large, scatter'd and spread over Hill and Dale, (for 'tis a mountainous Country) as the Convenience of Water, Coal,

Coal, and other Things proper to their Manufacture obliges them ; fo that the whole Parifh, which is a Circle of twelve Miles diameter, is, as before, like a planted Garden, or a Colony where every Family lives as it were within it felf, and by it felf, for the propagating their Bufinefs ; and where, tho' the whole Country is infinitely populous, yet, if you pafs in the middle of the Day thro' the Villages, and by the ftraggling Houfes on the Road, you fhall hardly fee any Body to ask the Way of : But if you go in the Evening, after working Hours, you are furpriz'd at the Multitude of the People every where to be feen.

Having taken a View of thefe Countries, let the fame Perfon take a Tour through thofe few Counties in *England*, where Trade has the leaft Concern, and where the Inhabitants confift chiefly of Landlord and Tenant, the Gentry and Husbandmen; and tho' there you fee no want of needful People to cultivate the Ground, or to difpatch the neceffary Labours of the Place; yet the Face of Things differs extremely, and the following Particulars difcover it.

1. The Market Towns are few and fmall, compar'd with fuch as I have nam'd, and compar'd with the general Bulk of the fmaller Towns, not fit to rank with thofe great ones nam'd ; nay, the Villages in thofe manufacturing Countries, are equal to the Market Towns in thefe.

2. The

2. THE Villages are diftant and remote, fmall and thinly inhabited ; and as for the open Country, you fee here and there a Farm-houfe, and a Cottage indeed, but nothing like the numerous Dwellings which fpread the enclofed Counties mention'd above, and where the Roads as you travel are like one continued Street, for fometimes twenty or thirty Miles together, and full of Inhabitants.

3. IN thefe unemploy'd Counties, you fee the Women and Children idle, and out of Bufinefs ; thefe fitting at their Doors, and thofe playing in the Streets ; even in the Market Towns, and the moft populous Villages, where they might be fuppofed to be employ'd, the Poor by the Rich, yet there 'tis the fame, much more in the fingle fcattering Villages, where they have no Bufinefs but their own.

WHEREAS, in the manufacturing Counties, you fee the Wheel going almoft at every Door, the Wool and the Yarn hanging up at every Window ; the Looms, the Winders, the Combers, the Carders, the Dyers, the Dreffers, all bufy ; and the very Children, as well as Women, conftantly employ'd.

4. As is the Labour, fo is the Living ; for where the Poor are full of Work, they are never empty of Wages ; they eat while the others ftarve ; and have a tolerable Plenty ; while in the unemploy'd
Coun-

Counties it goes very hard with them:
And whence is all this? Look to the
Lands, and confequently to the Eftates of
the Gentry, the manufacturing Counties
are calculated for Bufinefs, the unemploy'd
Counties for Pleafure; the firft are throng'd
with Villages and great Towns, the laft
with Parks and great Forrefts; the firft are
ftored with People, the laft with Game; the
firft are rich and fertil, the laft wafte and
barren; the diligent Part of the People are
fled to the firft, the idler Part are left at the
laft; in a Word, the rich and thriving
Tradefmen live in the firft, the decaying
wafting Gentry in the laft.

THE Product of the firft, tho' improv'd
by Diligence and Application, is all confumed among themfelves; the Product of
the laft, tho' not half what it might be, is
carried away for want of Money to the
Markets of the firft; *the firft* eat the Fat
and the Kernel of all, and enjoy the Soft, being by their Diligence made able to buy it;
and *the laft* eat the Husk, the courfe, and
the hard; pinch, and live miferable, being
without Employment, except meer Drudg-
ing, and confequently without Money.

THE Reafon of the Thing anfwers for
it felf; a poor labouring Man that goes a-
broad to his Day Work, and Husbandry,
Hedging, Ditching, Threfhing, Carting,
&c. and brings home his Week's Wages,
fuppofe at eight Pence to twelve Pence a
Day

Day, or in fome Counties lefs; if he has
a Wife and three or four Children to feed,
and who get little or nothing for themfelves, muft fare hard, and live poorly;
'tis eafy to fuppofe it muft be fo.

But if this Man's Wife and Children
can at the fame Time get Employment, if
at next Door, or at the next Village
there lives a Clothier, or a Bay Maker, or
a Stuff or Drugget Weaver; the Manufacturer fends the poor Woman comb'd
Wool, or carded Wool every Week to
fpin, and fhe gets eight Pence or nine
Pence a Day at home; the Weaver fends
for her two little Children, and they work
by the Loom, winding, filling Quills, &c.
and the two bigger Girls fpin at home with
their Mother, and thefe earn three Pence
or four Pence a Day each: So that put it
together, the Family at Home gets as
much as the Father gets Abroad, and generally more.

This alters the Cafe extremely, the Family feels it, they all feed better, are
cloth'd warmer, and do not fo eafily nor
fo often fall into Mifery and Diftrefs; the
Father gets them Food, and the Mother
gets them Clothes; and as they grow,
they do not run away to be Footmen and
Soldiers, Thieves and Beggars, or fell
themfelves to the Plantations, to avoid
the Goal and the Gallows, but have a

Trade

Trade at their Hands, and every one can get their Bread.

N. B. I once went through a large populous manufacturing Town in *England*, and obferv'd, that an Officer planted there, with a Serjeant and two Drums, had been beating up a long Time, and could get no Recruits, except two or three Sots, who they had drawn in to be drunk, and fo lifted when they were not themfelves, and knew not what they did.

Enquiring the Reafon of it, an honeft Clothier of the Town anfwered me effectually thus, *The Cafe is plain,* fays he, thus, there is at this Time a brisk Demand for Goods, we have 1100 Looms, *added he,* in this Town, and the Villages about it, and not one of them want Work; and there is not a poor Child in the Town of above four Years old, but can earn his own Bread; befides, there being fo good a Trade at this Time, caufes us to advance Wages a little, and the Weaver and the Spinner get more than they ufed to do; and while it is fo, they may beat the Heads of their Drums out, if they will, they'll get no Soldiers here; but let them come when Trade is dead, and the People want Work, and they may get Soldiers enough; the Gentleman

Officer

Officer took the Hint, and went off with his Drums, to try his Luck in the Counties where there was no Manufacture, and there he pick'd up young Fellows enough, where they were Poor and Proud, Idle and Lazy, as among the Farmers, Horfe-Breakers, Gentlemens Servants, &c.

IN a Word, 'tis Poverty and Starving that fills Armies, not Trade and Manufacturing; and therefore the *Swifs* and the *Grifons,* the *Danes,* and the *Lunenburghers,* the *Heffians,* and the *Pruffians,* are glad when they hear the Drums beat, and rejoice when other Nations will hire their Troops, and entertain their Men for Soldiers; for their Numbers are their Grievance: And for the fame Reafon, the *Scots* and the *French* are found difperfed over all the Nations of *Europe,* and indeed of the World, to feek Employment, either as Soldiers or Slaves (that is Servants) merely for want of Entertainment at Home; whereas on the other Hand, in *England,* in *Holland,* and *Flanders,* where the People have Manufacturing, and are well employ'd at Home, nothing is more difficult than to raife Men upon any extraordinary Occafion; it was found fo here, in the late War with *France,* after a few of the firft Campaigns had carried off the loofe Fellows that a long Peace had left among us; then they were oblig'd to make Acts of

Par-

Parliament to empower the Juſtices to ſend away all the poor Fellows they could pick up, and force them into the Service.

Nor would this do neither; in the next Reign the War being renewed, Men were ſo hard to be had, the Queen was oblig'd to hire Troops from all the neighbouring Princes, to form her Armies; ſuch as *Saxons, Heſſians, Danes, Lunenburghers,* and the like, few *Engliſh* could be had without the utmoſt Violence and Compulſion; even the *Scots* themſelves, what with Diſaffection, and better Buſineſs, were not able to ſupply any ſufficient Numbers; the Reaſon was plain; Trade flouriſh'd, the Manufactures were in Demand, the Merchants gave out large Orders, and the Men were full of Buſineſs: Indeed what poor Man in his Senſes, that could get nine Shillings, ten Shillings, and twelve Shillings a Week at his Loom, and at the Comb-Pot, or at the Clothworking, Dreſſing, *&c.* of the Manufactures, and live at home warm, eaſy, and ſafe, would go abroad and ſtarve in a Camp, or be knock'd on the Head on the Counterſcarp, at the Rate of three Shillings and ſix Pence a Week?

And here give me Leave to remind you of a Piece of Hiſtory recent in every Man's Head, and full to my Purpoſe. There was, one Year of the late War with *France,* a very terrible Scarcity of Corn throughout the whole Kingdom of *France,* ſuch a Scarcity,
that

that had it not been for the Merchants, who, as we might fay, rumaged the World for Corn, many Thoufands of People muft have perifh'd more than did, for many died of meer Want.

It happen'd that there having been three terrible Blows given to the *French* King the Year before, and his Armies having been routed on feveral great Occafions, as at the Relief of *Barcelona*, the Battle of *Turin*, and the Battle of *Ramellies* in *Flanders*, all in one Campaign, the King of *France* found himfelf greatly embarrafs'd with the Difficulty of recruiting his Armies, and it was the Opinion of moft of the Confederates, that the Fate of *France* was come; that the Fall of the *French* Empire was at Hand, for that his Armies were ruined, his Country threatned on all Hands, and his People ftarving, and ready to cut one another's Throats for Bread, fo that it feem'd impoffible for him to reftore his Troops.

In this Diftrefs the General Officers were almoft affraid to fpeak to the King, the old Monarch unacquainted with Misfortunes, was fo wayward, fo fretful, and fo full of Refentment, that none car'd to meddle with it, and yet they faw all was going to Wreck.

In the mean Time, the King publifh'd feveral Orders, and employ'd People, and iffued out Money every way for the amaffing Corn, from all the Quarters of the World; even

even from the outmoft Ports in the *Levant,*
to *Egypt,* to *Syria,* to *Cyprus,* to all the
Ifles of the Arches, to the *Gulph of Volo,*
to *Salonichi,* and even to *Conftantinople* it
felf, and great Quantities of Corn were procured, which the King gave exprefs Orders
fhould be brought into the publick Magazines, for the fupply of his Troops; but took
not the leaft notice, nor fpoke one Word
about raifing Men to recruit his Regiments,
and replace the many whole Brigades that
had been loft and cut off in the unhappy
Campaign that was paft; nor did he order
his Finnanciers or Paymafters to iffue out any
Money for the Supply of that important
Article, as he was always wont to do.

At laft, fome of the *Marefchals* of
France, who prefumed upon their great Intereft in his Favour, and were greatly concern'd at the dangerous delay, as they
look'd on it to be, refolv'd to move it to
him : *His Majefty* forefaw the Errand they
came about, but began with them plea-
fantly upon other Bufinefs, entertaining
them fo warmly with other Difcourfe, that
he gave them no Opportunity to fpeak a
Word about the main thing they came for,
namely raifing Recruits, and augmenting
his Troops, his Difcourfe ftill running another Way.

PARTICULARLY, *His Majefty* enquired of
them feparately, how the People far'd in
their Provinces, and in thofe Provinces
he

he knew were particularly under their Government, with Refpect to the want of Corn ; and all agreed, that the Mifery was inexpreffible, and that many of the poor People perifh'd for Want. *But,* fays the King, *How do my Troops fare? are the Orders I gave for fupplying my poor Soldiers put in Execution?* Yes Sir, *fays one of the Marefchals,* and *I think it was* Monfieur *Villeroy,* fuch of your Majefty's Armies as are lifted, are taken care of. *I underftand you,* fays the King, *I have given no Orders for Recruits, nor do I intend it till next Spring,* and with that fpoke again of the Corn, *Are my Magafins kept full?* fays the King. They anfwered, Yes, the Magafins were well fupply'd, and were all kept full.

The Officers were furprized at what *his Majefty* had faid about Recruits ; but fuch was the fiery Difpofition of the *auguft Tyrant,* that no body cared to make the leaft Reply to it ; but with a profound Submiffion went away, as acquiefcing with the King's Meafures, tho' they thought them the moft ridiculous in the World, and thought the King little better than ftupid, or lunatick.

At their going away, the King repeated his Orders to them, to take effectual Care that his Troops might be fupply'd with Corn out of the publick Magafins in all the Provinces where they were refpectively quartered, and told them he would have it
publifh'd

publish'd that this was his Order, *That so
says the King,* my good Soldiers shall know
that if they suffer any Want, it is not my
Fault, but the Fault of the *Mareschals* of
France.

Accordingly, publick Notice was given
in Print for the Encouragement of the Troops,
that the King had given express Orders, that
the Soldiers should be supply'd with Corn out
of the publick Magasins, and the Regiments,
whose Quarters were remote from the Magasins, were forthwith removed, so as to be
near those Magasins for their supply.

This was no sooner done, and that it
was every where known, that the Soldiers
had plenty of Bread, but the *Mareschals*
complimented the Wisdom of the King,
which they did not understand before; for
the poor starving Peasants run every where
to the Army, and lifted so fast, that tho' the
Army wanted near 80000 Men, the Troops
were fill'd up without any Expence, and
twenty new Regiments were raised by way
of Augmentation; and all this with a sur-
prising Expedition.

This Story abundantly confirms what I
have said, and for that Reason I told it, *viz.*
that Poverty and Want raises Soldiers. Trade
is a Friend to Peace, and provides for the People a far better Way: Trade sets them to work
for their Bread, not to fight for it; and if we
want Men in *England,* 'tis not that the
Number

Number is deficient, but becaufe they live too well to go for Soldiers.

THIS alfo confirms what has been faid above, namely, that as the trading, middling fort of People in *England* are rich ; fo the labouring, manufacturing People under them are infinitely richer than the fame Clafs of People in any other Nation in the World.

As they are richer, fo they live better, fare better, wear better, and fpend more Money, than they do in other Countries ; and I make no doubt 'tis the fame in fome other Places in their Proportion, as well as here ; at leaft, in free Nations, where the People are not affraid to own their Circum-ftances, and to appear in good Condition when they are in good Condition : In fhort, the Tradefmen in *England* live in better Figure than moft of the meaner Gentry ; and I may add than fome of the fuperior Rank in foreign Countries ; nay, not to magnifie Things here, and leffen them Abroad, it is very evident that we have Tradefmen or Shop-keepers, of very ordi-nary Employments in *London*, fuch as *Cheefe-mongers, Grocers, Chandlers, Brafiers, Vpholfterers*, and the like, who are able to fpend more Money in their Families, and do actually fpend more than moft Gentle-men of from 300 to 500 Pounds a Year, and that with this remarkable Addition, that the Tradefman fhall fpend it, and grow rich, and encreafe under the Weight of the

Ex-

Expence ; whereas the Gentleman fpends to the Extent of his Revenue, and lays up nothing.

How many Shop-keepers, Ware-houfe-keepers, and Wholefale Traders, (to go a Step higher) have we feen in *London*, fuch as Drapers, Iron-Mongers, Salters, Haberdafhers, *Blackwell-hall*, and other Factors, *&c.* who fhall fpend 500 Pound a Year in their Houfekeeping, and other Incidents, and lay up 500 Pound a Year more, while a Gentleman of a Thoufand Pound a Year Eftate, can hardly bring both Ends together at the clofe of the Year, and not live in a much better Figure than the Tradefman, and not at all in better Credit?

How do our Merchants in *London*, *Briftol*, *Liverpole*, *Yarmouth*, *Hull*, and other trading Sea-Ports, appear in their Families, with the Splendor of the beft Gentlemen, and even grow rich, tho' with the Luxury and Expence of a Count of the Empire ! fo true it is, that *an Eftate is* but *a Pond*, but *Trade is a Spring*.

But to look at the meaner People (for among them, generally, the Wealth of which I am now fpeaking is lodg'd, becaufe their Number is fo exceeding great) thofe, it is evident, are in *England* fupported after a different manner from the People of equal Rank in Trade among other Nations ; let any Man that has feen how the trading People, and the labouring Poor live

Abroad

abroad, make the Comparifon, it is too evident to be difputed.

IT is upon thefe two Claffes of People, the Manufacturers and the Shopkeepers, that I build the Hypothefis which I have taken upon me to offer to the Publick, 'tis upon the Gain they make either by their Labour, or their Induftry in Trade, and upon their inconceivable Numbers, that the Home Confumption of our own Produce, and of the Produce of foreign Nations imported here, is fo exceeding great, and that our Trade is raifed up to fuch a Prodigy of Magnitude, as I fhall fhew it is.

I need not defcribe it at large, a few Words will give a Sketch of it, and a great Volume will not line it out compleatly: They eat well, and they drink well; for their eating, (*viz.*) of Flefh Meat, fuch as Beef, Mutton, Bacon, &c. in Proportion to their Circumftances, 'tis to a Fault, nay, even to Profufion; as to their Drink, 'tis generally ftout ftrong Beer, not to take notice of the Quantity, which is fometimes a little too much, or good Table Beer for their ordinary Diet; for the reft, we fee their Houfes and Lodgings tolerably furnifhed, at leaft ftuff'd well with ufeful and neceffary houfehold Goods: Even thofe we call poor People, Journey-men, working and Pains-taking People do thus; they lye warm, live in Plenty, work hard, and (need) know no Want.

THESE

THESE are the People that carry off the Grofs of your Confumption; 'tis for thefe your Markets are kept open late on *Saturday* Nights; becaufe they ufually receive their Week's Wages late: 'Tis by thefe the Number of Alehoufes fubfift, fo many Brewers get Eftates, and fuch a vaft Revenue of Excife is raifed; by thefe the vaft Quantity of Meal and Malt is confumed: And, in a Word, thefe are the Life of our whole Commerce, and all by their Multitude: Their Numbers are not Hundreds or Thoufands, or Hundreds of Thoufands, but Millions; 'tis by their Multitude, I fay, that all the Wheels of Trade are fet on Foot, the Manufacture and Produce of the Land and Sea, finifhed, cur'd, and fitted for the Markets Abroad; 'tis by the Largenefs of their Gettings, that they are fupported, and by the Largenefs of their Number the whole Country is fupported; by their Wages they are able to live plentifully, and it is by their expenfive, generous, free way of living, that the Home Confumption is rais'd to fuch a Bulk, as well of our own, as of foreign Production: If their Wages were low and defpicable, fo would be their Living; if they got little, they could fpend but little, and Trade would prefently feel it; as their Gain is more or lefs, the Wealth and Strength of the whole Kingdom would rife or fall: For as I faid above, upon their Wages it all depends; the Price of Provifions depends

on

on the Confumption of the Quantity; upon
the Rate of Provifions the Rent of Lands,
upon the Rent of Lands the Value of Taxes,
and upon the Value of Taxes, the Strength
and Power of the whole Body: So that
thefe are originally the firft Spring of all the
Motion.

I n like manner it affects foreign Trade;
if the Poors Wages abate, the Confumption
of Quantity alfo, as above, would abate;
if the Quantity abates, the foreign Importation would abate, the Brandy, the Oyl,
the Fruit, the Sugar, the Tobacco: For if
the Poor have not the Money, they can't
fpare it for Superfluities, as thofe foreign
Articles generally are, but muft preferve
it for Neceffity; upon their Neceffity depends the Confumption of the ordinary
Food, which is the Home Produce; and
upon their Superfluity depends the Confumption of their Extraordinaries, which is
the foreign Importation.

E v e n the Wine, the Spice, the Coffee
and the Tea, after the Gentry have taken
the nice and fine Species off, are beholding to
the mean, middling and trading People to
carry off the coarfer Part, and the Bulk of
the Quantity goes off that way too: So that
thefe are the People that are the Life of
Trade.

T h e Silk Manufactures are indeed a
Branch, the chief part of which the Gentry
may be faid to fupport, and to help out
Trade

Trade in : As to the Linen, they take indeed the fineſt Hollands, Cambricks, Muſlins, &c. But the middling Tradeſmen break in upon them, and follow them ſo at the Heels, that 'tis to be queſtioned, whether, as the Humour runs now, the Tradeſmen by the help of Numbers do not out go them, even there alſo ; not to mention the vaſt Quantity of Linens of other Kind, which they conſume every Day, imported from *Ireland, France, Ruſſia, Poland* and *Germany.*

Having thus mention'd the Subſtance of our Trade, and the Support of it, it remains to examine a little the Magnitude of theſe ſeveral Branches, as well of Exportation, as of Importation, in Order to make this Diſcourſe be according to my Title, a true *Plan of the Engliſh Commerce ;* and here it is neceſſary to make ſome little Proviſos, againſt the too forward Expectation of the Reader, as to Numbers and Calculations, in which it may be impoſſible to go the Length which may be unreaſonably expected.

There are many Things in our Commerce, as well Abroad as at Home, in which no exact Calculation can be made ; and yet perhaps our Eſtimates and Conjectures may not be ſo remote as ſome may imagine, or ſo, as that no probable Proſpect, no rational View of the Commerce may be made from them ; *For Example,*

I r

It is not poffible to make any Calculation of the Number of Shop-keepers in
Great Britain, or of the Number of Spinners, or of the Quantity of Wool, or of
the Bulk of the woollen Manufacture ;
and yet, from what has been, and fhall be
faid, I doubt not, we fhall form juft and
rational *Ideas* in our Thoughts, of the
Greatnefs of our Manufacture, and of our
home Trade ; and fo of many other Things
which we cannot otherwife judge of, than
by fuch general Eftimates.

The World muft be left in the dark,
concerning many ufeful Parts of Knowledge,
if we were to take no Meafures, and form
no Ideas of Things from the Lights that
are given ; tho' it fhould be true, that thofe
Lights do not amount to Demonftrations ;
and efpecially, in Matters of this Kind,
where the Foundations are fubject to various Changes, and where the whole is rather Matter of Obfervation, than real Intelligence of Fact.

We may make an Eftimate of many
Branches of Trade, without being able to
determine the Dimenfions of either the
Subject on which thofe Branches are founded, or of the particular Parts themfelves:
We may make juft Eftimates of the Returns of Treafure from the *Spanifh Weft-
Indies,* without enquiring into the Fund
of that Treafure, (*viz.*) how many Mines
there are difcovered, in which the Silver is
found,

found, or how much every Mine that is
difcover'd produces ; and thus we may entertain a true Notion of the Magnitude
of woollen Manufacture, and of the great
Advantage of it to this Nation, without being able to know, to what Value the Return
of it amounts in a Year : We may give
an Account of its being able to confume
the whole Quantity of the Growth of our
Wool in *England,* and of much from *Ireland* ; and we may bring this in Evidence
of the Magnitude of the whole Trade,
without being able to caft up how much
that Wool amounts to, *and fo of the reft.*

We may venture to fay in Publick, that
we are a moft powerful Nation in Shipping,
having the greateft Number of Ships and
Seamen, of any Nation in the World, without being able to give a particular Account
how many Ships we have, or how many
Seamen we employ.

Upon the fame Foundation, 'tis reafonable to fay, we may judge of the Magnitude
of our Commerce in general, by the feveral Circumftances of the particular Branches ; *for Example,* the Encreafe of the
Confumption of fuch and fuch Goods imported, which are abfolutely requifite for
fuch or fuch a Manufacture, is a juft Meafure, by which to conclude the Encreafe of
that Manufacture : In other Cafes we may
have plainer Rules to judge from, and to
make our Eftimates by ; and yet, even thofe
Rules

Rules are not fuch, as that we can afcertain thofe Eftimates upon that Foot, becaufe of feveral Incidents in Trade, which cannot be accounted for, any more than they can be avoided.

WE may judge of the Confumption of Wines in *England*, becaufe they are all imported from Abroad, and we can have an exaƈt Account of the annual Importation from the Cuftom-houfe Books; but we cannot pofitively afcertain the Confumption from that Importation, becaufe, tho' all that are enter'd at the Cuftom-houfe, are imported and confum'd, yet all that are confum'd may not be enter'd at the Cuftom-houfe; clandeftine Trade, and fmuggling has a great Stroke in it; and the like of foreign Brandy: *Of both which hereafter.*

THUS again, we may judge of the Confumption of Spirits, by the Quantity of Malt diftill'd, and the Spirits of the firft Extraƈtion gaug'd by the Excife-Man; but clandeftine Concealments have fo great a Share in that Trade, that we can never fay our Calculations are exaƈt.

UPON the whole, if our Calculations and Guefles are rational and probable, we hope in thefe Cafes it may be allow'd to be fufficient, becaufe it is as far as any Man can go. The Commerce of *England*, is an immenfe and almoft incredible Thing, and as we muft content our felves with being in fome Cafes in a difficulty as to Numbers

bers and Figures ; but in all fuch Cafes, we expect the Reader will be content with the utmoft poffible Inquiry, and the utmoft poffible Difcovery that we are able to make, and with fuch Reafons as may be drawn from what appears, to judge of what cannot be fully difcover'd.

Of

CHAP. III.

Of the first Rise, Growth and Encrease of the COMMERCE *of* England.

 T is something difficult to adjust the Terms of our first Part of this Work, they are set down in general in our Title, *viz.* the Rise, Growth, and Encrease of our Trade; all which Words, as they imply a Progreſſion, they neceſſarily imply a ſtated Period, like an Epocha of Time, from whence the Motion might be ſaid to begin like the ſtarting Poſt, or Place of a Race, where all that run, ſet out exactly upon an Equality, whatever Advantage is obtain'd afterwards, being the Effect of the Strength and Vigour of the Racers, whether Horſes or Men.

I ſuppoſe all Nations had ſome Trade, and all People ſome Dealing with one another from the Begining; that is, ever ſince they began to converſe; when mutual Convenience guided them to enquire what they might either want from, or ſpare

to

to each other for the Supply of common Occafions.

BUT this would lead us back into dull Speculations of the Nature and Original of Commerce; a dry ufelefs Subject, and therefore carefully avoided in my Title, where it may be obferv'd, that I do not call this Work a Hiftory of Trade, or a Hiftory of the *Englifh* Trade; but a Hiftory of the *Rife*, *Growth*, and *Increafe* of it; by which I mean as above, from the Time, *let that Time be when you will*, when ftanding upon the Square with the reft of the World, *England* gave it felf a Loofe, and got the Start of all the Nations about her in Trade; and having held it ever fince, her Commerce is by that Means arriv'd to that Prodigy for Magnitude, which it appears in at this Time, and in which 'tis acknowledg'd by all her Neighbours, fhe out-does all the Nations in the World, as we fhall fee in the next Chapter.

How to fix this Period without running out into foreign Enquiries, and giving a State of Things tedious in themfelves, and remote from our Defign, is the Thing we are now to attend to; and tho' I fhall do it my own Way, and may differ from the Opinion of fome wifer than my felf; yet, I fhall endeavour to fupport my Opinion with fuch Reafons, as fhall bring over fuch differing Judgments to agree with me; or

I

I ſhall, for want of it, ſubmit to theirs ; ſo that either way the End will be anſwer'd, and the Magnitude and Encreaſe of the Commerce of *England* be confirm'd and deſcrib'd, and the Time of it aſcertain'd.

England being an Iſland ſurrounded with the Sea, and with neighbouring powerful Nations ; her Converſe in Peace, and at other Times her Wars with thoſe Nations, made Shipping in particular exceedingly neceſſary to her ; and we find upon many Occaſions, the *Engliſh* Fleets not only very numerous, but very formidable ; yet Hiſtory is very barren on that Occaſion, nor is there the leaſt Fragment to be gather'd up, that intimates to us, when, how, or in what manner this Nation began their Acquaintance with the Sea.

WE gather ſome Negatives indeed from Hiſtory, as to this Part ; we are pretty well aſſured, that the *Britains* had no Knowledge of Navigation, nor do we read of any Ships in Uſe among them, when *Julius Cæſar* landed here with a great Navy.

THAT the *Romans* had Ships, and that the *Britans* had none, or none conſiderable, will, I believe, be granted ; and as the *Romans* afterwards conquer'd and poſſeſs'd the Iſland, as is evident from Hiſtory, nothing then can be more natural, than to ſuppoſe, that the *Romans*
firſt

firſt introduc'd the Knowledge of Navigation, and the Uſe of Ships in this
Iſland.

It is true, and we are told it from Hiſtory, that the *Phænicians* traded hither ſeveral Ages before the *Romans*, and with
their beſt Ships, no doubt ; but be that
ſo or no, we do not find that the *Britains*
learn'd any thing from them.

The *Danes*, after this, came in great
Fleets, and ravag'd the Coaſts, both of
England and *Normandy ;* what their Ships
were, we know not ; but 'tis evident, they
were ſuch, as neither the *Britains* or *Saxons* could cope with ; ſo that even after
the *Romans* were gone, the Knowledge of
Shipping and Navigation ſeems to be much
ſunk and decay'd in *England,* and even in
this whole Part of the World ; for according to Mr. *Cambden,* the *Saxons* themſelves
came over in ſtrange Boats; that is to
ſay, in Boats or Veſſels, as we may ſuppoſe,
built of Wood ; that is, of Timber and
Boards, or Planks, and cover'd with a
kind of Tarpawlin, or Canvas dipt in Tar
and Oil, which being nail'd upon the Plank,
ſerv'd inſtead of Caulking, to keep out the
Water.

If this is true, the northern World, who
at this Time ſo much out-do the reſt of
the Nations in the navigating Skill, came
very late into the Knowledge, either of
building

building of Ships, or of managing them when built.

THE *Danes,* we may suppofe, had better Veffels, tho' not fuch as would now deferve the Name of Ships, and were neither fit for Fight or Freight, for War or Trade ; only prepar'd to waft over a Parcel of Thieves and Rovers, who came in a defperate manner, to fight, plunder and deftroy, without any View or Defign of returning; and therefore, when they burnt their Ships, as fometimes they did, and fometimes the *Britains* or *British Saxons* rather did for them, they had no great Lofs, for fending but one Veffel Exprefs to *Norway,* or to the Coaft of *Juitland,* they prefently had as many more as they pleafed; but all this while, here was no Shipping for Trade, no nor much Bufinefs for Shipping, if they had been furnifh'd with Veffels to be employ'd.

ON the contrary, what Commerce there was carry'd on at that Time between *Britain* and any other Countries, the Particulars of which, it is very hard to know, was certainly carry'd on in foreign Bottoms, till the Encreafe of Commerce brought the *English* to build Ships, or the Encreafe of Shipping brought the Commerce ; take it which Way we will, one is as probable as the other.

IT is true, that *Julius Cæfar* tranfported his Army over hither in Ships and Gallies,

lies, from the Coaft of *France*, from *Gaul* as he calls it in his Commentaries ; but 'tis as true by the fame Commentary, that he caufed thofe Ships to be built by his own People, I mean, *Romans;* for we do not find that the *Gauls*, any more than the *Britains*, had any Ships before.

HE built the Ships it is faid in about two Months, fo that they could not be very great; and he tells fomething of it himfelf, that for the Gallies, when they were landed in *Britain*, they haul'd them up upon the Beach : What Ships were employ'd for Commerce, we cannot tell ; yet there was fome Trade at that Time too ; for *Cæfar* fays, the *Britains* had Intelligence of his Defign to invade them, by Merchants who frequented their Coafts : See *Cæf. Com.* Lib. IV. Cap. 9. But all this leaves us in the Dark, either as to their Commerce, or their Navigation ; what they traded in, or what Veffels they traded with ; 'tis certain, the *Britains* had very little Trade, and lefs Shipping, for we read of none of their Ships for many Ages afterward.

WHETHER therefore in fucceeding Ages, Navigation introduc'd Trade, or Trade Navigation, is a Difpute not much material here ; 'tis probable it may ftand thus, *(viz.)* Neceffity produc'd the Converfe of Nations one with another, for the Supply of their mutual Wants, exchanging the

Produce

Produce of their refpective Countries, as their Wants feverally directed.

THIS exchanging of the Produce of Countries, produced Commerce or Trade.

TRADE thus explain'd, neceffarily required a *Voiture* or Carriage of Goods, by Land or by Water ; the latter requir'd Veffels to carry them in, either to fail or to row, and this is Navigation.

IF I was to write a Hiftory of Navigation, I fhould go back here to the firft Invention of Boats to row, of which they tell us the *Phænicians* were the Inventers; and of Sails to make ufe of the Wind, of which they tell us the Fable of *Dedalus* and *Icarus* is a Reprefentation, *viz.* that *Dedalus* being a Prifoner at *Cyprus,* contriv'd a Sail to his Boat, and taking his Opportunity when the Wind blew frefh from the Shore, put boldly out to Sea in the Sight of all the People ; his Son *Icarus* doing the like in another Boat fitted out by his Father's Direction. That the People enraged to fee them attempt their Efcape even before their Faces, purfued them with Boats row'd with many Oars, laughing at the Madnefs of the Attempt. But that when they came out to Sea, *Dedalus* run two Foot for their one, *as the Seamen exprefs it ;* the Sea alfo being rough, and the Wind blowing a frefh Gale ; fo he made his Efcape from them all, which they called flying in the Air with waxen Wings. As for his Son *Icarus*, he

out-

outwent his Purfuers too, but impatient, and not content with his Efcape, but willing to go fafter, he crowding too much Sail, as the Seamen call it, or not having Judgment to fill, trim, and manage his Sails skilfully as his Father did, he over-fet his Boat, and was drown'd ; which the Fable reprefents, by foaring too high, and melting his Wings.

But thefe Things would lead me out of my Way, I am not writing of Navigation, but of Trade and Commerce: So I return to my Subject.

It feems the *Dutch,* (for the *Flemings* were all called *Dutch*) a diligent and laborious People were in Trade before us, and being in Search of proper Methods to improve and enrich themfelves, fell to Manufacturing. In this the firft of their Improvement, as I am affured by good Authority, was *making Linen,* which they fell into by the Inftruction of fome *Carthaginian* Merchants, who fled into *France* by Sea from the Fury of the Wars between the *Romans* and *Carthaginians,* which War afterwards ended in the Deftruction of their City.

It is well known, that the *Carthaginians* were great Friends to Trade, and Encouragers both of Merchants and of Manufacture (that is a Hiftory by it felf). Thefe I fay fled to *France,* and thence fome of them to *Flanders,* where the *Romans* had

had not made fo intire a Conqueft as in *France*.

HERE they fell to Trade and Manufacturing, and having planted the Flax, which they found the Country very proper to produce, they of Courfe fet the People to Work, inftructing them how to drefs the Flax, fpin the Yarn or Thread, weave the Cloth, bleach it afterwards, and then to fell it; and this I take to be a true Account of fetting up the Linen Manufacture in the feventeen Provinces.

> *N. B.* The *Dutch* had their Linen Manufacture from the *Carthaginians*, they from the *Tyrians* or *Phænicians*, of whom they were a Colony, and they from the *Egyptians*; the fine Linen of *Ægypt* is often mentioned in the Scripture Hiftory, and in others alfo, as the moft antient.

INDUSTRY feldom wants Bufinefs : The *Flemings* falling into the Manufacture of Linen, it led them as it were by the Hand into that of the Wool; and the fame *Carthaginian* Refugees put them upon that alfo, for the old *Numidians* had Wool in great Plenty, and the Wool of *Barbary* is good to this Day.

BUT here they were put to a Stop, for neither *Belgia (Holland* and *Flanders)* or *Gaul (France)* yielded any Wool : This balk'd their Undertaking for a while; but the diligent Tradefman never tires; it

was

was not long before, searching among the neighbouring Nations, they found that they had Wool in *Britain*, and that so fine and good, that no other Wool the World produced was equal to it, for their Business.

This encouraged them so, that they bought the Wool in *Britain*, manufactured it in *Belgia*, and supplied first themselves, and afterwards the neighbouring Countries with woollen Manufactures, to the great Encrease of the Wealth and Power of the *Netherlands* ; especially by drawing infinite Multitudes of People to them, so that they soon became, from a few fishing Towns, and a poor labouring People, to be a most populous, rich, and powerful Nation.

The *Britains* too, in their Degree, found the Sweetness of this Encrease of Commerce, and next to the *Flemings* had their Share of the Gain from the Wool of their Sheep : This Wool was but of small Value to them before ; for instead of manufacturing it as the *Flemings* did, they wore the Skins of their Sheep with the Wool on: But now the *Flemings* eagerly calling for the Wool, and giving a good Price for it, the *Britains* were not only encouraged to preserve it, but to nourish and take more Care of their Sheep, in order to encrease the Number of them, that they might, in the Consequence, encrease the Wool.

Thus

THUS began the *English Commerce,* and thus it may be said began the Opulence and Greatness of the *English* Nation ; for the *Flemings* took off their Wool in a prodigious Quantity, and gave also a prodigious Price for it.

N. B. WE find in King *Edward* the III's. Time they gave 40 *l.* a Pack for the *English* Wool, which by the Way was more than 200 *l.* a Pack, as Money goes now ; but of that in its Place.

THIS filled the Nation with Money, the Merchants grew rich, the Staple of the *English* Wool was erected at *Antwerp,* 50000 Packs of Wool was the least that was carried thither yearly, and the Fleets of Ships which carried over the Wool, and which went generally from *Southampton* and *London,* were such, that sometimes Fifty, Sixty, to 100 Sail, went off at a Time.

IT is to be doubted indeed, the Ships were most of them *Hollanders,* that is to say *Flemings,* or in general *Dutch,* for I do not find, but that as they were before us in Trade and Manufacture, so they were also before us in Shipping and Navigation ; tho' growing rich by the Wool, we soon fell in to building Ships too, especially as Trade encreased ; of which hereafter.

As the Quantity of the Wool was thus great, and the Price also, the Ballance of

Trade

Trade was neceffarily very great on our Side, I mean great to the Advantage of *Britain ;* for the *Britains* bought but little of any Goods from Abroad, for many Ages after this, and their Wool was generally paid for in Money ; nay, they had two feveral Products befide the Wool, which were peculiar to *Great Britain,* and which no other Nation in the World had, *(viz.)* their *Block Tin,* and their *Lead.*

We have very good Evidence, that both thefe Metals were found and dug by the antient *Britains,* long before this, and efpecially that the Tin was fetch'd from *Britain* by the *Phænicians,* many Ages before the Time I am now fpeaking of.

I take it, that at the firft of the Trade with the *Flemings,* the Importations of *Britain* were fo fmall, that the Export of *Tin* and *Lead* was fufficient to purchafe all that they wanted from Abroad : So that the Wool was neceffarily all paid for in Specie.

This I fay enrich'd the *Britifh* Nations to a very great Degree, fill'd them with ready Money, and efpecially the landed Men grew very rich and powerful by it, I mean the Barons, Knights, Gentlemen and other Degrees, for they were the Men that got the Money, the Wool and the Sheep being their own.

N. B.

N. B. WHEN I fay other Degrees of Men, I mean plainly the Clergy, for the religious Houfes had many, if not moft of their Rents paid in Wool ; and fome had large Flocks of Sheep of their own, kept by their own Shepherds, for the Supply of the Houfe, (that is the Fryars) and their large Attendants with Mutton, and for Supply of Money to their Coffers by the Wool; and we fee the Clergy tax'd in King *Edward* the III's Time, in fo much Wool to the King and his Wars.

I T is almoft incredible what immenfe Sums of Money came over yearly to this Kingdom for the Wool, and how rich and powerful *England* grew by this Means, even in the Time of the *Normans* Government ; and had they not been fo often exhaufted by foreign Wars, peel'd and pol'd by their tyrant Princes, ravag'd and wafted at home by one another, I mean in civil Diffentions, and plunder'd and emptied by the foolifh and ridiculous Zeal, or rather Fury, call'd *the Holy War*, they might have been infinitely richer than they were.

LET but any Man of Figures calculate the Commerce at that Time; the Wool only that was exported, at the Rate above mentioned, amounted to two Millions *Sterling* in Specie ; an immenfe Sum, and more

than

than Ten Millions *per Annum* would be now.

IT is indeed very ſtrange, that when every Thing elſe was ſo cheap, the Wool ſhould be ſo dear, and that now, when every Thing elſe is ſo dear, the Wool ſhould be ſo cheap; we only are left in ſome Un-certainty as to what was then called a Pack of Wool, and how they could give ſuch a Price for it; if the Pack was the ſame then as it is now, the Price was intolerable, perhaps it might be made up in ſuch large Packs, as we ſtill ſee ſometimes brought into *Norfolk,* one of which loads a Waggon, and is called a Poke of Wool, or a Pocket; but that we cannot now determine: But be the Bulk what it will, the Number of Packs was the ſame.

AGAIN, the Pack of Wool muſt be much larger than it is now, otherwiſe the Quan-tity of Wool produced in *England* was but trifling; for as to 50000 Packs of Wool to be the whole Crop, or the whole Product, 'tis ridiculous to ſuggeſt it, 'tis evident we import more than twice that Quantity now yearly from *Ireland,* in Wool or in Yarn; the Wool of *England* is more likely to amount to five Hundred Thou-ſand Packs, than to fifty Thouſand; and we are aſſured, as you will ſee, by a juſt Calculation in its Place, that the Sheep fed in *Rumney* Maſh only in *Kent,* make 2523 Packs of Wool every Year; which, were

the

the whole calculated, is not a two Hundredth Part of the Wool of the whole Country.

BUT to leave our Gueffes at the Magnitude of the Pack of Wool, I am ready to grant it muft be larger than ours are now, which are but two hundred and forty Pound Weight to a Pack, and could never be worth forty Pound Sterling; but if a Pack was a Poke, and weighed twenty Hundred Weight, as the Poke of Wool ftill does, and is called in fome Places a Load of Wool, becaufe 'tis *a Waggon Load,* then indeed it might yield fuch a Rate (tho' dear too) and it alfo agrees beft with the Growth or Crop of *Wool* in *England,* which would then be about 400000 Packs a Year, and it was an immenfe Bufinefs of its Kind too, for the Time of Day in Trade.

THAT this Trade was really a Prodigy for Magnitude, at that Time, appears by many Particular Circumftances ; and efpecially by this, that great Increafe of Wealth and People, which the Manufacturing of it brought to the *Netherlands,* that is, to the feventeen Provinces, whofe Greatnefs, as well as ours, began here.

NOR is it fo long ago that this Trade receiv'd a Turn, that we fhould want Evidence of the Fact, for it continued in the fame Situation to the Time of *Henry* the VII. and tho' we began then (by the Wifdom and Sagacity of the Prince) to break

in

in upon the *Flemings,* and to manufacture much of our Wool at home, yet we find no Prohibition of the Exportation of Wool, till the Reign of Queen *Elizabeth ;* for the Fifth of *Edward* VI. we find a large Fleet of *Flemings* laden with Wool, fail'd from *Southampton* for the *Scheld,* being above fixty Sail, that Wool being fent to pay the King's Debts.

I have met with fome who are of the Opinion, that the Trade of the *Netherlands* in the Woollen Manufacture, was much greater then, than it is now here, or than it has ever been fince; and they give thefe Reafons for it,

1. That if they had not had a moft extenfive confumption, they could never have been able to have confumed fuch a Quantity of Wool ; for *England* being not enclofed and cultivated then, as it is now, they fuppofe the Quantity of Wool was much greater, than it has been at any time fince.

2. That they had no Rivals in the Trade ; no other Nation, for many Ages, having any fuch thing as a woollen Manufacture among them ; and this gave them fuch a Command of the Trade, as to be able to give a Price for the Materials, and to fell the Manufacture when wrought at a Rate in Proportion.

3. That by the fame Rule they had all the Trade ; and tho' it is true, they had not extended the woollen Manufacture into *Turky,*

Turky, *Ruffia*, and to both the *Indies*, as it
is now, and to feveral other remote Countries; yet, on the other hand, they had the
whole Extent of *France*, *Spain*, and the
German Empire, *Poland*, *Sweden*, and *Denmark*, to fupply with Goods; none of thofe
Countries making any thing of a Woollen
Manufacture; and as at length, the Dominions of the *Netherlands* fell to the Houfe
of *Auftria*, and that *Spain*, *Germany*,
Italy, and the whole *feventeen Provinces*,
were united under one Head, in the Government of that great Monarch *Charles*
V. they were allowed an unlimited Commerce through all his Dominions, and had all
poffible Encouragement for their Goods, of
which I might give many Particulars.

THESE things confidered, it muft be granted, that their Trade was exceeding great;
whether it was equal or fuperior to our
Trade of the fame kind now, is what no
body can make any Calculation of: And
therefore I fhall not attempt to form any
Plan or View of Trade upon thofe remote
Gueffes.

THE Turn given to this Trade afterward,
and the Wealth raifed upon it in *England*
in fo fhort a Space, as was feen in *Queen
Elizabeth*'s Time, may give us fome Idea of
what it was before; and this part indeed
cannot without a Breach in our Work, as it
is propofed in my Title, be quite pafs'd
over; but I fhall be as brief in it as I can.

THAT

That King *Henry* VII. was the firſt Prince that put the *Engliſh* upon the Thought of manufacturing their own Wool, muſt be acknowledged to his Memory ; we ſhould not do him Juſtice, if we did not mention it, as often as the Original of our Woollen Manufacture is ſpoken of.

He had been a kind of a Refugee in the Court of his Aunt the Dutcheſs of *Burgundy*, being forc'd to make his Eſcape from *Bretagne*, where he firſt harbour'd ; while he was here, he had opportunity to ſee as well as hear of the mighty Increaſe and Improvement of the Commerce of thoſe Countries ; how populous their Cities, how rich their Burghers, how great their Merchants, how all the People were buſy, and employ'd ; hardly a Child above five Years old, but could do ſomething to gain its Bread ; and particularly, it could not eſcape his Obſervation, that all this Commerce, all this Wealth, all this Imployment of the People depended entirely upon the Supply of the Materials, *viz.* The *Wool* and *Fullers Earth* from *England* ; that they had not a Pack of Wool of their own in the whole Country, and if that Source ſhould by any Accident be ſtopped, they ſhould be all ruin'd, their Trade would be at a full Stop, and in a Word, that the Manufacture could not be carried on without it.

To a Prince of ſuch Penetration as he was, it could not but occur after he came to
the

the Crown, that certainly *England* was much in the wrong, to let their Wool go out of the Country thus unmanufactur'd, and to let Strangers be made rich by the working of it, while his own People fat idle and unemployed, and confequently ftarving the Poor.

THAT without doubt, where the Principals and Materials of the Manufacture were only to be found, there Nature feem'd to direct the making of the Manufacture it felf, and there it might be wrought with the greateft Advantage ; that, at leaft, it would be an Advantage to his own Kingdom, and that he could fee no Reafon why that Advantage fhould be given away. In fhort, he refolved, that if he could prevent it, Strangers fhould no longer eat the Bread out of the Mouths of his own Subjects.

I need not enter here into the particular Meafures the King took to put this happy Refolve of his in Execution ; 'tis enough to mention it here, that in Perfuit of thefe Obfervations, he immediately fet about the Work, applied himfelf to the finding out proper Inftruments for the carrying it on, and fet the Manufacture of Wool on Foot in feveral Parts of his Country, as particularly at *Wakefield, Leeds* and *Hallifax,* in the Weft Riding of *Yorkfhire,* a Country pitch'd upon for its particular Situation, adapted to the Work, being fill'd with innumerable Springs of Water, Pits of Coal, and other Things

Things proper for carrying on fuch a Bufinefs, and where it remains and thrives to
this Day.

But not, I fay, to enter into the Particulars of this hiftorically, which would be too
tedious, 'tis fufficient to fay, the anxious
Care of this Prince for the Profperity of his
People has been followed with fuch a glorious Succefs, that the Example is perfectly
fitted to fire the Breaft of any fucceeding
Monarch, who defires the Good of his
Subjects with the fame paternal Warmth for
the general Improvement ; and for this End
I mention it, and for this End thefe Sheets
are thus addreffed to the fupreme Powers of
the *Britifh* Government, and at this Time
too ; becaufe, being affur'd that his prefent Majefty has the fame Ardour and Affe-
ction, the fame improving Genius, and the
Advantage of a much greater Fund of Wealth
and Power for the advancing the Intereft of
his People, nothing may be wanting to lay
open the feveral Profpects for the farther
improving the Commerce and extending the
Manufactures of *England* which yet remain,
and which perhaps have not been fo tho-
rowly confider'd of by any other Hand.

Tho' *King Henry* acted with a Vigor
becoming a Prince, and one that knew how
to execute, as well as how to refolve, for the
Advantage of his own Dominions; yet he
knew withal, that it was an Attempt of
fuch a Magnitude, as well deferv'd the ut-
                                      moft

moft Prudence and Caution, that as it was
not to be attempted rafhly ; fo it was not
to be pufh'd with too much Warmth: And
therefore, tho' he did not fail to encourage
his People in working and manufacturing,
and at a confiderable Expence, fecretly procured a great many Foreigners, who were
perfectly skill'd in the Manufacture, to come
over and inftruct his own People here in
their Beginnings ; yet he did not immediately prohibit the exporting the Wool to the
Flemings, neither did he, till fome Years
after, load the Exportation of it with any
more Duties than he had before.

NAY, fo far was the King from being able
to compleat his Defign, that he could never come to a total Prohibition of exporting the Wool in his Reign ; he did indeed
offer at it, but found, that if he had pro-
ceeded, his People were not Mafters enough
of the Trade to work up the whole Quantity of the Wool, and confume the Growth;
that the *Flemings* were old in the Bufinefs,
long experienc'd, and turn'd their Hands
this Way and that Way, to new Sorts and
Kinds of Goods, which the *Englifh* could
not prefently know, and when known, had
not Skill prefently to imitate : And that
therefore they muft proceed gradually.

BESIDES, if in fome Years the *Englifh* were
able to fupply themfelves, and make Goods
enough for the Home Confumption, fo that
they had no need to buy from the *Flemings*
the

the Manufactures of their own Wool, This was a great Point gain'd, and was a Step sufficient for the first Ages of the Manufacture ; whereas, to have prohibited the Wool being carry'd out while they were not able to supply the Markets abroad, was to ruin the Trade in general, and stop the Confumption of the Wool too.

On the contrary, the King acted like a wife and warlike Prince, befieging a City, who tho' he attacks the Garrifon, and batters the Out-works with the utmoft Fury, yet fpares the Inhabitants, and forbears as much as he can ruining the City, which he expects to make his own : So the King feem'd willing to let the *Flemings* keep up the Trade, till his Subjects were thoro'ly enabled to take it into their own Hands, and not deftroy a Commerce, which he knew would one Time or other be his own.

Upon this Foot, I fay, the prudent Prince went on by Meafures perfectly well adjufted, and particularly adapted to the End which he aim'd at ; and tho' he did once pretend to ftop the Exportation of the Wool, he conniv'd at the Breach of his Order, and afterwards took off the Prohibition entirely, leaving the Succefs of his Undertaking, to the Induftry of his People, who, he perceiv'd, to his great Satisfaction, went on with Courage and Chearfulnefs, improv'd daily, and would

at

at laft entirely carry the Bufinefs from the *Flemings*, by the meer Courfe of Things.

In this Manner the Manufacture began, and thus gradually it encreas'd ; nor was it much lefs than one hundred Years, before *England* came to fuch a Perfection, as to be able to claim the Property of it to themfelves, and to prohibit the Exportation of the Wool, which was never effectually done, till the *Spanifh* Tyranny under the Duke *d'Alva* finifh'd the ruin of the Commerce of the *Netherlands*, by driving the *Dutch* into a Common-Wealth, to caft off entirely the *Spanifh* Government ; and by forcing the Proteftant *Flemings*, who, indeed, were the chief Manufacturers, to take Shelter in *England*, where they prefently erected all the feveral Species of the Manufacture, which were not fet up before.

Thus it was, from the Year 1489, when King *Henry* VII. began to encourage the Manufacture in *England*, to the Year 1587, when Queen *Elizabeth* may be faid to fee it arriv'd to its Perfection, that this great Work was gradually encreafing and bringing forward.

It is worth obferving here, in how fhort a Time the Queen having fully ftop'd the Stream of Wool which fupported the Manufacture in *Flanders*, fpread the Commerce of *England*, into the remoteft Parts of the then known World, and carry'd
the

the Trade of the woollen Manufacture of *England*, into every Part which the *Flemings* had supply'd before, and to many Places where they had no Busineſs.

1. THE *Dutch*, who were erected into a ſeparate State under the Queen's Protection, and who breaking off from the *Flemings*, that is, from the *Spaniards*, had no Commerce with them, meddled not with Manufacturing, but apply'd themſelves to their fiſhing Trade, and to foreign Merchandize ; and having before a very great Correſpondence by their Rivers, *viz.* the *Maes*, the *Rhyne*, and other Rivers into *Germany*, they naturally apply'd to *England* for the woollen Manufacture, which they had formerly been ſupply'd with from *Flanders*, and were, as we may call them, our firſt Cuſtomers for them Abroad.

2. THE *Queen* heartily engag'd in the Intereſt of her People, and particularly eſpouſing her Merchants, ſent formal Embaſſies, with ſplendid Retinues, and in the moſt honourable Manner, for the opening the Sluices of Trade to her Subjects ; 1. To the *Grand Seignior* ; 2. To the *Great Duke*, or Emperor of *Ruſſia* or *Muſcovy* ; 3. To the *Great Mogul* ; 4. To the King of *Perſia*, and in a Word, to every other Place, whither her enterpriſing Subjects deſir'd her ; for it was at that Time an enterpriſing Age, and the *Engliſh* Merchants ſpread the Seas with

with their Ships, as the Poet expreffes it, every where as far

> *As Winds could carry, or as Waters roll.*

3. UNDER her Majefty's Conduct, and by her particular Encouragement, her fortunate Navigators, her Merchants, and other Adventurers began to fhew themfelves, not experienc'd only in, but Patrons and Improvers of Navigation, beyond all the Trades of the World ; they rang'd about the Seas having then no Rivals ; fearching the Globe for Difcoveries, planting Colonies, and fettling Factories in all Parts of the World : But I muft come to fpeak of this Part again more at large.

By this laft Part of the Queen's Management, *(viz.)* prohibiting the Exportation of the Wool, the woollen Manufacture in the *Netherlands* receiv'd its fatal Wound ; the *Spanifh* cruelty fcatter'd the chief Manufacturers, and the Prohibition ftarv'd thofe that were left ; for now having no more Wool to work up, the Work it felf ftop'd at once, the Trade expir'd and dy'd : Nor has it been able fince that to revive, no not in the leaft Degree ; for as it depended before entirely, upon the Supply of Wool from *England* for its Support, when that Stream fail'd, when that Chanel ftop'd, it could no more fubfift, than a Body with-

out

out Food, or Life without Sprits: In a word, the *Flemings* impoverifh'd and poor, difperfed and fled; their great Cities, fuch as *Antwerp, Ghent, Lifle,* and other Places wafted and decay'd; the People went away into other Parts to feek Peace and Employment; the populous Towns became thin of Inhabitants, compar'd to what they were; and the new eftablifh'd Common-Wealth of *Holland* became populous and rich, out of their Ruins.

The People who remain'd, and who are yet numerous, tho' not like what they were before, apply'd to other Works, fuch as Lace, Linen, and particularly fine Thread, fine Cambricks, and whatever elfe offer'd, for it muft be own'd they are a moft induftrious People.

They are now further reduc'd in their Bounds by the *French,* who have taken from them the whole Province of *Artois,* and great Part of *Flanders,* and *Hainault*; and efpecially, the Port of *Dunkirk,* and the great Cities of *Arras, Cambray, Doway, Lifle,* St. *Omers,* and many others, fo that the remaining Part, which is now call'd the *Netherlands,* is but fmall, compar'd to what it was; and their Trade is chiefly confin'd to the merchandizing Part, which they carry on by the River Navigation with *Holland* on one Side, and with *France* on the other, and by the Manufacture as above, of Lace and Linen: As to the woollen

len Manufactures, they are oblig'd to give them over, and to buy them of their Supplanters the *English*, to whom they formerly fold them.

THIS being the antient State of our Commerce, and from which it deriv'd its Being, I thought it abfolutely neceffary to give this Summary of it, that we may have no Occafion to look back any more, but begin the Plan of its fubfequent Improvements at this general *Epocha*, as from its real Fountain Head, and as it is properly an *English* Commerce.

THE Improvements of our Trade from this Time are no lefs wonderful ; its prefent Magnitude I call a Prodigy, and I think it well deferves that Name. How it come to arrive to fuch a Height, and how it may be farther improved and increafed in Spite of all the Prohibitions and Encroachments of its Neighbours, remains to be difcours'd of.

CHAP.

Chap. IV.

Of the Encreaſe of the Engliſh *Commerce, from the Time of Queen* Elizab th's *breaking with the* Spaniard.

N the laſt Chapter, I mention'd the Inclination Queen *Elizabeth* had to propagate the Intereſt of her People ; and eſpecially, that of their Commerce. I muſt obſerve here, as an additional Remark, that this Warmth of the Queen their Sovereign, fir'd her Subjects with an inexpreſſible Ardor for new Diſcoveries, planting Colonies, finding out unknown Paſſages, ſettling Factories, engaging in new Correſpondences for Trade, and the like ; and in this Reign, and in purſuit of this new Principle, (for it was new at that Time,) they began ſeveral of the preſent moſt flouriſhing Branches of our preſent Commerce, and where our woollen Manufactures are now beſt eſtabliſh'd : *For Example,*

1. The Queen ſending an Embaſſy, as I have ſaid, to *Muſcovy*, the *Engliſh* Merchants

chants obtain'd Licenfes of the Great Duke
for a certain Number of them to pafs with
their Merchandize thro' his vaft Dominions
into *Perfia*, where they carried their *Englifh* Cloth, Kerfeys, Bays, Says, *&c.* and
fold them to great Advantage, and brought
back their Returns by the fame Way 2500
Miles upon the River *Wolga*, 800 Miles upon the *Dwina* to *Arch-Angel*; befides crof-
fing the *Cafpian* Sea, and befides their Journey by Land to *Ifpahan*. Thefe were afterwards call'd the *Ruffia Company*, and
indeed, they carry'd on a very noble and
gainful Commerce, as well to themfelves,
as to their Country, till it was afterwards
interrupted by the meer abfolute Tyranny
of the *Mufcovite* Emperor or Great Duke,
without any Offence given, and without
fo much as a Pretence of any.

THIS Journey, befides the Voyage by
Sea, between *London* and *Arch-Angel*,
then alfo newly difcover'd, was five Times
perform'd by one Merchant of *London*,
whofe Name was *Lancafter*, as may at
large be feen in *Huckluyt's Voyages*.

2. THE Queen having by an Ambaffador,
as I have faid, eftablifh'd a Treaty of Peace
and Commerce with *Solyman the magnifi-
cent*, the Great Emperor of the *Turks*; Her
Merchants immediately follow'd with their
Ships; and the *Turky* Company being by
that means erected and eftablifh'd, they fettled their Factories at *Conftantinople*, *Smir-
na*,

na, and at *Aleppo,* where the Trade flourifh'd and encreafed to a very great Magnitude, and continues to this Day.

3. THE War with *Spain* encouraging
her Majefty's Subjects to farther Adventures, partly for Reprifals upon the *Spaniard,* and partly for Difcoveries, Sir *Walter Raleigh, Drake, Smith,* and others,
upon the meer Account of Commerce, difcover'd and planted the great, and now
flourifhing Colonies of *Hudfon's-Bay, New-
England, Virginia,* and *Burmoodas,* with
the Fifhery of *Newfoundland ;* the Magnitude and Commerce of which Countries,
is not eafily to be defcribed; and to which
are fince then added, the Ifland Colonies
of *America,* called in common the *Weft-
Indies,* fuch as *Barbadoes, Nevis, Antegoa,*
St. *Chriftophers, &c.* and at laft *Jamaica ;*
and upon the Continent, *New-York,* with
Eaft and Weft *Jerfey,* obtain'd by Conqueft from the *Dutch,* and *Penfilvania*
and *Carolina,* obtain'd by more modern
and extended Difcoveries.

To and from thefe, the Advantage of
the *Englifh* Commerce is fuch at this Time
in the Confumption of *European* Goods
fent thither, and particularly the *Britifh* Product, and their Manufactures of Linen,
Woollen and Silk ; in the Numbers of Seamen and Ships employ'd, and in the Returns made from thence, as alfo the vaft
Wealth acquir'd there in Plantations, Buildings,

ings, Value of Lands, Slaves, &c. that it is a Doubt not eafily refolv'd, whether is greater in real Value, the Silver return'd to *Spain* yearly by the Galleons, or the Sugars, Ginger, Tobacco, Rice, Furrs, Fifh, and other Product of *America* returned to *England*, and to other Parts on *Englifh* Account.

To fuch an immenfe Greatnefs is the Trade grown, fuch a Confumption is made of the *Englifh* Merchandizes, fuch Cities and Towns are built, Countries, nay Kingdoms peopled and inhabited, and fuch a Fund of Wealth and Commerce is raifed, that it is not to be eftimated.

4. In the fame enterprifing Times, was the Trade to the *Gold Coaft* of *Africa* begun; a Trade founded upon the moft clear Principles of Commerce; namely, the meaneft Export exchang'd for the richeft Return; a Trade carry'd on with furprifing Succefs, while juftly countenanc'd by the Authority which own'd its beginning; and a Trade ftill holding up its Head, tho' fo ftrangely, unaccountably, and contrary to the true Intereft of Trade in general, as well as of *England* in particular, abandon'd and forfaken at laft! And I ask leave to fay, I think 'tis the only national Advantage in Commerce, which feems to be neglected in *England*; it waits, however, for better Times; and I cannot doubt, but as it is capable (were it freed from the Invafions of Interlopers) of being made the

moft

moft flourifhing Trade of its kind in the World ; fo it will ftill recover it felf, and flourifh in a manner few People expeĉt, becaufe they do not fee it poffible ; which however, I fhall demonftrate, upon proper Occafion, to be both poffible and eafy.

5. Besides all thefe particular Steps taken for the Encreafe of Trade, the Export of the *Englifh* Manufaĉtures to *Holland*, mention'd above, took its beginning in this Queen's Reign, by the natural Confequence of the commanding Influence the Queen had over all the Affairs, as well as in the Affeĉtions of the *Dutch:* The *Hollanders* ador'd the Queen, and efteem'd her, as fhe really was, their great Patronefs and Proteĉtor, and in Return, they omitted nothing that would oblige her, or her People ; and particularly the encouraging and propagating the Confumption of the *Englifh* Manufaĉture was their particular Care, knowing they cou'd do nothing that could oblige her Majefty more.

This Part was indeed one of the main Articles, in which the Growth of the Manufaĉture at that Time confifted ; for as to the reft, tho' they were Foundations on which the future Greatnefs of the Manufaĉture of Wool was very much rais'd ; yet, as I faid of King *Henry* VII's Part, fo it was here, it was many Years, and not till long after the Queen's Death, that the Harveft of that Spring Time of Trade was reap'd.

N. B.

N. B. The Succefs of thofe glorious Attempts for the Encreafe of Commerce, and the generous Care for the Profperity of the Nation, tho' the Iffue could not be feen, or the Advantage be reap'd till fome Ages after, is a noble Patern for the Princes, and for the Legiflature of the prefent Age; moving them to lay fuch Foundations, as prefent themfelves for the future Advantage of their Subjects, tho' the Benefit fhould not immediately be felt, and tho' the Profpect be fomething remote, of which fomething farther remains in the Defign of this Work.

These, I fay, were the Beginnings of foreign Trade in *England*, and from hence the home Manufacturers rais'd themfelves: Thefe were the Beginnings, upon which the immenfe Bufinefs carry'd on in *England* at this time has been rais'd: This was the Time, when (as I faid above) *England* gave herfelf a loofe in Trade, and got the Start of all her Neighbours, and like a ftrong Horfe in a Race, who having fhot a Head of the reft at their firft fetting out, by the Skill of the Rider, holds it all the way, by meer Strength, as well as Speed.

The Advantages gain'd by the War with *Spain*, gave *England* fuch a Start of her Neighbours in this fingle Reign, in matters of Commerce, as the whole World could never overtake her in to this Day;

the

the Difcoveries made in *America* are an
Example of this; *England* began, and being early, carv'd for her felf, nor did fhe
lofe her Time; the *French* put in as foon
as they perceiv'd it, but found all the
North Coaft of *America* gone, and poffeft
by the *Englifh*, and were glad to take up
with what was left, (*viz.*) to run into the
great and dangerous Gulph of St. *Law-
rence*, take up with the frozen and
wild Countries of *Canada*, and plant behind the *Englifh*, remote from the Sea, and
out of the Way of Commerce, except by
that one Port ; by all which Inconveniences
they have been always fo crampt in Trade,
they have made but mean Advances in a
Hundred and fifty Years Poffeffion: As to
their *Louifiana* and *Miffiffipi*, it has indeed
been made a Bubble at Home, and but little
better Abroad, having only ftarv'd, or o-
therwife devour'd moft of the People that
have been fent over to it.

AMONG the Iflands the *French* came a
little more timely, and fo got a better Share
than any other of their Neighbours, except
the *Englifh*; for they got *Martinico
Guadaloup, Tortuga*, and a part of St. *Chriftopher*'s, and feveral other Places, which
they profitably hold to this Day.

THE *Dutch* came laft, got little upon
the Continent, and loft that little they had
got to the *Englifh*, *viz. New York*, and Eaft
and Weft *Jerfy* ; fo that they have nothing
to

to call their own on that Side; no, nor have
they one Iſland of any Conſequence ; they
got a footing in the *Braſils* indeed, and
held it above twenty Years, but were driven
out of it again by plain Force, even by the
Portugueſe : Thoſe very People, who on
other Occaſions they ſo much contemned,
and who, in other Places, they drove before
them, as Wolves diſperſe a Flock of Sheep.

ALL they have now left in *America,* is
the two ſmall Colonies of *Surinam* and
Curacao, of no Import, or worth naming,
and hardly worth their keeping, except for a
clandeſtine Trade carried on there with the
Spaniard on the Coaſt of *Caraccas* ; which is
now alſo likely to be entirely loſt, and then
the Intrinſick of the Product will be their
only Benefit, which will appear very ſmall.

ON the contrary, How are theſe Colonies of the *Engliſh* increas'd and improv'd,
even to ſuch a Degree, that ſome have ſuggeſted, tho' not for Want of Ignorance, a
Danger of their revolting from the *Engliſh*
Government, and ſetting up an Indepen-
dency of Power for themſelves.

IT is true, the Notion is abſurd, and
without Foundation, but ſerves to confirm
what I have ſaid above of the real Encreaſe of thoſe Colonies, and of the flouriſhing Condition of the Commerce carried on there.

HOW great a Conſumption of the *Britiſh* Manufacture has the Encreaſe of theſe

Co-

Colonies been to this Nation? Let the yearly Export of all Kinds of Goods from hence
to *New-England, Virginia, Barbadoes,*
and *Jamaica,* besides all the lesser Colonies, be a Proof of it: Above a Thousand
Sail of stout Ships are constantly running between *England* and those Countries, above
another Thousand are employed in coasting
and traversing the Seas between the Islands
and the Continent, including the Fishing
Trade; besides the Numbers of Sloops continually waiting upon the Trade in *Virginia,* which they tell us are double the
Number of all the rest.

I have omitted the Trade to *India,* as
an Article made so much less advantageous
to *England,* by our own Mismanagement,
than it might have been, that I see but little
to boast of in it: But the general Commerce is my Business, especially in those
Parts where our Manufactures are particularly concerned.

THE next to the *Dutch,* (with whom we
carry on such an immense Trade, that it
was affirm'd to the Parliament in a particular Debate upon that Subject, that they
took off two Millions yearly of our Woollen Manufacture only) I say, next to these
our Trade with *Hamburgh* and the *Baltick*
has been carried on to such an exceeding
Degree, and so encreased of late, that notwithstanding several Prohibitions and Invasions upon the Manufacture lately appearing

in

in *Germany*, in Bar of our Manufacture, our Trade thither is yet superior to all the other Nations ; and in a Word is so great, as perhaps is beyond all Conjecture.

THE *Turkey* Trade has been carried on in the most regular Manner imaginable, from its first Establishment spoken of above : Its Encrease is visible, and as the Returns are to be duly estimated, and we can make it appear to be encreased from thirty or forty Thousand Pound *Sterling* a Year, to upwards of 300000 *l.* Value in a Year.

THE Export of our Manufacture to *Italy*, *France* and *Spain*, and particularly to *Portugal*, how are they advanc'd upon the first Establishment made in Queen *Elizabeth*'s Time : It is true, *France*, by our egregious Folly, is lost to us in some Sense ; but how it is in *Portugal*, by the Encrease of their Colonies in the *Brasils*, and on both the Coasts of *Africa* South of the Line ; I say, how has the Consumption of the *British* Woollen Manufacture encreased among them ; so that I am assur'd the *Portuguese* alone take off more *English* Woollen Manufacture at this Time, than ever *Spain* and *France*, put together, took off from us before.

THE Trade to *Italy*, especially to *Leghorn* and *Genoa*, *Messina* and *Venice*, is the same, and under the same Proportion of Improvement. To this Prodigy of Magnitude is the *British* Manufacture arriv'd, and

and all built upon the folid Foundations
layd by that glorious Princefs: She opened
all thefe Doors, fhe fent out all thofe Adventurers, fhe planted all thofe Colonies,
or made Way for the planting them; fhe
circled the Globe by her Mariners, fhe
founded the Commerce of both the *Indies,*
of *Africa,* of *Holland,* and *Hamburgh,* the
Levant, and the *Baltick* Seas.

SHE did not live indeed to fee the Ani-
mofity of the *Spanifh* War abated, much
lefs brought to an End, or the Haughtinefs
of that proud Nation humbled into a fettled
Friendfhip and Commerce, as was afterwards done; but it was all founded on
her Conduct; for Example,

ON the Foot of her Eftablifhments, the
American Colonies are fince brought to
that flourifhing State in which we now fee
they ftand; on her laying the Foundation
of the *Turkey,* the *Eaft India,* the *Holland,* and the *Eaft Country* Trades, they
are grown up to what we now fee them.

BUT above all, and what I have not
mentioned before, the Naval Glory of *England,* is all raifed upon her prudent exerting
her Strength at Sea; fhe fhew'd the *Spaniard,* that however fuperior his Forces were
on Shore (and it muft be allowed his Armies were at that Time formidable, and
his Troops, as well as his Generals, the beft
in the World) yet, *I fay,* her Majefty fhew'd him, that her Wooden Walls were
her

her fufficient Defence ; that fhe built her Strength for War as well as for Commerce, upon the invincible Power of her Fleets, and the Courage and Bravery of her Seamen. By this fhe carried her Arms to the Doors of her Enemies, and vifited them with her Terrors in their remoteft Situation.

By thefe fhe took *Cadiz*, burnt the *Galleons*, with twenty Millions of Treafure in them, infulted *Lisbon*, (then in the Hands of *Spain*) ravaged the Coaft of *Galitia*, and in a Word made all *Spain* tremble : By thefe fhe feiz'd the Iflands and planted the Continent, landed upon the Coafts, plundered the Cities, deftroyed the Shipping, and took immenfe Wealth from the *Spaniards* in *America*

In a Word, fhe cover'd the Seas with her Men of War, and like King *George*, let the Enemies of *England* fee, that they that command the Sea, awe the World, and that to be Mafters of the marine Power, is to be Mafters of all the Power, and all the Commerce in *Europe*, *Afia*, *Africa*, and *America*.

Nor was this all, but the *Queen* by thus exerting her Naval Power, encreas'd it ; nay, fhe took the beft and the only Way to enlarge and encreafe it ; the Succefs at Sea made Seamen, as her Succefs in Trade made Merchants : To fpeak the Truth, all her Subjects were fir'd with new Thoughts ; the very Nobility.

bility, and firft Rate Gentlemen, fell into it, the *Cliffords* Earls of *Cumberland,* Sir *John Hawkins,* Sir *Thomas Cavendifh,* Sir *Richard Greenville* of the *Devonfhire* Family, fince Earls of *Bath,* the Earl of *Effex,* Sir *Walter Raleigh,* and Multitudes more: Some commanded Ships, fome Troops ; fome planted Colonies, fome fupply'd Stocks ; fome ventur'd their Lives, fome their Eftates ; all fomething : The Trade, the War, the Sea, emulated one another ; all the Nation was in a kind of Flame.

THE Seamen returned enriched with the Plunder, not of Ships, but of Fleets, Loaden with Silver; they went out Beggars, and came home Gentlemen ; nay, the Wealth they brought Home, not only enrich'd themfelves, but the whole Nation.

THIS made the People run to Sea, as Country Folks to a Fair ; and all the young Fellows turn'd Seamen as naturally as if they had been born fo : The Multitude of Ships and Sailors in *England* grew fo great, that, in a Word, they, as it were, covered the Seas ; every Part of the World was vifited, and the Queen reign'd as it were Miftrefs of the Ocean ; nor do we learn by Hiftory or Tradition, that the Queen ever preft any Seamen ; Her glorious Succeffes at Sea both in publick and private Adventures, animated her People fo, that they crouded into the Service on all Hands; and whatever

Ad-

Adventure was on Foot, they never wanted Hands.

THUS the Queen, I fay, by exerting her Naval Strength, encreafed it; and that to fuch a Degree, that no Power on Earth, during her whole Reign, was able to match her at Sea; nay, I believe I do not carry it too far, if I fay, fhe was at that Time able to have fought all the Maritime Powers of Chriftendom at Sea, had they been all in Confederacy together; and this I fpeak of the Number of her Seamen and Ships, not at all infifting on the Goodnefs of her Seamen; tho' it muft be allow'd, that her Seamen, flufh'd with *Spanifh* Prizes, were the beft and the boldeft at that Time, of any Sailors in the World : But that is a Subject by it felf.

I return to the Subject ; as it is now, fo it was then; *Spain* could not bring home her *American* Treafures, without her Majefty's Leave; and with this addition too, that almoft as often as they ventur'd to do it, they mifcarried; which has not yet been our Cafe.

HERE began the formidable Strength, as well as Trade of *England*, to fhew it felf, the World fcarce ever heard of an *Englifh* Navy till then; the Emperor *Charles* the fifth had powerful Fleets, when he carried on his Wars with fo much Glory againft *France*, againft the *Turks* (then very formidable at Sea) and againft the Rovers of

Tunis

Tunis and *Algier;* and his Son King *Philip*
had indeed great Navies, when he carried on his Wars againſt the *Dutch*, not
then form'd into a State; and when he fitted that terrible Fleet againſt *England,*
called *Invincible*, and which had been
truly invincible, had not Heaven and
Earth, as it were, fought againſt it in Conjunction.

Bu T the World ſcarce ever heard of an
Engliſh Man of War (ſo by the Iniquity
of Cuſtom we call our Ships of War)
much leſs of an *Engliſh* Navy till Queen
Elizabeth.

W I T H our naval Power grew up our
Commerce, as if like Twins they were born
together, and not to live aſunder : What
had been all her new ſettled Plantations,
all her Infant Colonies ? they had Difficulties almoſt unſurmountable in their very
Beginning, Difficulties found in the very
Nature of their Undertakings, and which
follow'd in the Conſequence of the Thing ;
(*viz.*) planting among the barbarous Nations,
and lying at the Mercy of the Savages : How
often famiſh'd, and frozen to Death by the
Severity of the Climates, and Want of Supplies ? How often maſſacred by the treacherous Natives ? How often driven, to abandon the Settlements they had made ? And
had the *Spaniard* too been able to have attack'd them by Sea, had not the Queen always kept herſelf in a Condition to defend
them,

them, and to protect their Commerce, all the Difcoveries they had made, and the Colonies they had planted, like ill Births had been ftrangled in the bringing forth; and all had fallen back to the *Spaniard*, by the meer Confequence of their Naval Power.

BUT the Queen was the Life of all that Glory ; her adventurous Subjects found out the Places, planted and fettled them, and as well as they could, fortified themfelves a-gainft the Bow and Arrow Enemies, which they found in the Place.

BUT 'twas the Queen's *Naval Strength* that was their Security; by this fhe kept the *Spaniards* Hands full, that they had no Time to beftow in attacking the newly planted Merchants ; nor had they Ships to fpare, they were met with in every Cor-ner, fought with on every Coaft, and which was more, beaten almoft as often as fought with, on whatever Occafion.

UNDER this Protection the Commerce encreafed, Trade got Ground, the *Englijh* Nation fwelled into an Empire of Nations, and the *Englijh* Merchants carried a ge-neral Negoce to all the Quarters of the World.

HAVING thus look'd back a little upon Things paft, I fhall fay a Word or two to Things prefent, and conclude with Things yet to come.

CHAP.

Chap. V.

Of the present State of the English Commerce, especially that Part of it which relates to the woollen Manufacture; the Prodigy of its Magnitude, and some Enquiry into how it may be call'd great, and what that Magnitude really is.

Y what has been said, we are a little let into the Beginning of Things, and *English* Men of Trade may see their glorious Original; how they receiv'd Life, as we may call it, from the Powerful Influences, and Paternal Concern of their sagacious Princes; and how they became a trading Nation. Take a Summary of it again in the following Abstract.

HEAVEN bestow'd the Wool upon them, the Life and Soul, the Original of all their Commerce; he gave it them, and gave it exclusive of all the Nations in the World; for none comes up to it.

Their

Their King (*Henry* VII.) open'd their Eyes to the Bleffing, and put them upon manufacturing it, after they had, for almoft a Thoufand Years of Ignorance, fold it to the diligent *Flemings* ; and even bought their own Cloaths of them again, after they were made with it Abroad.

Their glorious *Queen, (Elizabeth)* fhewed them the Way to find a Market for it, when manufactur'd ; fhe open'd the Sluices of Trade to them, and Trade open'd the Sluices of Money. In a Word, fhe made them a Trading Nation, and that has made them a rich Nation, as we fee them at this Time.

But I am called upon to defcribe the Magnitude of this Commerce, and fhew the World, that we do not boaft of its Greatnefs without Caufe ; that Strangers may know, what we fay of it, is not made up of Blufter and Wind, and that even thofe that read it among our own People, may be able to fupport and explain what they fhall, upon any Occafion, advance of the real Greatnefs of our Trade.

The Funds of Trade in any Nation, and upon which the Commerce that is rais'd, is with Propriety faid to be the Trade of that Nation, muft be contain'd in thefe Two.

The Produce of the Soil, and,

The Labour of the People.

Now

No w, if I make it appear, that in both thefe the Trade of *England* is greater than that of any other Nation, I hope I may be fuppofed fufficiently to have prov'd the Magnitude of it.

1. The Produce of the Soil.

And here, that I may make all Things plain and eafy as I go, and leave as little Room for Cavil as poffible, I demand to explain briefly the Term *Product* or Produce : By Produce, as to Trade, I am to be underftood to mean, not that Part of our Produce, be it of what Kind it will, that is confumed at Home, and is employ'd by our People; for this does not relate to the Trade of the Kingdom, as I underftand Trade in this Difcourfe ; that is to fay, Our foreign Trade: By this Exception I take out all the vaft Confumption of Corn, Cattle, Coal, Fifh, Fowl, or whatever of our own Growth is confum'd unmanufactur'd ; and tho' this makes an inexpreffible Sum, and employs a Multitude of thofe of our People we call Shop-keepers, Carriers, Coafting Sailors, with Servants, Labourers and Horfes; Ships, Barges Boats, Carts and Carriages innumerable, and that a vaft Wealth is raifed by this part of Trade ; yet, I fay, this is not the Article, or Branch of our Trade that I am in particular now defcribing: But by the Produce of the Soil here, I mean fuch part of its Growth as is exported beyond the

Seas.

Seas. What is confum'd at Home, will come under another Head. This includes,

1. WOOL, the greateft and beft of our trading Produce, the Soul and Life of our whole Commerce, and the Fund of all our Profperity and Succefs in that Commerce.

2. CORN, fo much as is exported only.

3. COALS and Leather, alfo exported.

4 TIN and Lead, Iron and Copper.

5. FISH and Salt.

I fuppofe no thinking Man will objeƈt that Fifh being the Produce of the Sea, and not of the Soil, is not to be call'd a Produce.

6. Tobacco, Sugars and Ginger.
7. Rum, Melaffes, Indigo.
8. Cocoa, Pimento, and Drugs.
9. Furrs and Skins of Beafts.
10 Turpentine, Rice, Cotton,
11. Timber, Mafts, and Planks.

THE Produce of our Colonies, which is the fame Thing as our own Produce.

THE Magnitude of our Trade, founded upon thefe Produƈtions, will appear, when they are confidered apart, and when the Labour of the People, being added to the Value, fhall fo far double and redouble the Sum,

Sum, as the Nature of the Things refpe-
&ively fhall admit.

THE *Labour of the People* is the next
Article. This is fuppofed to be rated according to the Thing they labour about, and
is to be added to the intrinfick Value of the
Materials ; which being fo join'd, the Work
finifh'd is call'd Manufacture.

1. The Wool, as it is the firft and greateft
Produce, fo it is the firft and principal Manufacture ; an Eftimate of its Value, as
Wool, is as difficult to be made, as of its
Quantity ; the Numbers of People it employs are not to be reckon'd by Thoufands,
but by Millions ; the Places in *Britain*
where the Work is managed and carried on,
are not to be meafured by Towns, and Di-
ftricts of Towns, Villages, or Lordfhips,
but by Counties, Provinces, Parts and
Quarters of the Ifland : As it is a Product
every where ; fo every where we fee more
or lefs of the People employ'd in it : The
beft Meafure we can take to give you an
Idea of its Magnitude, is to tell you, that
it works up, and confumes not only all the
Wool produced by the Sheep of this whole
Ifland, the *Cattle upon a thoufand Hills*,
but it calls for a prodigious quantity from
Abroad.

N. B. I fuppofe I am much within Compafs, when I fay, that in the Fleece
and in Yarn, we import 100000 Packs
of Wool every year from *Ireland*, befides

fides all the Wool of *Scotland*, which, fince the Union, is generally brought to *England*, to be manufactured ; and whofe Quantity, as reprefented at the Time of that Treaty, was rated in the Parliament there, to be worth 60000 Pound Sterling *per Annum*.

They that would examine into the Quantity of Wool ufed in *England*, muft make an Eftimate of the Numbers of the Sheep fed here, which it would be very hard to do ; but let them view the Country where thofe Sheep are generally rais'd and fed, or enquire of thofe who have view'd it critically, and let them fee the innumerable Flocks of Sheep fed conftantly in the feveral Parts of *England*, following.

1 *Romney Marfh*, an Extent of Land for about 20 Miles long, and 10 Miles broad, of the beft and richeft kind of Sheep Ground. I name this Place firft, becaufe I can give an authentick Account of its Extent, and from thence may give you likewife fomething more than a rough Guefs at the Produce of it in Wool.

THE Flat Country, commonly call'd *Romney Marfh*, includes fome other Lands of the fame Nature, and lying all in the fame Level, but of which *Romney* is the Chief, and therefore gives its Name to all the reft, the Quantities of Land they contain, and upon which they are rated in their Level Books, ftand thus.

Romney

	Acres.
Romney and *Walland Marſh*	40000
Gulford Marſh - - - - -	3000
Bromehill - - - - - - -	906
Denge Marſh - - - - -	2912
New Romney Level - - -	292
	47110

The ordinary Bounds of this great Level, are by Eſtimation, from *Rye Harbour,* or *Guldford Marſh,* Eaſt to the Town or Port of *Hithe* Weſt, 20 Miles, and from South to North; that is to ſay, from *Lyd* on the Sea Shore South, to *Warchorn* North, which is ſuppos'd to be a Medium of the Breadth, at leaſt ten Miles.

As all (or all to a Trifle of) this Land, is employ'd in breeding and feeding of Sheep, they reckon the ſtated Number of Sheep to Stock, the whole, that is to ſay, of Weathers and Ewes, which produce Fleece Wool, is three Sheep to an Acre.

N. B. The Lambs, of which a very great Number, are every Year ſold off, are not included.

So that the Number of Sheep, and conſequently the Number of Fleeces of Wool raiſed in this *Level,* is 141330 Fleeces.

Of theſe 'tis uſually reckon'd, that 14 Fleeces, one with another, make a Draft, and four Drafts make a Pack of Wool; ſo
that

that 56 Fleeces make a Pack, each Pack weighing 240 Pound ; and, thus

THE Total of the yearly Growth of Fleece Wool in this *Level,* is 2523 Packs 23 Fleeces.

I could give many more Eftimates of particular Places after the like manner; but, as all together will not amount to an exact Calculate, I fhall not trouble the Reader with Figures. This is fufficient to give you fome juft Ideas of the reft, after I have a little defcrib'd the Countries where the Principal Numbers of Sheep are kept.

2. THE South *Downs*; an Extent of Carpet Ground, reaching from *Bourn* in *Suffex,* to near *Chichefter,* and with fmall Intervals to *Poft Down* in *Hampfhire,* being at leaft 65 Miles in length, and generally 5 or 6 Miles broad at a Medium ; all covered with Sheep of a fmaller Size, but of the fineft Wool ; in which Compafs I find there is eftimated above 70000 Acres.

3. THE *Downs* and *Plains,* vulgarly call'd *Salisbury Plains,* but extending from about 10 Miles on this fide *Winchefter,* to the *Divizes* Eaft and Weft, and from *Andover* on the Edge of *Berkfhire,* through the whole Counties of *Wilts* and *Dorfet* to the Sea at *Weymouth,* North and South; containing all, or the moft Part of the large Counties of *Southampton*; befides, as above, that of *Wilts* and *Dorfet,* the Number of Acres not to be

be eftimated, and the Sheep not to be gueffed at.

4. THE *Cotfwould* Hills and the Plains adjoining, in the Counties of *Worcefter, Gloucefter* and *Oxford*; all thefe laft Counties breed an infinite Number of Sheep.

5. THE County of *Surry* breeds a very great Number on *Banfted Downs*; and alfo on the vaft extended Commons and Heaths on the Weft Part of the fame Country, towards *Farnham, Guildford,* and the *Hind Head Hills,* all to be feen on the Road to *Portfmouth.*

6. THE two rich feeding Counties of *Lincoln* and *Leicefter,* where the largeft Sheep in *England* are bred, and from whence comes that innumerable Store which fupplies the Markets of *London* with their Flefh, whofe Number admits of no Calculation.

7. *Newmarket Heath,* and all thofe Downs and Heaths adjoining in the Counties of *Suffolk* and *Norfolk,* which reach from *Bourn Bridge* on the fide of *Effex* to *Thetford* North Eaft, and on by *Brandon* and to *Lyn* North Weft, and to the Sea due North, where an innumerable Number of Sheep are fed, noted for having all white Wool, but black Faces.

I forbear to examine the Mountains of *Wales,* the fine Wool of *Leominfter,* the *Woulds* in the Eaft Riding of *Yorkfhire,* the Bank of *Tees* in the Bifhoprick of *Durham,* where are the largeft Breed of

Sheep

Sheep in the whole Ifland ; even larger than in *Leicefterfkire,* or *Romney Marfh*; and laft of all the *Northumberland* Sheep, where, and in *Cumberland* their Number is fo great, that they are brought Southward to be fold, even to *London* it felf.

ADD to all thefe, that at leaft there is brought from *Scotland* 120000 Sheep every Year, with the Wool upon their Backs, befides Wool, as I faid before, of all the numberlefs Flocks that are left behind, in the Shires of *Galloway*, *Air*, *Nithfdale*, *Tiviotdale*, and other Parts of *Scotland*.

IT would be foreign to our purpofe, to mention thefe particular Sheep Countries, if there were not fomething material in it, to thofe *Englifh* Men who are acquainted a little with their own Country ; and who by reflecting on the Quantities of Sheep, may make fome Guefs at the prodigious Quantity of Wool produced by them ; as an Illuftration of which, be pleas'd to obferve.

1. THAT at *Dorchefter*, the County Town of *Dorfetfhire* abovemention'd, I was told by very grave and creditable Perfons, Inhabitants of that Town, that upon a Wager decided, it was made appear, that within a Circle drawn round the Town, fix Miles every Way ; that is, twelve Miles Diameter, placing the Town exclufive in the Center, there were 600000 Sheep
feeding

feeding at that one Time, *viz.* in *June*, *Anno* 1673.

2. THAT at *Salisbury*, I received an Account from Perfons alike grave and judicious, that there were fold, or brought to be fold, at one Time at *Wey-hill* Fair, 400000 Sheep ; and at *Burford* Fair in *Dorfetfhire*, the fame Year, upwards of 600000.

THE Sum of this Account is, that as the Number of Sheep, which are conftantly kept in this Ifland, is fo exceeding great, and as we may fay, numberlefs ; fo muft the Growth of the Wool be yearly in Proportion ; and how great then muft be the Manufacture, which not only works the Wool always up, but receives fuch immenfe Quantities from *Ireland* and from *Scotland* ?

THE next Confideration upon which, to form an Idea of the Greatnefs of our woollen Manufacture, is the Exportation of it, and the feveral Markets where it is fold : For Example,

THE Markets for *Englifh* broad Cloths in *Turky*, viz. at *Conftantinople*, *Smyrna*, *Scanderoon*, *Aleppo*, and at *Alexandria* in *Egypt*.

THE Staple at *Hamburgh*, the Fairs at *Leipfic* and *Frankfort au Main*, and the Markets of *Ausburgh*, *Nuremburgh*, *Ulm*, and many of the moft confiderable Cities of the upper, as well as the lower *Germany*.

THE

THE great Quantity of *Englijh* Manufacture fold yearly at *Lubec*, *Gottenburgh*, *Stockholm, Straelfand, Stetin, Koningsburgh, Dantzick, Riga* and *Petersburgh* ; and this, notwithstanding all the Prohibitions, and pretended Imitations of our Manufacture in *Sweden*, *Pruffia*, *Saxony* and *Switzerland.*

THE incredible Vent for the woollen Manufacture of *England*, which is now actually in *Holland*, as well at *Rotterdam* as at *Amfterdam* ; and from thence it is fent to all the Provinces and Counties of *Germany* ; which, as I have faid above, is faid to amount to above two Millions Sterling *per Annum.*

THE lately encreas'd Market at *Lisbon,* where, notwithstanding all that has been faid of the *French* fupplying them, we have fo great a Vent for the woollen Manufacture, that 'tis faid, the *Portugal* Trade is at this Time the beft, and moft entire Trade we have.

THE Trade to *Spain*, as well old as new, and to *Italy*; however, the firft has been interrupted, either by clandeftine or Permiffion'd Traders : I fay, it is very confiderable ; and it is obfervable, that our Importation of woollen Manufactures into old *Spain*, much over-ballances all the Goods we bring back from the *Spaniard*, their Bullion only excepted.

THE

THE Trade to *India*, with all its Faults, in which the Company oblige themselves to export yearly, the Value of 100000 Pound in woollen Manufacture.

ADD to all this, the Consumption in our own Colonies and Plantations, which, as has been already observ'd, is beyond the reach of all Calculation.

THUS far relates to the first Article of the Employment or Labour of the Poor, *viz.* the woollen Manufacture only.

2. THE Silk Manufacture; this is en- creas'd in *England* within a few Years to such a Degree, that whereas it was assert- ed by the late Dr. *d'Avenant*, and others, that in the Years 1680, 1681, 1682, there was imported yearly, by a Medium of three Years, above 1200000 Pound *per Annum*, Sterling in Value, in wrought Silks from *France* and *Italy ;* I am assured, that at this Time, there are not twelve thousand Pounds first Cost, imported in a Year from *France*, and from *Italy* less than ever, ex- cept what may be run in by Smuggling, which, we have Reason to believe, is not considerable : It is true, this is a Manu- facture wrought from foreign Materials ; but it has two Particulars attending, ex- tremely advantageous in Trade, and which ballances all that can be said against it.

1. THAT the foreign Materials are such as are imported manifestly in Return for our Manufacture exported; as particularly

the

the Raw-Silk from *Turky* and the *Levant*, and the Thrown-Silk from *Italy* and *Sicily*.

2. THAT the Labour of our own People is employ'd on the making thofe Goods, which, however they may be confum'd at Home, yet, would otherwife be bought from Foreigners with our Money ; fo that by this Labour of our People, the Sum of more than a Million Sterling *per Annum* is fav'd; if it is not gain'd, 'tis kept at home, inftead of being fent abroad, and the Ballance of our foreign Trade turn'd fo much the more in our Favour.

THUS far the Confumption at home is made a Branch of our Gain; and the Labour of the People, tho' expended by the fame People, is made a means to keep a Million of Money at home, which would otherwife go aboad in Levity and Trifles.

BUT I return to foreign Trade.

3. THE Labour of our People is concern'd in foreign Trade, in all our Hard-Ware Manufactures, fo far as thofe Hard-Ware Manufactures are exported ; and this, if caft up in Form, and containing all our wrought Iron, Copper and Brafs, and wrought Pewter, is a very great Article in the general Commerce ; befides the many thoufand Families employ'd in the Mines, in digging Lead, Tin, Iron, Copper and Coal, for Exportation; that is to fay, the Lead in Sows or Pigs, call it as you pleafe, the
Tin

Tin in Blocks, and the Copper in Bars and Plates.

4. The Labour of the People in the Fishery of all Sorts, in which, tho' we do not come up to the *Dutch*, who they tell us employ 10000 Seamen every Year in the Whale Fishing, and 10000 more in the Herring Fishing, and 10000 more in all their other Fishing, including the fetching Salt from St. *Uvies* ; yet, it is certain, that next to the *Dutch*, we have more Men employ'd in the taking and curing of Fish, including the *Newfoundland*, and *New-England* Fishing, than all the World befides.

5. Add to this, that *England* employs, without Queftion, more Shipping than any other Nation, even than the *Dutch* themfelves; and confequently more Seamen, and Builders of Ships ; for tho' the *Dutch* have an infinite Number of fmall Craft, fuch as Galliots, Hoys, Buffes, and Bylanders or Hoys, for their River Navigation, in which they and the *Flemings* out-do all the *European* World ; yet for great Ships, and Ships of Force for the Merchants Trade, they cannot come near us ; our coafting Trade for Coals, our *Weft-India*, *Spanifh*, and *Straits* Trade, which is all carry'd on in large Ships, carrying from ten to thirty Guns, or able to carry fo many, and fome 36 to 40 Guns, efpecially the Trade to *Virginia*, *Jamaica*, *Barbadoes*, *Spain*, *Italy* and

and *Turkey*, in which many Ships are employ'd, which, in times of a fudden Rupture, have been hir'd and taken up for Ships of War, and are very fit to be fo.

HERE the Strength, as well as the Wealth of this Ifland, is difcovered; and I need not add, that out of this extraordinary Number of Ships employ'd in our Commerce, the Government, with very little Compulfion, and lefs now than ever, is able to man any Squadron of Ships of War; nay, if need be, the whole royal Navy with unexampled Expedition.

And this is another unanfwerable convincing Argument to prove the Magnitude of the *Englifh* Commerce, (*viz.*) that if the King wants 20000 to 30000 Seamen for the Fleet, they are always to be had; the Trade fupplies them, and the continued Train of homeward bound Ships produces them, and yet the Merchants always find Men for their Bufinefs; on the other hand, if Peace returns, and the Royal Navy lies up, if 20000 Seamen are difmifs'd and paid off, they are gone in a few Minutes, they find a Birth, (as they call it) in Trade, the Merchants fit out the more Ships, and good Seamen never want Bufinefs.

THIS could never be, if the *Britifh* Trade was not a Prodigy for its Magnitude; what Difficulties was the late King of *France*, a Prince born to furmount all Difficulties, I fay, what Shifts was he put to to find, or
rather

rather to make Seamen to man his Ships at the beginning of his late fatal Greatnefs? How did he oblige all his Merchant Ships to carry more Men than their Complement (or Compleatment) to Sea upon every Voyage? and befides that, a certain Number ftill more upon the King's Account, and paid by the Royal Treafury, that thofe Men being inur'd to the Sea, might be afterwards fit for his Service.

How did he invite foreign Sailors, efpecially *Irifh* and *Scots,* to ferve in his Fleet, by Offers of Preferment, and extraordinary Wages, manning his beft Ships with fuch, becaufe he found them better and more experienc'd Seamen than his own Subjects?

Even the *Dutch* themfelves, if a War prefents, as was the Cafe more than once in their former Wars with *England,* and was in 1689, and 1690, are oblig'd to ftop their *Greenland* Fleet, and even fometimes their Herring Fifhery, or, at leaft, to fhorten the Number, in order to man their Fleets.

Whereas the *Englifh,* fome fmall Embargoes excepted, for a Week or ten Days at a Time, never put a full Stop to any general Head of Trade, for want of Seamen; on the contrary, in the hotteft Prefs, and when Seamen are wanting on any fudden Expedition, yet they grant Exemptions and Protections, upon the ordinary Reprefentations of the Merchants and of the Cities and Towns; as, to the Coal Trade from
New-

Newcaftle, the Mackrel and Herring-Fifh-ing Smacks in their Seafons, and to their outward bound Merchants on many Occa-fions: And this was done in the late King *William's* Time, even when the Govern-ment required 40000 Seamen to man the Fleet, and when two or three Hundred Ships at a Time were employed in the Tranfport Service to *Ireland,* and other Places.

How could this be, if the Magnitude of the *English* Trade was not, as I have faid, a Kind of Prodigy in the World, fuch as is no where now to be equalled, or was ever before heard of?

THESE I take to be folid Proofs of the general Propofition; they are no Rhodo-montades or Boafts; the Cafe does not want fuch mean Helps to fet it out; the Thing is not private and conceal'd, for a few to know and be called upon to give in Evidence, the whole World are Witnefles; where to the Southward of our Channel is the Port or the Place of Trade, in *Europe, Africa* or *America,* where among all fo-reign Ships that enter their Harbours, the *English* are not the moft in Number? at *Lif-bon,* at *Cadiz,* at *Malaga,* at *Meffina,* at *Leghorn,* at *Genoa,* at *Zant,* at *Venice;* read any of the publick Advices, there is ordinarily more *English* Ships, not only than of any other Nation, but generally more than of all the other Nations

put

put together. The laſt Account I ſaw went thus,

Lisbon	French Ships — — —	18
	Dutch — — — — —	5
	Swedes — — — — —	2
	Hamburghers — — —	1
	Engliſh — — — —	50
Cadiz	French — — — —	12
	Dutch — — — — —	3
	Hamburghers — — —	2
	Swedes — — — —	1
	Engliſh — — — —	18
Leghorn	French — — — —	5
	Dutch — — — —	2
	Engliſh — — — —	8

And ſo of ſeveral other Ports.

As for *America*, we ſee hardly any *French* or *Dutch* in any of the Ports or Places of the Country, except the *French* Bankers off of *Newfoundland*, and a few Ships at *Canada ;* the *Dutch,* with all their powerful Commerce, have ſcarce any Thing to do there.

THESE I call Demonſtrations of the Greatneſs of our Commerce in general ; 'tis true it is not a Detail of Particulars, neither is it needful to our Subject.

I have met with ſome who have pretended to be critical in thoſe Things, and have made Eſtimates of the Value of the Woollen Manufacture in the whole ; and they
have

have told us, that they allow it to be five Millions *Sterling* exported, and two Millions *Sterling* the Home Confumption. Thefe Calculations I take to be much of a Piece with thofe general Gueffes formerly made at the Value of our old Coin ; fome would have it to be three Millions, and others four; and the laft pretended to fpeak with Judgment, and with a Kind of Authority, and took upon them to make the World believe they knew fomething more than common.

FROM this affuming pofitive Way they went on, to make a Judgment of other publick Things, as the Proportion of People, the Value of Lands, the Number of Acres in *England*, and what fuch and fuch Taxes might raife ; by all which it paft with the World as a juft Calculation, that the current Coin was 4 Millions of Silver Money ; and when upon thefe Prefumptions they adventur'd upon that great Work of reforming the Coin, and calling in the old Money, they found the Sum nearer to twelve Millions than to four ; which Miftake plung'd the famous Mr. *Montague*, afterwards Lord *H-----x*, into unexpected Difficulties, which required his utmoft Skill to go thro', and which a Genius lefs than his, would have been in Danger to have been funk under.

CALCULATIONS in Cafes where there is no Principle to calculate from, no given
Number

Number or Rule to begin at, fhould never obtain too much upon us; the judging by or from fuch Calculations leads Men, of otherwife great Penetration, oftentimes into fatal Miftakes, fuch as at leaft touch the Reputation of their Underftandings and Judgment; and fometimes fuch as expofe them to Contempt; fuch were the Gueffes of that great Pretender to politick Arithmetick, Sir *William Petty*, whofe Calculations of the Numbers of the Houfes, and Families, and Inhabitants in *London*, and other populous Cities, were not erroneous only, but we may fay have been fince prov'd abfurd, and even ridiculous.

I give therefore no Heed to thofe Gueffes of five Millions and two Millions, in the Account of the Value of our Manufacture, there being no Rule or Foundation to make fuch an Eftimate upon, and it may be too little or too much, none knows whether.

But all this, without Impeachment of my general Propofition, *viz.* that the Magnitude of our Woollen Manufacture is a Prodigy in Trade.

I muft therefore be allowed here to enter into fome Comparifons, and to talk by Allufion in Behalf of this particular Branch of our Commerce, and that is, that it is not only prodigious great, but that it by far out-does, and goes beyond any fingle Branch of Trade, or any particular Manufacture
of

of any other Nation, at leaſt in theſe Parts of the World.

It is true, the Linen Manufacture is a Thing ſo univerſally uſeful, ſo wanted and called for in all Parts, that if any Thing in the World out-does our Wool, it is the Flax, and this I might grant, without Prejudice I ſay to my general Propoſition.

For this is not a national Manufacture, but a Manufacture of many Nations; and I might almoſt ſay of all Nations, even from *Egypt* in the *Levant,* where we have Reaſon to believe it began, to *Ruſſia* at the Bottom of the *Baltick*; whereas the Woollen Manufacture, as now deſcrib'd, is a *Noſtrum*, a Peculiarity to *England,* and to no other Country in the World, except *Ireland,* which is our own.

The Wool, as I have ſaid, is an excluſive Grant from Heaven to *Great Britain,* 'tis peculiar to this Country, and no other Nation has it, or any thing equal to it in the World ; and the Manufacture is of Conſequence ſingular to us alſo; nor do all the Depredations made upon it by Imitation, by Application for the getting Wool either from us by Stealth, or from remote Countries, as *Saxony, Sileſia, Poland, Barbary,* and the like, amount to much ; far from ſo much as *England* need be concerned at them; while ſhe has the Wool, her Trade is invulnerable, at leaſt no mortal, final, deſtructive

Blow

Blow can be given it; of which I fhall fay more in its Place.

AGAIN, the Callico and the Silk Manufactures in the Eaft *Indies* are (at leaft for *Afia*) an univerfal Manufacture; fo great, that fpreading into *Europe*, they become a general Grievance, and are already prohibited from being imported in feveral Kingdoms and Countries in *Europe*, the Quantity is fo great.

BUT thefe again are the Manufactures of many Nations, Kingdoms, nay Empires of Nations, fuch as the Empire of *China*, and of the great *Mogul*, the Kingdoms of *Golconda*, of *Siam*, of *Cochinchina*, and many more, too long to reckon up.

BUT the Woollen Manufacture, as above, is fingular to our Nation, no People in the World can come up to us in the Workmanfhip, or have the Materials; not that I am, or will be partial to my Countrymen, as if they were the Nonparels of the World for manufacturing of Wool; 'tis evident, other Nations would go a great Way with them in it, if not outdo them, if they had the Wool, the main Principle of the Manufacture to work upon; but it cannot be, they have it not, nor can have it, the whole World cannot fupply it; they may get fome Wool in one Country, and fome in another, and too much they get clandeftinely from *England*, and much too much, from *Ireland*; and with this the *French* make fome Things
very

very well, nor fhould I deny this Juftice to
that diligent Nation to own, that confidering the Shifts they are put to for Wool, they
fhew themfelves but too good Manufacturers in making fuch Things as they do.

But what does it amount to? they fupply
themfelves perhaps, and 'tis a great Step, if
they can do that ; but it muft be remem-
bred, that it is becaufe their Government
obliges them to make Shift with it, and to
wear their own Works, however defective;
a Wifdom we cannot arrive to, tho' we have
the Manufacture in its utmoft Perfection:
Of which in its Order.

But after all, they do not fupply themfelves neither, and in Spite of the fevereft
Prohibition, in Spite of Tyranny, and the
Terror of an abfolute Government, they do,
and will get *Englifh* Manufactures in, and
do import very great Quantities too, as I
could demonftrate by undeniable Evidences
of Fact.

What elfe means the great and fudden
Export of *Englifh* Goods to *Leghorn*, more
juft after the Stop of the *Englifh* Commerce
with *France* than ever before ? what the
continued Export of the fame Goods to
Dunkirk? and above all, what means the
Commerce between *Holland* and *France* by
the *Maes* and the *Sambre*, and by the *Lys*
and the *Scheld,*

And why? if the *French* make their Manufactures equal to others, I fay, Why is it,
that

that when the *French* Gentlemen make a Tour over hither to fee the Country, or to vifit the Court, they bring no more Clothes with them, than thofe on their Backs, but make them more Clothes as foon as they come hither, and always carry feveral Suits of Clothes Home with them ?

On the contrary, if an *Englifh* Gentleman goes Abroad into *France* to travel, he always makes himfelf new Clothes, and carries them with him; I fpeak now of the Gentlemen of Quality that do not want Clothes, or Money to buy them.

The Reafon is plain, the *Frenchman* can get none fo good at Home as he can buy Abroad, and the *Englifhman* can get none fo good Abroad, as he can buy at Home.

It is the like with the Linen and Lace in *Holland* and *Flanders*, if an *Englifh* Gentleman travels into *Flanders* or *Holland*, he carries as little Linen as poffible out with him, but gets all he wants made there ; and when he comes back, he is fure to make himfelf two or three Dozen of fine Shirts, and to lace them at the Neck and Hands with fine Bone Lace.

On the contrary, if a *Dutch-man*, or *French Gentleman* comes over to *England*, he is always well furnifh'd with Linen and Lace before he comes.

The Reafons are juft the reverfe of what is faid above ; the *Dutch-man* or *Fleming* can get none fo cheap Abroad as he can buy

at

at Home, and the *English-man* can get none fo cheap at Home, as he can buy Abroad.

I give this Inftance of the *French*, becaufe they are the People who are faid to have made the moft confiderable Advances in the Woollen Manufacture ; and much has been faid, and much fruitlefs Pains taken to infinuate, that the *French* make our Goods to Perfection; nay, fome will tell you, the *French* out-do us, and underfell us at Market; which is a great Miftake, and even in the *Turkey* Trade, which is the Top of their Performance, and the Goods they fend thither are certainly the beft of their Performance; yet I appeal to the Men of Experience even in that Trade, whether they out-do us; whether, as is mention'd in our firft Chapter, a Bale of *their Cloth* will weigh as much, or fell for as much at Market, as a Bale of *English* Cloth? and whether in general, the *English* Cloth is not rather bought, tho' at a dearer Price, by the *Turkish* and *Armenian* Merchants, I mean thofe who are the chief Dealers in thofe Goods, than a Bale of the *French*.

It is true, there are in all Markets a fort of Buyers, who take up with the Goods of an inferior Quality, for the Sake of a cheap Price, and thefe will buy the *French* Cloths: And the worft Goods will find a Chapman, as well as the beft, if the Price be accordingly.

IT

I<small>T</small> is true alfo, the *French* Cloths carry as good a Face as the *Englifh*, are as well drefl, as well pack'd and fet off, and the Colours are as fine ; fo that it is not hard to deceive the unexperienc'd Buyer: And this is not the only Example of the fuperficial Performances of that Nation, who are very rarely wanting in Outfides, whatever they are within ; but the Subftance is wanting, the real intrinfick Worth of the Goods is found in the *Englifh* Cloths, and in them only ; there is all the Beauty of Colour, and the Ornament of Drefs, and the Subftance too ; and this, whether the firft Buyer can difcover it or no, the laft Buyer and Confumer, the *Turkifh* or *Perfian* Gentleman, *Aga* or *Baffa* that wears it, finds it out prefently ; one will wear firm and fmooth, and folid to the laft; the other wears rough, light, fpungy, and into Rags ; and when this Man buys again, he calls for *Englifh* Cloth, he will have no more *French* Cloth, for it did him no Service, it did not wear well.

I<small>F</small> I did not fpeak this from the Experience and perfonal Knowledge of thofe that have been upon the Spot, and been Witneffes to the very Fact, I fhould not take upon me to affirm it thus pofitively ; but I may appeal for the Truth of it to unanfwerable Evidence, nor is there Room to difpute it ; the Nature of the Thing fpeaks it, the *French* Cloth, with all its fuperficial *French* Glofs upon it, is fine, but thin and fpungy,

and

and will do the Wearer neither Credit or Service, while the *English* Cloth wears to the laſt like a Board, firm and ſtrong, and has a kind of Beauty even in its Rags.

HENCE I infer, we have no ſuch Reaſon to terrify our ſelves with the Apprehenſions of other Nations ruining our Trade, and out-doing us in our woollen Manufacture; let us but keep our Wool at Home, and we need be in no Pain for our Manufacture any where: *But of that hereafter.*

I return to the Magnitude of our Woollen Manufacture; which, as I have ſaid above, I inſiſt is the greateſt ſingle Manufacture, and occaſions the greateſt Trade both Abroad and at Home, of any Manufacture that is to be found in any particular Nation in the World, be that Nation otherwiſe as much greater, richer, or more populous than we are, as you will.

BUT there is yet another thing to be conſidered in the *English* Woollen Manufacture, which is above all our Boaſts; and were we to uſe the utmoſt Partiality, and the utmoſt Art to compliment our own Country, and ſet out the Beauty and Uſefulneſs of our Manufacture, nothing could be equal to this.

IT is not only great from the prodigious Quantity of the Wool, the Numbers of the People employ'd in it, the vaſt Quantity of Goods made, and the Beauty and Perfection of the Performance: But the Extenſiveneſs of its Conſumption, is another Prodigy

digy in Trade; and I cannot pass it without some Notice: I'll be as brief as I can.

LINEN is a Thing universally worn and wanted; and few People of any tolerable Figure or Fashion in the World are, or can be without it: But then, more or less, all the Nations of *Europe* make it; and all they have to do, is only as it were to exchange Sorts with one another.

THE Silk Manufacture is very great, and in all Nations some or other of it is made use of; but then, 'tis made in many Countries, and is exported from one to another in Trade several Ways, the *French*, the *Italians*, the *Venetians*, the *Dutch*, the *Flemings*, and now the *English*, make all their own, and carefully exclude the *East Indian* Silks from their Countries.

THE *Russian* and *Turkish* Empire are supply'd from *Persia*, and the *Spaniards* and *Africans* South, and the *Germans* and *Swedes* North, from *India*, the Variety spreads as the Situation of the Countries, and as the Commerce directs.

THE Callicoes are sent from the *Indies* by Land into *Turky*, by Land and Inland Seas into *Muscovy* and *Tartary*, and about by long-Sea into *Europe* and *America*, till in general they are become a Grievance, and almost all the *European Nations* but the *Dutch*, restrain and prohibit them.

BUT take our *English* Woollen Manufacture, and go where you will you find it;

'tis

'tis in every Country, in every Market, in e-
very trading Place; and 'tis receiv'd, valued,
and made ufe of, nay, call'd for and wanted e-
very where. In a Word, all the World wears
it, all the World defires it, and all the World almoft envies us the Glory and Advantage of it.

Nor is it the Drefs of the Mean and the
Poor in the feveral Countries where it
fpreads, but of the Beft and Richeft: The
Princes, nay, at this Time I may fay, the
Kings of the Earth, are cloth'd with it. I
appeal to all his Majefty's Servants, who
have had the Honour of his Commiffion as
Ambaffadors, and Refidents in foreign Coun-
tries, and the Courts of Princes throughout
Europe, whether they have not feen the
Czar of *Mufcovy*, the Kings of *Sweden*,
Denmark, *Pruffia*, *Poland*; nay, even the
Emperor of *Germany* himfelf, cloathed in
Englifh Cloth.

The King of *Spain* vouchfafes, even on
his Days of Ceremony, to appear in a Bays
Cloak ; the *Grand Seignior*, Lord of the
whole *Turkifh* Empire, has his Robe of *Englifh Cloth*, and the *Sophy* of *Perfia*, amidft
all his *Perfian* and *Indian* Silks, wears his
long Gown of Crimfon *Broad Cloth*, and
efteems it, as it really is, the nobleft Drefs
in the World.

As it is with the Princes, it is, and ever
will be with the People, the Nobility, the
Gentlemen, and in a Word, the Burghers,
the beft and wealthieft of the People are
gene-

generally cloath'd with it; nay, fo far has it prevail'd, that in *Ruffia* and *Sweden*, and other cold Climates, it has been known, that thofe who could not go to the Price of *Englifh Cloth*, have bought the Lifts of it which the Taylors cut off, fowed them together, and lin'd them with Furs, to make them long Robes or Garments, which they wore in that Country, till the late *Czar* cut them fhorter for them.

AND this brings me back to the Imitations which the People of thefe feveral Countries are faid to run into, to the Prejudice of our Manufacture. 'Tis true, the *Swedes*, the *Pruffians*, and feveral other People, do imitate the *Englifh* Manufacture, and would gladly do it univerfally for the Advantage of their People; and we cannot blame them; nay, even this alone is a Document, an authentick Voucher to the Truth of what I have faid: For if our Woollen Manufacture were not neceffary to them, they would not buy it of us; and if not profitable, they would not attempt to mimick and make it.

BUT what does it all amount to? they are able indeed to make the coarfeft and meaneft of the Manufacture, and that juft enough to cover and cloath the Boors, and moft defpicable of their People; thofe whofe Clothing was our coarfe Duffells, Wadmill, Half thicks, and in general a kind of the coarfeft Kerfies, but a Degree or two above Blankets; or perhaps, the meaneft of our Dozens,

and

and what we call *Yorfhire* Cloths : And even this is done but indifferently neither.

BUT in all thefe Countries, the People of Fafhion ftill cloath with our *Englifh* fine broad Cloth; and 'tis ordinary to have a Ship bound to *Gottenburgh*, or to *Stockholm*, carry 500 or 1000 *Spanifh Cloths* at a Time into *Sweden* ; by *Spanifh* Cloths I mean the fine medly Cloths, fuch exactly as we wear here, which are mix'd with *Spanifh* Wool in the Making, and therefore call'd *Spanifh* Cloths.

IT is the fame at *Stetin* and *Koningfburgh, Straelfund* or *Dantzick,* notwithftanding the Kings of *Pruffia* and *Poland*, prohibiting our Cloths, and fetting their own People to Work.

To conclude ; our Manufacture is the general Wear, for therein the Argument is forcible ; 'tis not that fome of it is to be had everywhere, for fo might be faid of feveral other Things, as of the *French* fine Stuffs, Silks and Druggets, and other light fpungy Manufacture of Hair and Silk mingled with Wool, *&c.*

BUT the *Englifh* broad Cloth is the general Wear ; the Druggets, Serges, Du-roys, Kerfies, Camlets; in a Word, the Woollen Manufactures of *Great Britain* are the general Wear in all the Countries in *Europe.*

THE *Mufcovites*, as I have faid, wore them formerly in their long Vefts, the *Germans*, the *Poles*, the *Swedes* are clothed
with

with them univerſally ; witneſs the great
Marts or Fairs, of *Leipſick* and *Frankfort*,
where ſuch exceeding Quantities of them
are ſold every Year, as is ſaid above, and witneſs the Cities of *Hamburgh*, *Lubeck*, *Bremen* and *Embden*, by which all the Provinces of the lower *Germany* are ſupplied.

Not a capital City in the Empire, but
you may find the Shops of the Tradeſmen
ſtor'd with *Engliſh* Cloth, as far as the Navigation of the *Elb*, the *Oder*, or the *Weiſ-
ſel* can convey them; the *Rhine*, the *Maes*,
the *Moſelle*, the *Saar*, the *Main*, the
Neckar, the *Danube*, they all aſſiſt to hand
it on, not at *Prague* only, not at *Vienna*,
not at *Munich*, but even at *Buda* and *Bel-
grade*, it is to be ſold; and the beſt Gentlemen in the Country buy it, if they do not,
'tis for Want of Money, and not for Want
of Will.

From the Empire, and the northern
Countries, come away into the *Mediterranean*, I have mention'd the *Turkiſh* Court,
there you ſee the *Baſſas*, the *Agas*, the
Kadileſchars, and even the *Grand Seigni-
or*, cloth'd with *Engliſh* Cloth, even in
their Habits of Ceremony.

From thence you come to *Italy*, 'tis the
ſame there, and the great Fair at *Meſſina* is
an undeniable Evidence of it, where there is
ſeldom ſo little as an Hundred Thouſand
Pound Value, ſold in our *Engliſh* Woollen
Manufacture every Seaſon, ſuch as Druggets,

gets, Du-Roys, Sagathyes, Camlets, with all other Sorts of Mens Stuffs, and broad Cloth it felf; and tho' they have wrought Silks in fuch Abundance, and fo cheap, yet you fee the *Italians* generally clothed in *Englijh* Cloth or thin Stuffs; the Clergy in black Bays, the Nuns are vail'd with fine Says, and *Long Ells,* and even the noble *Venetians* wear our fine Cloth for their beft Drefs.

AT *Rome* it is the fame, the foreign Princes and Ambaffadors, and the *Italian* Princes themfelves, wear it at *Millan,* at *Turin,* at *Naples,* even at *Rome,* 'tis all the fame: As to *France,* I mention'd it already, and I fcarce need name the *Spaniards* and the *Portuguefe.*

WHAT one Manufacture like this can boaft of fo general a Reception, or of being the Favourite Drefs of the whole Chriftian World? If we fhould go over to *America,* whether to the *Brafils,* the flourifhing Colony of the *Portuguefe,* how many Hundred Thoufand Moyd'ors a Year do we receive from thence, for the *Englijh* Manufactures worn and confumed there, notwithftanding the intenfe Heat of the Place? 'tis the fame Thing at *Mexico,* the moft luxurious, extravagant, and profufe City and Country in the World; even there the utmoft Pride of the proudeft People upon Earth, is to be clothed in the *Englijh* Cloth, and to have their Waftcoats and

Breeches

Breeches of fine Camlets, and other Stuffs
of Crimfon and Scarlet ; and over all, a
Cloak of our *Eſſex Bays.*

'Tis the fame at *Cartagena,* at *Panama,* at *Lima* and St. *Jago,* the Capital
richeſt Cities of their ſeveral Countries;
ſome of them ſituate within ten Degrees of
the Equinox, and where the Heats are
almoſt unſufferable; which I mention to obſerve to you, how well our Manufactures
are adapted to all Countries, Climates, Perſons, and Qualities ; not too thin for the
frozen *Laplanders, Swedes,* and *Ruſſians,*
or too thick for the ſcorch'd *Americans*
and Inhabitants of *Peru* and *Brazil*; not
too light for the *Germans,* or too *heavy* for the *Italians.*

In Value 'tis the fame; not too cheap
for the Nobility, no not for the Kings and
the Emperors of the World ; not too dear
for the Burghers and the Tradeſmen, no
not for the Boors, and the Peaſants; not too
gay for the Men, not too grave for the
Ladies: We find in common, the *Britiſh*
Manufacture is the general Wear, as well
of Poor as rich; the higheſt Sovereign, and
the moſt retir'd Recluſe; 'tis the beſt Habit
of the beſt of their People, in every Nation
in *Europe, Aſia, Africa* and *America*; the
only Country where it is not ſo, is that Part
of *Aſia,* which we call the *Eaſt Indies,* where
the infinite Variety of their own Manufactures, and the little Time that the
Engliſh

Englifh have traded among them, has not yet made its Way ; yet we find it begins to be received in *China*, and alfo at the Court of the *Mogul ;* and as the Number of *Europeans* encreafe in the *Indies*, there is Room to believe the *Britifh* Manufactures will gain Ground among them too; It is evident, that at *Melinda*, and the other *Portuguefe* Settlements on the Eaft Coaft of *Africa*, beyond the Cape of *Good Hope*, where the *Portuguefe* have brought the Natives to wear Clothes, even within five Degrees of the Line; there the *Britifh* Manufacture, carried by the *Portuguefe* to them, are the general Habit, as well of the Natives, as of the *Portuguefe*, among whom they dwell.

WHAT can be more plain than thefe Facts, of which the whole World are Witneffes? And what can be a clearer Proof of the Magnitude of our Woollen Manufacture? I think I need fay no more about it.

WHAT Wonder then, that the feveral Nations endeavour to fet their own People to work to make it? How could any other be expected? That alfo is a farther Teftimony of its intrinfick Value, and the Neceffity of it in Ufe.

1*ft*, IT appears, that they cannot be without it.

2*dly,* THAT it is to be had no where elfe.

1. THEY

1. THEY cannot be without it ; if any other Sort of Goods would fupply, if their Linens would cloath the *Germans,* or their Silks the *Italians ;* if any Thing of their own Growth would be equivalent to them, why do they not prohibit ours, as they do the Silks and Callicoes of *India ?* I mean in general, as the *Spaniards* moft ridiculoufly did a few Months fince, without having any thing for their People to wear in the Room of them; which made their very Women laugh at them, and ask their Husbands where they would get Cloths.

IT is true fome Princes have prohibited fome of our Manufactures; that is to fay, fuch particular Sorts as their own Wool, and their own People can make ; but where is the Prince or People, Kingdom or Empire in the World, the *Indies* excepted, who will, or indeed can be wholly without our Woollen Manufacture ?

2. THAT it is not to be fupplied from any other Country, is as evident as the other ; for where is that Country, and why are they not as rich, as opulent, as powerful at Sea, and on Shore, as *England* is ?

WHERE is the Country ? if there is not a Country, as I have prov'd above, that has or can have an equivalent Manufacture, or that does not buy from us, How fhould there be a Country that can fupply its Neighbours?

BUT

BUT why do not fome of the Nations, who envy the Profits and Advantages of this Manufacture to us, and who would be careful to keep at home the immenfe Sums of Money, which this (to us happy) Article draws from them; I fay, Why do they not publifh a general Prohibition, not of this or that particular Sort of our Goods, but of all Woollen Goods whatfoever, and from what Country foever?

I s it poffible, that they can find out no Equipment for themfelves? Might not the Men in *Italy* and *Spain* cloath themfelves in thick Silks, Velvets, and ftrong *Paduafoys*? and in the North, might not the *Poles,* the *Ruffians,* the *Swedes,* the *Danes,* the *Pruffians,* the *Saxons* drefs themfelves in rich Furrs, Skins of Beafts, fuch as the Sables and Ermines, Beaver, Otter, and black Fox Skins, the latter more valuable than Ermines?

METHINKS the *Germans*, and *Italians*, who are fuch Mafters of the Linen and Silk Manufactures, and have the Advantage of fuch Quantities of Furrs as the *Ruffians* could furnifh them with, might improve them into fome Form, and turn them into fome Shape, fo as to fupply their Want of Clothes, and not impoverifh themfelves and their Country to buy Foreign Manufactures: The reverend grave Sables, and the royal Ornaments of Ermines, might ferve to gratify their Vanity, and make them all, like thofe Cor-
poration-

poration-Princes, called Aldermen; and they might cloath as rich in Furs and Fox-Skins as they pleas'd, if the Outfide was plain, the Infide would be great and rich, and the Climate would reconcile them to the Warmth of the Drefs.

But 'tis impoffible; it will not do; nothing can anfwer all the Ends of Drefs, but good *Englifh* broad Cloth, fine Camlets, Druggets, Serges, and fuch like; thefe they muft have, and with thefe none but *England* can fupply them; Be their Country hot or cold, torrid or frigid, 'tis the fame Thing, near the Equinox, or near the Pole, the *Englifh* Woollen Manufacture clothes them all; here it covers them warm, from the freezing Breath of the Northern *Bear*; and there it fhades them, and keeps them cool from the fcorching Beams of a perpendicular Sun.

Let no Man wonder, that the Woollen Manufacture of *England* is arriv'd to fuch a Magnitude, when in a Word it may be faid to cloath the World; there are but three Sorts of People in the World that do not ufe it.

1*ft*, Those that cloath altogether with Callicoes, and Silks, as in *India ;* the Manufactures of their own Country.

2*dly*, Those that living in fome hot Countries, wear no Cloths at all. And,

3*dly*, Those who are fo very poor and defpicable, that they cannot get it.

CHAP.

CHAP. VI.

Of the Magnitude of the British *Commerce, as it respects the Consumption of foreign Goods imported from abroad, as well as of our own Product and Manufacture at home.*

S our Manufactures, and other Exportations are thus great, and the Consumption and Export of our own, whether Product or Manufactures, are so much a Prodigy for their Magnitude, and are thus extended to all Parts of the World, our Importations are no less prodigious ; and this the rather, because of the great Consumption of those Importations among our selves, as well as their Exportation as Merchandize.

I T must be acknowledg'd, that the Trade of the *Dutch* by foreign Importations, is also very great, and may be said to exceed the Importations of *England* ; and I believe in many Articles they do so, if we consider their *East Country* Fleets, their *Greenland*
Fleets,

Fleets, their *Eaſt India,* their *French* Wine, and their Herring Fleets, and all their other Branches of Trade to *Turky,* and to the *Mediterranean;* and eſpecially their Importations of *woollen Manufacture, Sugars, Tobaccos,* wrought and other Plantation Goods; *Lead, Tin, Iron,* and *Braſs;* *Drugs, Dye Stuffs, Corn,* &c. from *England.*

But then the *Dutch* muſt be underſtood to be as they really are, the *Carryers of the World,* the middle Perſons in Trade, the Factors and Brokers of *Europe:* That, as is ſaid above, they *buy* to *ſell* again, *take* in to *ſend* out; and the greateſt Part of their vaſt Commerce conſiſts in being ſupply'd from all Parts of the World, that they may ſupply all the World again: Thus they ſupply ſome Nations with Corn, others with Ships, or Naval Stores for Ships; others with Arms and Ammunition of all kinds; ſuch as Powder, Shot, Shells, Lead, Iron, Copper, Cannon, Mortars, *&c.* others with Fiſh, others with woollen Manufactures, *and the like;* and yet, they have neither Corn, Hemp, Tar, Timber, Lead, Iron, Arms, Ammunition, woollen Manufacture, or Fiſh of their own Growth; the Product of their own Land or Seas, or Labour of their own People, other than as Navigators and Seamen, to fetch, find, and carry them.

Nor is their home Conſumption of foreign Importations great, except of Corn
and

woollen Manufacture ; their People are few, compar'd to foreign Nations, tho' many compar'd to the Country where they dwell ; their Way of Living is fparing, their Exceffes few and mean, and their Oftentation or Gayety very low priz'd.

BUT in *England,* the Country is large, populous, rich, fruitful ; the Way of Living, large, luxurious, vain and expenfive, even to a Profufion, the Temper of the People gay, oftentatious, vicious, and full of Exceffes ; even criminally fo in fome Things, and too much encreafing in them all.

HENCE comes as a Confequence, a vaft Importation of foreign Growth of every kind, either for Eating or Drinking, for Fancy or Fafhions, and this fo great, as not to be equall'd in any Part of the World ; the Fact feems a Charge, tho' not defign'd as fuch, but to illuftrate the Subject : But I muft defcend a little to Particulars, to make it out.

I am credibly inform'd, and firmly believe it to be true, that take all the maritime Nations of *Europe,* where no Wine is made, and caft them up together, they do not import fo much Wine as the Subjects of **Great Britain** do, for we have not a Drop of our own Growth ; and this, notwithftanding a very great Confumption of Malt-Liquors, Malt and Melaffes Spirits, brew'd and diftill'd at Home ; and notwithftanding

ftanding a vaft Quantity of Cyder and Perry, Mead, Rum, and other Liquors; much of it fpent in meer Extravagance and Profufion; and in fpite of a moft exceffive Duty upon the Importation of the Wine, as well as an Excife upon the Confumption of the brew'd Liquors of our own.

The Importation of Wines of all Kinds, and Brandy included, from abroad, have been often calculated by juft Mediums of Years, and is lately caft up for the Year 1721, at 60000 Pipes, or 30000 Ton *per Annum.*

But then let me add by Way of Supplement, That as I underftand it,

1. All this Account is exclufive of the Wines and Brandy imported in *Scotland* and *Ireland,* and the *Ifle of Man*; and of all the *Madera* and *Canary* Wines imported in our Colonies, the *Madera* Wine being at leaft 1000 Ton *per Annum ;* and the Wine imported in *Scotland* and *Ireland,* &c. cannot be fo little as 3000 Ton more, which makes it 40000 Ton in all.

2. It is exclufive of all the *French* Wines and Brandy run on Shore by the Smugglers, in all the three Kingdoms, and efpecially in *Scotland* and *Ireland,* where I have fome particular Reafons to believe, not 1-6th Part (of the Brandy, efpecially) pays the Duty.

3. It is exclufive of all the Rum diftilled in the *Weft India* Colonies, and confum'd

fum'd in thofe Colonies, as well in the Iflands, as on the Continent.

THESE are all to be call'd Importations, and the Sum total is prodigious; let any Man that may think me fevere, in faying we are a luxurious, expenfive People, calculate the annual Confumption of Wine and ftrong Liquors in his Majefty's Dominions at this Time ; and then judge impartially, whether I do Juftice to the People or no.

WERE Wine the ordinary Drink of the People, or were ftrong Beer and Ale the needful Table-Liquors for the Support of Life, it were quite another Cafe ; but if Wine were the ordinary Drink, it would be mingled in the drinking with Water, as it is in the ufual drinking of the Countries where it grows, as in *Spain, Italy, France,* &c. where fcarce any Wine is drank without Water, and very little to Excefs.

N. B. IN *France* and *Spain,* Wine mingled with Water, is the ordinary Beverage or Drink for meer Neceffity, as Food ; but if they take any Thing to exhilerate or raife the Spirits, it is Brandy ; which yet, they very rarely drink to Excefs ; whereas here ; all, as well Brandy as Wine, and all our ftrong compounded Drinks, fuch as ftout Ale, Punch, Double-Beer, Fine-Ale, *&c.* are all drank to Excefs, and that to
such

fuch a Degree, as to become the Poifon, as well of our Health as of our Morals ; fatal to the Body, to Principles, and even to the Underftanding ; and we fee daily Examples of Men of ftrong Bodies drinking themfelves into the Grave ; and which is ftill worfe, Men of ftrong Heads, and good Judgment, drinking themfelves into Idiotifm and Stupidity : But that by the way ; I return to the Difcourfe, as it is the Subject of Trade ; Wine, and all the ftrong Liquors mention'd above, are not our Drink, but our Excefs ; not our needful, but our fuperfluous Drink.

O n the other Hand, our *Table Beer*, which is the wholefome, ufeful, and neceffary Liquor of the Country, made for Family-Supply, and ufed as fuch by the fober Part of our People, is excluded from the Account : Nor is there a Gallon of Water mingled with a Hogfhead of Wine, one with another, for all the Wine we drink.

I am not going to launch out here into a Satyr upon our Country, or to dip into the Scandal of our common Vices ; the immenfe Greatnefs of our Trade is the Subject ; but our Vices are fo unhappily mingled with our Intereft in Trade, that as a late Author, writing on that Subject, fays well, *Our Luxury is become a Virtue in*
                                 Com-

Commerce, and our Extravagancies are the Life and Soul of our Trade.

As I propofed to judge of the Greatnefs of our Manufactures, by the Quantity of the Wool which is confum'd in making them ; fo we may take fome View of the Confumption of Liquor among us, from the Quantity of Malt confum'd in *Great Britain* and *Ireland,* that being the Fund or Principle from whence they are produc'd.

I fhall not enter here into a Cloud of Figures, to deduce the long Account ; but tell you in the Grofs, and at one View, that calculating the Quantity of Drink brew'd from the Quantity of Malt made, and taking that from the Foot of the Excife, *or Duty* paid on the Malt, called in general the *Malt Tax,* I venture to affirm, there are forty Millions of Bufhels of Malt brew'd or diftill'd in his Majefty's Dominions every Year, exclufive of what is exported in Trade to foreign Countries.

It remains only to deduct out of this Reckoning, the *fmall Beer* ; that is to fay, the Quantity yearly made Ufe of in Table Beer for Family-Ufes ; and fhould I take out one fourth Part for neceffary Beer, as I call it ; that is, fmall Table-Beer, which, I think, is a great deal too much, there would ftill remain thirty Millions of Bufhels to be brew'd in ftrong Beer, which it muft be acknowledged, is much of it Luxury

ury and Extravagance, much of it Vice and Intemperance.

REDUCE this again into Drink, and allow three Bushels of Malt to every Barrel of strong Beer ; this makes no less than ten Millions of Barrels of strong Beer consum'd at Home, in this sober Nation in a Year.

THE only Exception to this Account that I can meet with, which has any weight in it, is, that some of this Malt is distill'd into Spirits ; and suppose I allow 200000 Quarter *per Annum*, so consum'd, that is, one Million, 600000 Bushel; it will be answer'd, 1*st*, That this is of the worst of the Malt, and of a Kind which would not make good Beer, if it was brew'd, and that much of it is not fit to be brew'd at all : But then, 2*d*, It will be said, that this cannot be plac'd to the Account of our Temperance, or taken off from the Luxury spoken of, since 'tis generally brew'd into a worse Liquor, and apply'd to worse uses, which it is not my Business at this Time to talk of, and which it would be better, were it entirely forgotten (if that could be) then spoken of at all.

IF this Consumption of Liquors in the King's Dominions were to be calculated in the whole, and the Value were to be cast up in Money, what an immense Sum would it amount to ? And what an Article would

would it make in the Magnitude of our Trade?

1. TAKE the Wine and Brandy confum'd in the whole, and fuppofe the Quantity to be no more, than what is legally imported, not reckoning the fo much greater Quantity of what is clandeftinely run on Shore by Smuggling, and other Frauds: If the legally imported Quantity of Wine and Brandy amounts to 40000 Ton, the Rum confum'd in the Plantations not included, which is a very great Quantity.

LET this be brought to the Pint Pot; that is, to the Retailer, and reduce it thus, 1. The Price of almoft all Sorts of Wine and Brandy, is at leaft to a Confumer, fold at two Shillings *per* Quart; the *French* Wine, the Canary, the Rhenifh, the Sherry, all at more than two Shillings; and the Brandy by retail, generally at double the Price: But take it one with another, at two Shillings *per* Quart, which is eight Shillings *per* Gallon, and make a reafonable Allowance for Bottoms and Leakage, as ufual; yet to what an immenfe Sum does the Confumption of imported Liquors in the *Britifh* Dominions amount to?

252 Gallons is a Ton, this at 8 *s. per* Gallon, (the Retailers Price) amounts to 100 *l.* 16 *s. per* Ton; but abating 12 Gallons in every Ton for Bottoms and Leakage: And fuppofe it to be but 240 Gallons Nett Wine *per* Ton, at 8 *s. per* Gallon, it is 96 *l. per* Ton.

40000

```
Ton.
40000  of Wine and Brandy imported
   96  yearly at 96 l. per Ton, a-
———————  mounts to 3.840000 l.
240000
360000
———————
l. 3.840000.
```

N. B. THERE is no need at all of the Abatement for Bottoms and Leakage, the Vintners making effectual Provision for it in their short Measure; and if that is not taken out, it amounts to just four Millions Sterling *per Annum;* besides all the Wine and Brandy really imported in the dark; *that is*, by clandestine Trade, Smuggling, *&c.*

THUS much is calculated upon the legal Importation; and as we may call it, the known, and avow'd Consumption of Wines and Brandy in the Dominions of *Great Britain;* what we may suppose to be clandestinely brought on Shore, is hard to determine: But they who know as I do, how common, how plentiful Brandy is, I mean *French* Brandy, known and acknowledg'd to be such on all the Sea Coasts of *England*, in all Parts of *Scotland* and *Ireland*, and how much it is us'd. They who'd know, that but a few Years ago, 5000 Ton

of

of Brandy was faid to be brought into the Ifles of *Jerfey* and *Guernfey*, from *France* in one Year. They who have had any Knowledge of the prodigious Quantity of Wine and Brandy conftantly brought to, and manag'd (fo it feems 'tis call'd) in the *Ifle of Man*, for fome Years paft, and by which that whole Ifland is vifibly enrich'd, to a furprifing Degree : I fay, thofe who have had any Infight in thefe Things, will not think it unreafonable to allow, at leaft one fourth Part more of Wine and Brandy to this Account.

BUT it is enough to mention it only ; I believe, it will be readily admitted, that what is faid above, is very likely to be true, *viz.* That the *Britifh* Dominions import more Wine, than all the Countries of *Europe*, who are without Wine of their own Import, put them all together.

IT may be true, that fome of thofe Countries import more Brandy than we do, in Proportion to their Trade ; but it is to be allow'd, only, becaufe we have loaded the foreign Brandy with heavy Duties, in order to encourage the Confumption of our own Malt Spirits.

2. I might in the next Place calculate here the Value, as I have already the Quantity of our home Confumption of ftrong Beer and Ale, among our own People ; and it would not be difficult to do it, either from the Quantity of Malt confum'd

in

in the whole, (as well for Sale, as for private Ufe) as alfo from the Rate of Excife : But the Sum would be fo great, it would furprife the Reader.

I T is true, the Beer, or Ale brew'd in Gentlemens Houfes for private Ufe, does not coft fo much as the Beer brew'd for Sale, becaufe of the Excife ; but then, if we fhould abate reckoning the Beer and Ale retail'd, at the Price paid by the Confumer, which is the manner of Reckoning we are now going upon, and is the true way, when we are to examine the Magnitude of an Expence, on the Foot of Trade ; *I fay then,* if we fhould abate the retailing Price of the Beer and Ale retail'd, in Ballance of the Quantity confum'd in private Families, which I think is giving up a very manifeft Odds ; upon this Equality, we might bring it to a Head, by rating all the ftrong Beer, and Ale confum'd in *England,* at the Rate of twenty Shillings, upon every three Bufhels of Malt. If there are any Objections to be made againft the Calculation, I believe they would be eafily anfwer'd ; but if they cannot, they may be ballanc'd by Abatement ; for as by this Calculation, the Confumption of ftrong Drink amounts to no lefs than ten Millions Sterling *per Annum,* if we fhould abate a quarter Part of it ; 'tis an immenfe and almoft incredible Sum, and what no other Nation in the World can expend in one fingle Article.

Now,

NOW to examine this a little another Way, let any Man that is admitted to fuch a Liberty, caft up the Books of the Excife, and tell us how much the Excife upon ftrong Beer amounts to in *Great Britain* and *Ireland*, and from thence fome Eftimate may be made.

SUPPOSE then, for Example, the Duty, as collected; for in this Account, we are not to caft up and deduct the Charges of the Collection, the Eftablifhment of the Office, the Incidents, &c. but how much is collected from the Brewer; I fay, fuppofe this amounts in *England, Scotland,* and *Ireland,* and all his Majefty's Dominions, where the Excife is payable, to 800000 *l. per Annum :* I doubt not, but it amounts to much more; but let the critical Enquirer do Juftice on that Account, as he finds the Cafe will demand; I have good Grounds to fay it may be caft up thus, till a Reafon is produc'd why it fhould not.

IF the Excife then, at four Shillings and nine Pence *per* Barrel upon ftrong Beer, collects 800000 *l. per Annum ;* the Beer being fold to the Retailer, at twenty Shillings *per* Barrel, muft then amount to above four Times the Sum : We need not in fuch a conjectural Eftimate as this, caft up the Fractions of three Pence *per* Barrel, it would but add to the Sum, which you may evidently fee, I do not feek to make greater than it is.

THIS

THIS then brings the Value of the Beer, as fold to the Retailer, to be three Millions two hundred thoufand Pounds *per Annum*.

ADD to this then, the Value of the ftrong Beer brew'd for private Families, which, as before, I take to be equal to the other, (under the Difadvantage of its being under rated, *viz.* to the Retailer, and not to the Confumer) but to avoid Cavils, I'll ftate it at half that Sum : The Expence then of ftrong Beer in thefe Dominions, rifes to four Millions nine hundred thoufand Pounds *per Annum.*

I could fupport thefe Eftimates, by a ftricter comparing the Quantity brew'd, with the Quantity of Malt made ; but 'tis needlefs here, there is a manifeft Difference between exact critical Examination, and a general Eftimate, after the manner of an Hypothefis ; it is the latter that is before me now ; wherein, however, the Advantage is fo great, that it fully anfwers the End of the Argument, if I fhould throw in a Million or two of Pounds Sterling, in the whole, and take it at fo much lefs than it really amounts to, as I am well *affur'd I do in this Account : For Example,* if according to the propofed Principle, I am cafting up the Value of the ftrong Liquors which the Nation confumes, and ought to take it (for the purpofe) at the Rate it cofts the Confumer, as I did in the Wine, it would

would ftand thus. Every Barrel of ftrong Beer retailed by the Victuallers, meafures him out by the Quart Pot 36 Gallons; this fold at 3 *d. per* Quart, the ordinary Price, (tho' the general Rate is now 4 *d.*) is 36 *s.* the Barrel, befides the Advantage of the felling much of it at 2 *d. per* Pint, and befides the Half, which the Victualler finds in fhort Meafure.

   N. B. THIS is evident in the Suttlers and others, who draw Drink in Garrifons; and the Tapfters, who take Cellars and Tap-houfes in great Inns, who frequently allow the Governours and Mafters of fuch Houfes, 30 to 35 *s.* and fome 40 *s. per* Barrel for the Drink they draw under them; fo that if I calculate all the ftrong Beer at the Rate of but 20 *s. per* Barrel, it will allow for all the Objections that can be made againft any other Part, feeing it cannot amount to much above half the Value which the Confumer pays.

   UPON the Whole, I take upon me to fay, without any Hazard of being confuted, that there is confumed in his Majefty's Dominions, of all the following Liquors, exclufive of fmall Beer, no lefs, reckoning it at the Value paid by the Confumer to the Retailer, and including the ftrong Beer brew'd for private Ufe, than the full Value of eight Millions *per Annum.*

                           THE

The Liquors included in this Account, are as follows.

Wine of all Sorts, } Imported.
Brandy,

Strong Beer, and all } Brew'd at Home.
Cyder and Perry,

Malt and Melasses Spirits } Distill'd at
Cyder Spirits   Home.

Rum distill'd from Sugar and } in the Plan-
Beer and Ale brew'd   tations.

The Plantations, as being Part of our felves, are always in Accounts of Trade, to be caft up with our other Accounts; and as their Produce is efteem'd our own: So their Confumption fhould be alfo, and is fo in all juft Calculations; and for this Reafon, the Importations from thence are not reckon'd as foreign Importations, but as a Home Produce.

The next Article of the Importation of foreign Goods is Linen, and this, it muft be acknowledg'd, relates more efpecially to *England*, and to the Confumption here, and in the *Englifh* Colonies in *America*.

Of this Confumption, it may indeed be faid *it is a Prodigy*; and tho' there is a confiderable Quantity of Linen made in fome Parts of *England*, efpecially in the North
Parts,

Parts, as in *Lancashire*, *Cheshire*, *Yorkshire*, and the four other Northern Countries, infomuch, that at one Market in *Lancashire* 'tis faid, there is the Value of 500 *l.* a Week fold in Hukabacks only; yet this Quantity is fo little worth mention, that this fort of Linen is fcarce feen at *London*; but *England* does as it were ravage the whole fpinning World for Linen and Linen Yarn and Lace, which is Linen alfo.

THE principal Importations of Linen are indeed from our neighbouring Countries; but fuch is the exceeding Confumption of Linen here, that it feems as if all the World were not able to fupply us; and this not only of the coarfer Kinds of Linen from the Northern Nations, but fuch is the Demand of fine Linens, *Hollands*, *Cambricks*, and the fineft of other Country Linen, that it is advanc'd to me for a certain Truth, by a Perfon experienc'd in thofe Trades, that *England* alone wears and confumes as much fine Linen; nay, his Words are, *More of the fineft Linen* than all the Kingdom of *France*, the *Auftrian Netherlands*, and the *united Provinces* put together, where the fine Linen is chiefly made.

I need not enter critically into the Enqui-whether this is literally true or no; but when I come to look into our Cuftom-houfe Entries, and fee by the Books the exceeding Quantity of Linen, as well fine as coarfe, impor-

imported into *England* from all Parts, it is really furprifing. *For Example,*

COARSE *Ruffia Linen,* properly fo call'd, from *Petersburgh* and *Narva, Revel, Riga, &c. Canvas* and *Polifh* Linen from *Dantfick, Koningsberg, Stetin* and *Straelfund, &c.* and *Diapers, Damasks* and *Lawns* ; from *Silefia* and *Lufatia,* and *Saxony* by way of *Hamburgh* ; alfo other *Germany* Linens, including a multitude of Sorts of middling Finefs, fuch as are the Manufactures of feveral Countries upon the *Elbe,* imported likewife from *Hamburgh.*

> *N. B.* THE Quantity of *German Linen* imported from *Hamburgh,* is paft all Calculation, and is fuppofed to amount to many Hundred thoufand Pounds Sterling a Year, fomething more than two Millions.

COARSER Linens, fuch as *Heffens, Ofnabrigs, Hinderlands,* and feveral other Sorts from *Bremen* and *Embden,* the Manufacture of the Circle of *Weftphalia,* and the Countries of *Ofnaburgh, Hannover* and *Lunenburgh.*

FINE *Hollands* for Shifts and Sheets, and fuch like fine Ufes, of all Prices and Denominations, from 1 *s.* to 12 *s. per* Ell ; as alfo the beft Sail Cloth, call'd *Duck,* all from *Holland.*

FINE *Ghentifh Hollands* of feveral Sorts from *Bruges* and *Ghent,* generally from 2 *s.* to 4 *s.* 6 *d.* and 5 *s. per* Ell.

FINE

FINE Cambricks and fine Lace from *Lifle*, *Bruffels*, *Valentiennes*, *Mecklen*, all the upper *Flanders*, and the *Paiys Conquis* the Cambricks to fuch a Degree of Trade, that *England* and *Ireland* are faid to take off juft now above 200000 *l. Sterling per Annum* in Cambricks only, the Quantity exceedingly encreafed by the Wear of Muflin growing out of Fafhion.

DOWLAS *Lockrams*, and *Vitry Canvas* from *France*, the Quantity formerly prodigious great, not lefs than 100 Ships Loadings a Year, and now encreafing again, notwithftanding the high Duties, it is imported from *Morlaix*, and feveral other Ports in *Normandy* and *Bretaigne*.

ALL thefe, befides *Irifh* and *Scots Linen*, the Quantity of which, efpecially fince the Encouragement given to their Importation, by the printing of Linen, is fo much, that the Importation of *Irifh Linen*, amounts to at leaft 2000000 Yards in a Year, and is ftill exceedingly encreafing; being fo in Demand, that if the Ships are but a little Wind bound, there is frequently not a Yard of *Irifh Linen* to be had in the Town.

LET any one judge, whether we do not as it were ravage the World for Linen, and whether I have exceeded in faying, we import more Linen than any one Nation in the World.

IT is true, that a very great Quantity of Linen of all Kinds is fhip'd off again from hence.

hence. But it is anfwered, That it is chiefly, if not wholly to our own Colonies in *America*, which, as I faid above, is juftly to be efteemed our own Confumption, as being all confumed by our own People.

It is indeed impoffible to make an Efti-mate of the Quantity of Linen imported from all thefe places into *Great Britain* and *Ireland:* For notwithftanding the Quanti-ties made either in *Scotland* or *Ireland*, there are yet great Quantities of fine Hol-lands, Cambricks, and other Sorts imported in both thofe Countries. I fay, there can be no Eftimate made of the Value. But having thus defcrib'd the Trade in its feve-ral Branches, I leave it under this General, namely, that there is more Linen as well in Bulk as in Value imported from other Coun-tries, into the *Britifh* Dominions, than any, or than all the Nations of *Europe* put to-gether import befides us.

I could run over all the Kingdoms and Pro-vinces of *Europe* by Name, and from their par-ticular Circumftances give Reafons to prove this. It is certain, that thro' all the *German* Empire, *Italy, France, Flanders, Holland*, all thofe Kingdoms and Provinces, either make their own Linen, fome fmall Quanti-ty of particular Sorts excepted, or make more than they ufe, and fend it abroad.

It is alfo certain, that thofe Countries where the Linen they make is of an inferior Quality, as in *Poland, Ruffia, Pruffia*,

Pome-

Pomerania, &c. Either they ufe a very little Quantity of *Linen*, compar'd to what is made Ufe of in *England*, or make Shift with the meaner Quality and Kinds, which their own Countries produce; and except the Courts and Princes in thofe Countries, they call for very little from abroad.

FOR Proof of this, we are able to give a known Example of all the Northern Parts of the Empire in Particular ; where 'tis evident, tho' they buy neither from *Holland*, *France*, or *Flanders*, they are in no Want; but the Gentry, and even the Princes and Nobility are fupplied with fine Linen, at leaft the fineft that they ufe from their own Manufacture ; that is to fay, from *Silefia*, and the Provinces of *Lufatia*, *Bohemia*, *Moravia*, and the Countries adjoining ; fo that all that Part of the World may be faid to make Linen even more than fufficient to themfelves.

NOR can we defire a better Evidence of this, than is to be found in the two following Articles,

I. THAT as I faid above, we import into *England* a great deal of fine Linen from thofe Countries, fuch as fine *Lawns*, equal to fome of the Cambricks which are made in *Flanders*, alfo fine Diapers and Damasks; and it cannot be doubted, but thofe Provinces which fupply thofe Sorts to us at fuch a Diftance, are able to fupply themfelves; for I call all the *German* Provinces on that

Side,

Side, *themselves* ; being all the Dominions of the fame Sovereign, fpeaking the fame Language, and lying contiguous to one another.

2. The *Dutch* themfelves, who make thofe fine Hollands which we import here, and which we give fuch a Price for, buy the fineft of the Yarn, with which thofe Hollands are made, from thofe very Provinces; and it cannot be queftion'd, but that the *Silefians,* who fupply the *Dutch* with fuch fine Yarn, are able to fupply themfelves, and the Provinces about them, with all the fineft Sorts of Linen they have Occafion to buy.

This Example is fufficient, and for this Reafon I bring it; to prove that all thefe northern Countries fupply themfelves with Linen fufficient for their own Ufes; no Nation but *Britain,* nay, but *England,* buys and imports the Grofs of their Linen from Abroad; and yet at the fame Time, no People in *Europe* wear and confume fo great a Quantity of Linen, and that Quantity fo fine in its Quality, as the *Englifh* do.

It is true, that *Spain* and *Portugal* import great Quantities of Linen, having very little of their own ; but 'tis not worth Mention, in Comparifon with *England* ; nor do the *Spaniards* wear any Proportion in *Quantity* to the *Englifh* ; as may be determined from the Certainty and Same-

nefs

nefs of their Drefs: So I need fay no more
to that Part.

A s to *Italy* in all its Parts, from *Na-*
ples to *Turin, Rome* and *Venice,* they
not only do not ufe fo much in Proportion as the *Englifh*; but what they do make,
they (efpecially the *Venetians*) make in
their own Countries.

INDEED it cannot be fuppofed, that the
Venetians, who for fo many Ages were
famous for making the fineft Lace, and
confequently muft have a fufficient Quantity of the fineft Thread, could want a Manufacture of the fineft Linen ; and it is
known, that they do not want it, but on
the contrary, export it to the Iflands in
the *Archipelague,* and other Parts among
the *Greeks,* who have much Cotton, but
little or no Flax.

THUS I think I may have accounted for
all the Linen-wearing World ; that every
where but in *Italy* and *Spain,* they wear
lefs Linen, or make more than in *England*;
and in moft of thofe Countries, make fufficient for their own Ufe : There might be
fome Exceptions to this general Head, *that*
is to fay, that in *Sweden, Norway* and
Denmark, they do not make any large
Quantity of *Linen,* and that the City of
Lubec carries on the Linen Trade to *Swe-*
den, as the City of *Hamburgh* does to *Eng-*
land; but the Objection is not worth the
Anfwer ; it is provided for before; I do

not

not fay no other Nation imports any Linen, or ufe any, but what they make of their own; but I do fay and infift on it, that all thofe Nations put together, do not import the Quantity that *England* and the other *Britifh* Dominions do import.

I have quitted this Article, without mentioning alfo, that befides the Quantity of Linen we confume, which as above, is beyond all Calculation, we import from *Holland*, *Hamburgh*, and efpecially of late from *Ruffia*, very great Quantities of Linen-Yarn, for our own People to manufacture, and weave into Linen at Home; much of which Yarn is made ufe of in the Homemade Cloth, which as I have faid, our People make in the northern Parts of *England*; and in the Linfey Woolfey Manufactures at *Kiderminfter*, *Manchefter*, &c.

Nor is this Importation fmall and inconfiderable, tho' in Comparifon of the Linen it is fo indeed ; but all join together, to let us fee what a Prodigy of Trade, the Confumption of Linen in this Nation really is ; the Account of which is, without Doubt, many Millions yearly.

N. B. Whereas I omit the *Turks*, and and all the eaftern and fouthern Nations in *Europe*, in the Account of the Linen Trade Abroad ; the Anfwer is, That all thofe eaftern Nations are fupplied with Cotton and Callicoe, inftead

ftead of Linen, and very little Linen is ufed among them.

THE next Capital Head of our Importation I call FRUIT, and this confifts of a great Variety of fmall Articles, which however, being put together, will appear to be not only very confiderable, but in a Word exceeding great in Trade.

PERHAPS I may be cavill'd at for the Term FRUIT, the Product being fo various, and in its Appearance trifling; but as 'tis juft to bring all fuch fmaller Articles under one general Head, as they are a Merchandize; and that they are all really the Product and Growth of the Plants, which come under the Denomination of Vegetables, I think it will be a needlefs Objection: The Particulars are as follows, *viz.*

1. Raifins,	THESE are all, except the Oyl (which notwithftanding is fo too) ufually called Fruit, by the Merchants that import them; and even all thefe have this Particular attending them, as a Trade, *viz.* that they are ufed in no Nation in *Europe*, in Proportion to what is ufed in *England.*
2. Currants,	
3. Figs,	
4. Oranges and Lemons,	
5. Almonds,	
6. Oyl.	

N. B.

N. B. These are brought from several Countries, but chiefly from the *Mediterranean, viz.*

Raisins from $\begin{cases} Alicant \\ Malaga \\ Lipari \end{cases}$ and some small Ports adjacent.

Currants from $\begin{cases} Zant \\ Cephalonia \end{cases}$ and some small Ports in the *Morea.*

Figs from $\begin{cases} Algarve, \text{ sc. } Faro \text{ and} \\ Figuera, \text{ and from } Barbary. \end{cases}$

Oranges and Lemons $\begin{cases} Malaga \\ Sevillia \\ Lisbon \\ Oporto \end{cases}$ and some from *Genoa.*

Almonds from $\begin{cases} Barbary, \\ Spain. \end{cases}$

Oyl from $\begin{cases} Lisbon \text{ and } Oporto, \\ Faro \text{ and } Figuera, \\ Sevil \text{ and } Cadiz, \\ Leghorn \text{ and } Gallipoli. \end{cases}$

7 Coffee

7. Coffee,
{ All from *Mocca* or *Mocha* in the *Red Sea*, either by Way of *Alexandria*, or about by *Long Sea*, round the *Cape of Good Hope*.

8. Tea,
{ All from *China*, or from *Japon*, by Way of *China*.

9. Cocao,
{ From *Jamaica*, the Coast of the *Carracas*, the Gulph of *Honduras*, and other Parts in the *West Indies*.

10. Spice,
{
Nutmegs, Cloves, Mace, } From the *Indies* by Way of *Holland*, and (*as it happens*) no other Way.

Cinnamon, } From *Ceylon* by the same Hands.

Pepper, } from { *Malabar*, *Sumatra*, } by our own Shipping.

Piemento, From *New Spain*.

11. Pickles such as { Capers, Olives, *&c.* from *Leghorn*. *Lucca* and *Seville*.

12. *Add to these* Anchovies, } From *Leghorn ;* tho' this is indeed a Fish, not a Fruit, and is the only Fish we import from any Part of the World, except *Sturgeon*; but I add it here, as not sufficient for a Head by it self.

THEY

THEY that at firſt Sight look upon this Article under the Head of Fruit, will perhaps think it a trifling Thing, and that Oranges, Lemons, Raiſins, Almonds, &c. are all Trifles.

BUT let them go thro' all the Articles, and bring them into one Head of Importation, and they will have three Things to obſerve, which bring them to our preſent purpoſe.

1. THAT they are really ſo far from being ſmall, and of little Importance, that on the contrary, they are very conſiderable, and that many Ways.

2. THAT no Nation in *Europe* imports an equal Quantity of any of them, much leſs of all of them together, as we do.

THEY are a wonderful Teſtimony of the Greatneſs of the *Britiſh* Commerce, in that thoſe twelve Articles of petty Trade, (as they may, and would be eſteem'd any where elſe) are by our Conſumption of Quantity made ſo conſiderable ; that as I am aſſur'd by thoſe who have made Eſtimates of the Value, the Coffee, Tea, and Chocolate only, are equal in Trade, to the Spices of the *Dutch.*

IT is worth Notice alſo, what Numbers of ſtout Ships theſe particular Articles, tho' ſmall in themſelves, conſtantly employ ; for beſides the Pipiners, as they call the running Fregats, and which are a little Fleet of ſmall Ships, that in the Sea-

fon fetch Oranges from *Sevil*, and Lemons
from *Malaga* ; I fay, befides thefe, the
Trade for Raifins and Currants only, does
not freight lefs than forty to fifty good
Ships every Year from the Coaft of *Spain* and
Italy, including the Ifland of *Zant*.

THE Oyl from *Gallipoli* fourteen or fifteen more; and fo in Proportion thofe
Things which do not come fingle ; as the
Coffee and the *Tea*, and all the fmaller Kinds
of Goods from *Leghorn*, and other Ports,
tho' they are little feparately, yet together, are very great Articles in the Freight
of Ships, and encourage and fupport the
Navigation in its moft confiderable Parts.

IT would be furprifing, if the Confumption of thofe few Articles once thought fo
trifling, and formerly fo entirely unknown,
were caft up into Money, and their Value
brought together, what Sums they would
amount to : To caft up the Tea, Coffee,
and Pepper only, three Articles of the Eaft
India Trade ; how often do we fee in the
Cargoes of the Eaft *India* Ships 500000 *l.*
Weight of Tea in one Ship, fix or feven
hundred thoufand Pound Weight, when
two Ships come in together ? We cannot
fuppofe this fold cheaper than from 10 to 16 *s.*
per Pound to the Retailer; 300 to 400 Tun
of Coffee comes frequently Home in one
Ship; Pepper indeed is of lefs Value, and
not much of it confum'd in *England*; but
the Quantity is great, and the Chocolate

makes

makes up the Value of the reft to be a mon-
ftrous Sum, confidering it all as a Superfluity.

THE Importation of Silk is an Article of
home Confumption, grown up now to a
prodigious Height, and is the more profitable to this Nation, in that,

1. IT is all manufactur'd within our
felves; and as it is now grown up to fuch a
Magnitude as was never known before, employs abundance of our Poor, who, by Decay of other Branches of Commerce, began
to be threatn'd with want of Employment.

2. AND efpecially, as it now fupplies the
Nation with thofe fine Silk Manufactures,
by the Induftry of our own Poor, which it
has been publickly prov'd, coft us (as above)
Twelve hundred thoufand Pounds a Year
to purchafe them of the *French*, the *Flemings,* the *Dutch* and *Italians.*

THIS Importation of raw Silk, and
thrown Silk has been lately calculated to
amount to about 500000 *l.* a Year from

> *Turky,*
> *Italy,* and
> *India.*

HERE I fhould mention, and I fhall but
mention it, the great Importation of Drugs
and Dye Stuffs, in which, put together, no
Nation can confume, or does import alike
Quantity as *England,* fuch as,

Brafil

Brafil, and Brafilletta Wood.
Fuftic.
Logwood,
Sumach,
Red-wood,
Red Earth,
Gauls,
Madder,
Woad,
Indico,
Turmerick,
Cocheneal,
Cantharides,
Bark *Peru.*
Gums of many Kinds,
Civet, Aloes, Caffia.
Turkey Drugs, ⎫
African Drugs, ⎬Innumerable.
Eaft *India* Drugs,⎭
Rhubarb, Saffafras, *cum aliis.*

I might go on here to mention the other
Importations from *India* ; and the late Addition made to our Commerce by the Trade
to the South Seas; but as the laft is only an
Abatement of Commerce in one Part of the
World, for an Encreafe in another, the *Affiento* Contract only excepted ; and the other,
an unhappy Trade, to fay no worfe of it,
and efpecially made fo, by being unhappily
managed, I fhall omit entring upon them
in this Part of the Difcourfe of Trade, as
being no Addition to the Magnitude of the
Britifh

British Commerce in general, whether it be not a Leſſening and Abatement of the Commerce, or, at leaſt, injurious and ruinous to it, I ſhall not enquire here.

BUT I muſt not omit another Branch of Importation, which is great in it ſelf, and neceſſary too: And this is the Importations of Naval and building Stores from the Eaſt *Indies,* and North Seas, ſuch as,

Tar,
Hemp, } From the *Ruſſian* Dominions.
Flax,

Iron,
Copper, } From *Sweden,* and ſome of the
Deals,   firſt from *Spain.*

Deals,
Timber and
Fir (ſmall) Wood, } From *Norway.*
Maſts, *&c.*

Canvas,
Sail Cloth
Eaſt Country Plank, } From *Dantſick*
Clap-Board and   *Momel* and
Wainſcots   *Koninsbro'*

Oyl — — } From *Greenland.*
Sulphur or
Brimſtone } From (*Denmark*) *Iſceland* and
Roſin   *Italy.*

To

To make an Eftimate of the Value, or of the Confumption of all thefe Things, would be in fome Meafure to enquire into the Number of our Shipping, of Ships built yearly, (and which is ftill more as to the Confumption) Ships repairing and fitting out; an Article, when join'd together, too great to make any Calculation upon.

I might mention here, how unaccountably to blame we are in this Trade; that whereas a full Supply might be had of all thofe things, *I may fay, Every one of them* from our own Colonies, the Product of the *Britijh* proper Dominions, the Labour of the *Britijh* People, and which is equal to it, all brought by our own Ships, to the vaft Encreafe of the *Britijh* Navigation, it fhould miferably be neglected or omitted, and the Goods be bought with our ready Money, great Part of them brought Home in foreign Bottoms, and the whole Trade managed in a wrong Place; or, as we may fay, running in a wrong Channel, to the infinite Advantage of the *Danes, Swedes, Poles, Pruffians* and *Mufcovites,* and to the enriching the (otherwife) pooreft and moft worthlefs, and I had almoft faid, the moft beggarly Nations in the World. But I fhall fpeak farther of this by it felf.

I have not in all this Account mentioned any thing of our Importations from *Holland,*
except

except only that Particular of the Spice Trade, and Linens, which I call their own.

BUT this is not, that our Importations from thence are not exceeding great, only that we do not import any thing material or confiderable from thence, that is of their own Growth or Manufacture; but that by importing from them, we only bring in the Goods of almoft all Countries in the World thro' their Hands: So that, tho' we are faid to fell them the Value of two Millions *per Annum* in our own Manufacture; yet 'tis certain, we take off again a prodigious Quantity of Goods of other Nations thro' their Hands; fo that 'tis hard to determine which Way the Balance turns, either for us, or againft us, and I make no Difficulty in affirming, that it may be fometimes one Way, fometimes another.

PARTICULARLY, fuppofe a dear Year of Corn in *England,* fo that the Exportation comes to be prohibited. This putting a Stop at once to fo confiderable a Branch of our Exports to *Holland,* would go a great Way in fhortning our Credit, in the general Account of Trade with the *Dutch for that Year,* and confequently might give a turn to the Balance; we at the fame Time not abating our Demand of foreign Goods from them.

AGAIN, fuppofe for a further Example, a Scarcity of Sugars and Tobacco in the *Britifh Colonies* for the fame Year; for at the

fame

Time that a common Sterility, or failing of the Crop of Corn fhould happen in *England*, the Crop of Sugars might (*as it often does*) fail in *Barbadoes*, *Jamaica*, and the other Iflands and Colonies of *America*, and the Crop of Tobacco alfo in *Virginia*.

ADD to this, that in fuch a Year, it being probable the diftilling of Corn might be forbidden in *England*, as no doubt it would for fuch an Occafion ; the Confequence of which would be the allowing a greater Importation of Brandy from *Holland*, which they would pour in upon us, infinitely to their Advantage, we being pleafed at this Time to allow the bringing in *Brandy* by way of *Holland*, at the fame Time loading it with an infupportable Duty, if direftly brought from other Places, tho' we might perhaps put all the Gain which the *Dutch* make now of it, into our own Pockets.

IN thefe, and many other Cafes, it is eafie to fuppofe, that the Ballance of Trade may, and fometimes does turn againft *England*, by our general Commerce with the *Dutch*.

NOR can it be doubted, but that even at this Time, tho' the Exportation of Corn, and of Sugars, and Tobacco, has no Interruption ; yet the late Encreafe of the Importations from *Holland*, fuch as fine Hollands and Linen of all Sorts, and admitting Brandy from thence, as above, has infinitely

nitely encreaſed the Debt of Trade on our Side, and at leaſt turn'd the Ballance very much in favour of the *Dutch.*

THE Sum of all theſe Explanations, and more, which might be mentioned, may be drawn up into theſe Heads.

1. THAT the Magnitude of the *Engliſh* Exportations, as they conſiſt only of our own Growth and Manufacture (including that of our Colonies as our own) is greacer than that of any other ſingle Nation in the World.

2. THAT the Conſumption in *England* of foreign Importations, and of the improv'd Product of our own Country; that is to ſay, our Woollen and other Manufactures, is likewiſe infinitely greater than the Home Conſumption of any other Nation.

FROM both which Articles, as they have been explain'd in the laſt two Chapters, I think I have ſufficiently made out what I ſaid in my Title, of the Magnitude of the *Engliſh* Commerce, and that it is a Prodigy of its Kind, the like of which is not to be ſeen any where in *Europe,* if it may be in any Part of the World.

THERE are ſome other Heads of Trade neceſſary to be ſpoken to, in order to make this Work a compleat Plan of the *Britiſh* Commerce.

1. WITH Relation to *Home Trade,* I ſhould make ſome Eſtimates of the natural

ral Product of the Land and Sea in this Island, *viz.*

The Corn,   The Mines,   The Timber,
The Cattle,   The Minerals,   The Stone.

HERE I should describe the Manner of breeding and managing our Cattle, the prodigious Consumption, especially of their Flesh, and the Employment of them; that is, of Oxen and Horses in Labour for the carrying on of Trade.

N. B. ALSO I might assert, and (fully prove my Assertion by unanswerable Reasons) that notwithstanding in general, it is the Advantage of Commerce, to have all Things done as cheap as possible; yet that *as* it is the grand Support of Wealth and Trade in *England*, to have our Product consum'd, and in order to it, to have our People and Cattle employ'd; So, it is not always the Advantage of *England*, to lessen the Labour of the said People and Cattle, by the Encrease of River-Navigation; and some Examples which might confirm this might be brought, which amount to a Demonstration.

2. WITH Relation to the Shipping and Navigation of *England*, the Number of Ships built and employ'd in *Great Britain*, and in that Article two other, *viz.* (1.) the Number of Trades depending upon the
buil-

building and repairing, fitting and furnifhing of thofe Ships, (2.) The Number
of Mariners who are bred up and employ'd
in thofe Ships, to the great Encreafe of Navigation, and furnifhing a conftant Supply
of able Seamen, the Strength and Glory of
the whole Nation.

In both thefe Heads, I have ftill the fame
General to maintain, and that without the
leaft Boaft, (namely) that *England* out-does
the whole Trading World, and that there is
no Nation, except *Great Britain,* that can
carry on fuch a Trade ; and this that I may
not be fuppos'd to fpeak in the Grofs, and
leave it unfupported, I fhall explain in the
Particulars following.

> *N. B.* Before I defcend to thefe Particu-
> lars I am to note, That I think it is no
> Boaft to infift upon the Article of Ship-
> ping as an extraordinary Branch of our
> Commerce, not only as it is exceeding
> great, but as fo great a Quantity of
> the Materials are of our own Growth
> and Produce, and almoft all of our
> own Manufacture, whereas the Ship-
> ping in *Holland* has hardly any Thing
> belonging to it produced at Home,
> no not the Provifions which victual
> the Ships.

Here

Here follows a Repetition of the Particulars in the Trade, in which I infift it is already proved that we exceed other Countries. *Take it as follows,* viz. That there is not any one Nation in *Europe,*

1. That confumes the like Quantity of Flefh Meat, and Malt Liquor.
2. That having no Wine of their own Production, confumes the like Quantity of Wine imported from Abroad.
3. That having fo little Linen of their own Product confume the like Quantity of Linen imported from Abroad, or that wear fo much Linen, efpecially of the fineft that is or can be made.
4. That have fuch a Prodigious Quantity, or fo good a kind of Wool.
5. That export an equal Quantity of, or Value in any one Manufacture of their own, let it be of what kind it will, as *England* does of her Woollen Manufacture
6. That build and employ in their own Bufinefs a like Number of Ships, and maintain a like Number of able Seamen.
7. That have a like Variety of Nature's Productions, fingular to themfelves, or fo fingular, as that they are not to be had in Quantities for Commerce in any other Country ; fuch as

1. Block

1. Block Tin,   4. Lapis Calliminaris,
2. Lead,   5. Allom
3. Coal,   6. Wool, &c.

I cannot enlarge on every Particular.

CHAP. VII.

Of the Magnitude of our Trade, as it relates to our other Exportations, and particularly what we call Re-exportation, or Exporting by Certificate; including the Exports of Goods first imported from our own Colonies, and Factories Abroad.

 H O' all I have said of the Greatness of our woollen Manufacture is prov'd, and how great soever the Consumption of it is in the World, I would not be understood to mean, that this was the whole of our Commerce, either one Way or other : On the contrary, this is but one Branch of it : It is true, it

is

is the moft confiderable Branch; that I muft always grant, and is indeed the Wheel within the Wheel of all the reft; That which fets all the Wheels of Trade in Motion; I mean of the *Britijh* Trade; 'tis the Life of all the reft.

But we have feveral Branches of Commerce, very confiderable befides this, and that for Exportation too : *For Example,*

The Exportation of Corn, Salt, Fifh, and Flefh, I put thefe four Articles together, for Reafons which we fhall fee in the Courfe of this Work; they are all very great Heads of Trade and Employ in *Great Britain,* a great Number of our Ships, more perhaps than will be thought probable at firft Sight.

This Article, indeed, includes *Ireland,* of which I have yet faid nothing; tho' as we are one Government, the Trade of the whole ought to come under one Head of Commerce : However, I fhall not meddle with the Trade of *Ireland* here, any farther than as it is blended with the *Britijh* Commerce, and carried on together, as in this Article it is, and is infeparable from it.

Corn is chiefly exported from *England* to *Holland;* tho' *Great Britain,* which may truly be call'd a Corn Country, is always ready to fend it, wherever they can find a Market; fo that wherever the Harveft happens to fail abroad, whether in *France, Spain,*

Spain, Portugal, or even in *Italy* it felf, we are always at Hand to fupply them; it being very rare that *England* and *Scotland* has a general Scarcity, fo as to ftop the Exportation.

As it is certainly true, that whatever Corn can be fpared for Exportation out of *Great Britain,* above what is neceffary for fubfifting our own People, is clear Gain to the publick Wealth of the Nation : So this Article of exporting Corn, is one of the moft advantageous Parts of our Commerce, in Proportion to its Magnitude.

Nor is the Dearnefs of the Price of Corn at Home, any real Detriment to the Generality, or any Abatement of the publick Stock, provided we admit none from Abroad; for tho' it may be a Damage to fome particular Perfons, and may pinch the Poor, who yet, for ought I fee, are always alike poor, in Plenty, as in Scarcity ; of which hereafter ; yet, I fay, 'tis no lofs to the publick Stock, becaufe it is all paid among our felves; The general Body of the People have but one publick Stock of Wealth, whereof every individual is trufted with a Part ; and what they pay to, or get from one another, no way leffens or encreafes that Stock, only leffens and encreafes the particular Part, which this or that particular Perfon was fo entrufted with ; as if ten Men, having each a hundred Guineas in their Pockets, go together into

into a Room or Houfe to play ; 1*ft*, take the Room in which they play, to contain a publick Stock of the whole thoufand Guineas ; fuppofe then, after fome Time of play, one or two of the ten win all the Money, and break the reft : There are eight Men left empty and poor, and two Men grown full and rich ; but the Money is all in the Room ftill, the thoufand Guineas are not diminifh'd at all, the Stock they play'd with is neither leffen'd or encreas'd.

THIS is too plain to dwell upon : It is the fame Thing in the Rife and Fall of the Rate of Corn confum'd at Home.

ON the other Hand, if Corn bears a great Price in *Portugal* or *Spain*, or any where Abroad, all that Advance of Price, except only the Labour of the People in carrying it, is clear Gain ; and even all their Labour too, except the Provifions which they confum'd in the Voyage, is fo much added to the publick Stock.

I am a profefs'd Oppofer of all fortuitous Calculations, making Eftimates by guefs Work, of the Quantities and Value of any Trade or Exportation, where, as I faid before, there is no given Number or Rule to raife thofe Eftimates upon ; and as this is one of the Cafes, in which there is no Certainty to calculate from, and efpecially having not the Cuftom-Houfe Books to refer to, I therefore decline it.

AND

AND yet, I would not have been without some probable Grounds of Calculation from the Cuftom-Houfe Books, if I had not found that there is no judging of the Exportation of one Year, from the Quantities exported in another, for the Reafons following.

1. BECAUSE our Exportation of Corn depends upon the Crop we have had the Harveft before, and by Confequence on the Price the Corn bears at Market, whether dear or cheap, according to which the Merchant is limited from, or encourag'd to the Exportation.

2. BECAUSE likewife, tho' the utmoft Encouragement was given at Home for the Exportation, the Quantity exported will depend alfo upon the Plenty or Scarcity of Corn Abroad. It is true, that dear or cheap, Corn always finds a Market in *Holland:* But then, 'tis as true, that if the *Dutch* find a forc'd Exportation, they, like all expert Merchants, will buy cheap, and perhaps to lofs, or not buy at all : So that in fhort, it is no Market at all : To fell to Lofs, is not to be call'd Trade, but a Stop or Check to Trade ; for the Seller finding no Profit, is fure to come there no more, till he is fatisfied by his Intelligence of a better Market.

THE Quantity exported therefore depending upon fuch precarious Circumftances, it would be of no Importance to make

Calcu-

Calculations upon Uncertainties, that is to fay, upon fuch evident Uncertainties; There may be 500000 Quarters of Corn exported in one Year, and not one Bufhel the next; as was the Cafe among our felves but a few Years ago, when there was not lefs than a Thoufand Quarters of Wheat a Day entred at the Cuftom-houfe in *London* for a great while together, to be exported to *Ireland*, befides an immenfe Quantity fhipt off on all the Weft Coaft of *England*, from *Chefter Water* as far North as the *Clyde* in *Scotland*, A great Scarcity happening that Year in *Ireland*.

IT would be laying a prepofterous Foundation to calculate from hence what might be yearly exported that Way, when perhaps for twenty Years before, *Ireland*, which generally is more able to fpare Corn, than likely to want it, had not called for a Quarter of Corn, and perhaps may not again, for twenty Years to come.

IT may be the like in *France*, and often is, that in one Year they fhall take two or three Hundred Thoufand Quarters of Corn from *England*, if they can get it; and the next Year or two would give nothing for it (fpeaking comparatively) if you would carry it them.

UPON the whole, I fay there is no Calculation to be made of the Quantity of Corn exported; only that in general it is always very great, *(except as before)*

The

THE Eaſt and South Coaſt of *Britain* is chiefly concerned in this Trade from the *Firth* of *Edinburgh,* to the Mouth of the *Thames ;* more eſpecially the Ports of the *Humber,* the Coaſt of *Norfolk,* from *Lyn* to *Yarmouth,* and the Coaſt of *Suffolk* alſo, from *Yarmouth* excluſive, to *Ipſwich* incluſive.

₂*dly,* THE Fiſh; there is ſomething more of Certainty in our Calculations of the Exportation of Fiſh, than of moſt other Goods; particularly of the Herring, Pilchards, and white Fiſh, and to take this by the Merchants Calculations, rather than by that of the Cuſtom-houſe, becauſe the former can give an Eſtimate where the latter cannot, I mean Abroad. To begin North,

THE *Scots* are ſaid to cure ſixty Thouſand Barrels of Herrings for Exportation, one Year with another, including the Weſt of *Scotland* as well as the Eaſt Side ; I think they that calculated the *Scots* Herring-fiſhing at ſixty Thouſand Laſt, which is ten Times the Quantity, had no Gueſs with them, but ſpoke by Way of Bluſter, (tho' in Print) it being more than the *Dutch* take one Year with another ; at leaſt in their firſt Part of the Fiſhery : Sixty thouſand Barrels is a large Quantity.

THE next Part of the Herring-fiſhing on the *Britiſh* Coaſt is at *Yarmouth,* for the red Herring Trade; the Towns of *Yarmouth*

mouth and *Leoftoff* are fuppofed, if they have a good Fair, as they call it; that is a good fifhing Seafon, to cure four Thoufand Laft of Herrings, that is, forty Thoufand Barrels a Year, the greateft Part of which is exported to *Holland, France, Spain* and *Italy.*

NEXT to *Yarmouth,* the Fifhing for Herrings for the *London* Market comes in, and for prefent Confumption, and this is a confiderable Article; but being all for Home Bufinefs, it weighs nothing in the Scale of our foreign Commerce: Thefe Fifh are ordinarily taken in the Mouth of the *Thames.*

IN the Weft of *England,* on the Coafts of *Dorfet* and *Devonfhire,* and fometimes of *Cornwal,* the *Pilchards* are a particular Fifhery, fingular to that Coaft, and found no where elfe in thofe Seas, or in this Part of the World; it is computed, that the ufual Quantity of *Pilchards* cur'd in thofe Seas in a Year, are from a Thoufand to twelve Hundred Laft.

ADD to thefe the Herring-fifhing in the *Briftol Channel,* about *Bidiford, Barnftaple,* and thofe Parts, where in a good Year they ufually cure about the fame Quantity of *Herrings,* as the other Side cures of *Pilchards.*

THIS is the Sum of the fifhing for Herring on the feveral Coafts of *Great Britain,* the Merchants of *Belfaft,* and of *London-Derry* in *Ireland,* have, as we are told, a
Con-

confiderable Share alfo in this Herring-
fifhing; but I have not learn'd any Thing
of the Quantity they take.

UPON the whole, the *Britifh* Fifhing (for
Herring and Pilchards only) amounts not
to lefs than fifteen Thoufand Lafts, or a
Hundred and fifty Thoufand Barrels, befides the Home Confumption of the Fifh
uncur'd.

THE next Branch of our Fifhery is the
white Fifh, which may be divided into
four Parts,

1*ft*. THE *Englifh* Fifhing for Cod in the
North Seas, and which are therefore called
the *North Sea Cod*; the Fifh taken here is
generally brought to *London*, and to the
Sea Ports on the Coaft, and is ufed princi-
pally in victualling of Ships, Coafters, and
others, for fhort Voyages; as alfo for home
Confumption: So that this I take no notice
of in Trade.

2. THE fecond is, The *Scots* white Fifh,
as they call it, which is the fame kind of
Fifh, and are taken upon the Eaftern Coaft
of *Scotland*, from *Heymouth* to *Dunbar*,
and into the Mouth of the Firth: But neither is the Quantity great on *this* Side.

3. THE Third is, The Fifhing for Cod on
the North Weft of *Scotland*, and among the
Weftward Iflands, which lie about the *Lewze*
and the *Orkneys*, where the *Glafgow* Merchants, as alfo the *London-Dery* Merchants
take them; and thefe are ufually exported to
Spain.

Spain, but not in great Quantities, that Fishery being not improv'd to the Extent, as it might be, for want of sufficient Adventurers.

4. THE Fishing for Cod in *Newfoundland*.

5. THE like Fishing on the Northern Coast of *New-England*.

THESE Fisheries cure a very great Quantity of Fish; and if we may credit their own Accounts, there are not less than 200000 Quintals of Fish cur'd by them every Year: Most of which is sent to *Bilbo* in *Spain*, to *Oporto* and *Lisbon*, to *Cadiz*, and to all the Ports of *Spain* and *Italy* in the *Mediterranean*, but especially to *Leghorn*, and also to our other Colonies in *America*, besides what is sent to the *Canaries*, *Maderas*, and *Cape de Verde* Islands.

THERE are two remaining Fisheries belonging to *Great Britain*, I mean for Trade, and these are,

1. THE Whale Fishing carried on, (1.) for some Years on the Coast of *Long Island*, and *Rhode Island*, and *New York*; and now, within about three Years, by the South Sea Company at *Greenland*.

2. THE Salmond Fishing for barrelling up and exporting them: And this is done,

1. AT *Aberdeen* in the North of *Scotland*.

2. AT *Berwick* upon *Tweed* on the Border of *England* towards *Scotland*.

3. AT

3. At *Newfoundland* (that is) within the Rivers on the Ifland of *Newfoundland,* where they take pretty great Quantities, and the Trade encreafes every Year : But neither of thefe are yet very confiderable.

Thus far the *Fifhing Trade* in which the *Dutch* are faid to go beyond us as to the Herrings and the Whales, but not to come near us in that of the white Fifh.

N. B. The white Fifh or Cod is a very improving and encreafing Trade, and employs at leaft 200 or 300 Sail of Ships or Ketches, befides fmall fifhing Veflels, without Number,

As for the Exporting of Flefh; it confifts of two Parts, (*viz.*) The Exporting of Beef from *Ireland,* as well to our Colonies in the Weft *Indies,* as to *France.*

2. The Exporting barrelled Pork from *Aberdeen,* chiefly brought by the Dutch for victualling their Ships to the Eaft *Indies,* and other long Voyages.

3. The Exporting of Tallow, Butter, and Hides from *Ireland* to *Flanders,* by the Ports of *Dunkirk* and *Oftend,* thefe are properly annexed to the Flefh, as being Part of its Subftance.

These, put together, amount to a very great Sum, efpecially the *Irifh* Beef, of which we can make no Eftimate here.

3. Our next confiderable Article for Exportation, is the Product of our Colonies; that is to fay, fuch of them as being firft

impor-

imported from the *Englifh* Plantations in *America*, or from the *Britifh* Factories in the Eaft *Indies* in our own Ships, and having been already affiftant to our Navigation; but being more than our Home Confumption calls for, are exported again by Certificate. The Goods thus imported, are, chiefly

1. From the Eaft *Indies*.
   Pepper,   Coffee,
   Painted Callicoes,   Tea,
   Wrought Silks,   Indigo, Drugs, &c.

2. From *America*.
   Hides,   Molaffes, Logwood,
   Virginia Tobacco,   Cotton and Indigo,
   Sugar, Ginger,   Rice, Drugs, &c.

Of thefe the main Articles for Re-exportation are,

1. PEPPER, moft of which is exported again; our Home Confumption being fmall, 'tis exported chiefly to *Italy*, *viz.* to *Leghorn*, *Genoa* and *Venice*, and to *France*, the Quantity ufed at Home, is about 6000 Bags a Year. The reft is fent Abroad.

2. TOBACCO, the Quantity exported by Certificate, generally fpeaking, may be eftimated at about 30000 Hogfheads, and the Quantity confum'd in *Great Britain* and *Ireland*, to 50000 more, in which I am fure to be a great deal within Compafs. We are told, that fince the late Peace, *France* alone

alone has taken off 10000 Hogſheads of Tobacco in a Year, and ſometimes more; the reſt is exported to *Holland*, to *Germany*, *Norway*, and the *Baltick*.

>   *N. B.* By the Word *Germany*, I am to be underſtood now, and at other Times, when ſpeaking of Marine or Trading Affairs, the Coaſt of *Germany*, from the *Embs* to the *Elb* incluſive, which takes in the Cities of *Embden*, *Bremen*, *Hamburg*, and all the Ports in and between thoſe Rivers, with the Coaſt of *Holſtein* or *Holſatia*, the River *Eider* to *Huſum*, and the Coaſt of *Juitland*.

3. Sugars, Indigo, Ginger and Rice: Theſe, and the Tobacco alſo, as they are the Growth of the *Britiſh* Colonies, and the Returns for all the Exportations thither, not from *England* and *Scotland* only, but from *Ireland*, and from the Coaſt of *Afric* alſo, are in the Language of Trade, to be eſteemed as Exportations from *Great Britain*, and are, without Diſpute, Branches of the *Britiſh Commerce :* The Value of theſe is hard to determine; the Quantity of Sugar and Rice is exceeding great, the Sugars eſpecially which are ſhipp'd off to *Holland*, and *Hamburgh*, and *Venice*, where they are us'd by the Sugar Bakers, as we ſimply call them; for they ought to be called Sugar Boilers, but are more properly called Abroad, Sugar Refiners.

We

W E are ſuppoſed to export more than 40000 Hogſheads of Sugar a Year, one Year with another; ſome times much more, as the Crops of Sugar Abroad may yield, which are often very different.

As to the Rice, it is a new Trade, being the Product of one Colony only, namely of *Carolina*, and has been brought over in Quantity but a few Years; but it is an encreaſing Trade, and is now ſpread into *Penſylvania,* and other Places: But be the Quantity what it will, it goes moſt of it Abroad again, and is a very acceptable Merchandize to *Holland* and *Germany*, (underſtood as above) and is likely to be a very great Article in our *American* Returns.

4. W E muſt not omit here the *African* Trade, as it regards the exporting Slaves from thence to the *Britiſh* Colonies in *America*, particularly to the Iſlands, and to *Virginia,* for the other *Britiſh* Colonies do not much make uſe of them, I mean, *New-England, New-York, Carolina,* &c. As theſe Slaves are the Produce of the Britiſh Commerce in their *African* Factories; they are ſo far a Branch of the *Britiſh* Exportation, juſt as if they were firſt brought to *England,* landed here, and then ſent Abroad again, or exported by Certificate (for it would be the ſame thing) to the *Weſt Indies,* or by the South-Sea Company to *New Spain.*

THE

THE Number of thefe is very great, and the Value of them very confiderable. The Rate of *Negroes* in *America,* as it is of late Years rifen in all the Colonies, is from 20 to 25 to 30 *l.* a Head, according to the Age, the Growth, and the Sex of the Negroes; and if we allow 30000 to 40 and 50000 Negroes a Year to be carried away, as (if the Trade was uninterrupted) would be the Cafe; then the Value of this Trade at a Medium of 25 *l. per Head* upon all the *Negroes,* amounts to no lefs than One Million two hundred and fifty thoufand Pound *per Annum.*

THIS is a Trade of infinite Advantage, confidering that thefe Negroes do not coft in the Country above 30 to 50 *s. per* Head; and if the Trade was uninterrupted, as it might, and I think indeed merits to be, we fhould, no doubt, including the *Affiento,* carry 40 to 50000 Slaves a Year from the Coaft of *Africa,* and find Bufinefs enough for them all in our encreafing Colonies.

THERE are feveral other Branches of Commerce which might enlarge the Subject, but I ftrive to contract it; and therefore fay no more to that Part.

PART

PART II.

CHAP. I.

A Solid Enquiry into that important Queſtion, whether our Trade in general, and our Woollen Manu-facture in particular, are ſunk and declined, or not.

E have been very much alar-med of late with publick Complaints of the Decay of our Trade; I think the Peo-ple who thus complain, ought to be ſeriouſly asked to ex-plain themſelves, *and to tell us,*

1ſt, WHETHER they mean in general, that the Bulk of our whole Commerce is

lcſſened

leffened and decayed, and that there was any Time formerly, when it was greater than it is now.

2*dly,* O R whether they mean in particular, that any of our Manufactures are under Decay, that their Confumption is lefs now Abroad, or at Home, than it has been; or that there is any Appearance that it may be fo.

IF they mean the *Firft,* they ought to tell us when that Time was, and how they prove the Fact? Then we might enter with them into a calm Examination of the Thing, judge of the Calculations they make; and by the Particulars, as they fhall lay them down, determine whether they complain with Reafon, or without.

WHILE inftead of this, they content themfelves with a meer Suggeftion, making a Complaint in general, claiming to have it be believed in the grofs, as they bring it, without farther Enquiry. This feems to be a Kind of Popery in Commerce, demanding our implicit Affent to what we cannot believe, or they demonftrate; begging the Queftion in the groffeft Senfe, and in fhort is rather a Clamour than a Complaint, and ought to be treated as fuch.

IF I fhould deal with thefe People, as they deal with us, I ought to anfwer them alfo in grofs, and affirm, which I believe I am much better furnifh'd with Arguments
ments

ments to prove, that the *English* or *British* Commerce is at this Time so far from a Decay, that it is encreafed to a Magnitude far greater than it ever was before, and is ftill encreafing more and more ; in a Word, that our Trade is in a more flourifhing Condition than the Trade of any other Nation in *Europe,* perhaps in the World.

It is true, that as this is affirming without Evidence, fo it is anfwering without Proof, and is only paying them back the fame Kind they bring ; but I fhall defcend to Particulars in its Place, and explain my felf at large ; at prefent I muft go on with the Complainers.

If they mean the *fecond,* that any particular Branch of our Commerce is decay'd, as efpecially our Manufactures, which is what they feem to point at, *they ought then* to have defcended to the Particulars of thofe Manufactures which they fay are decay'd, feeing 'tis evident fome of our Manufactures are exceedingly encreafed ; nay, the Trade, or general Term, *our Manufactures,* or the *British Manufactures,* are encreafed ; and we call feveral Manufactures our own, and juftly too, which never were fo before : Of which alfo in its Order.

N. B. Here I fhould obferve, that we ought to diftinguifh thus between the Decay of the general Commerce of a Nation, and the Decay of any particular Branch of it ; becaufe fome particular
cular

cular Manufacture may decay, and even wear out, in a Country, and some other may rise up in its Place; as the Custom, Fashions, and Fancies of the Times may influence and direct, and of which many Examples are just now to be seen among us; and yet at the same Time the general Commerce may not at all be decayed or decreased.

But to bring the Complaint mention'd above to a Point, and to understand it, as I suppose the Complainers would be understood, however lamely they express it: By the Decay of our Trade, they seem to mean this, and no more, namely, a Decay of the *English* Woollen Manufacture.

This they alledge is in a declining Condition, and they tell us for Proof of it, That the Consumption is lessened, both *Abroad* and at *Home*.

1. That *'tis lessen'd;* this they say is evident, by other Nations falling into the Way of manufacturing their own Wool; imitating our Manufacture to great Perfection; their People underworking ours, and their Tradesmen therefore underselling ours in Price at Market; their Governments respectively, for Encouragement of their own Poor, pressing the Consumption of those Manufactures among themselves, and prohibiting the *English* Manufactures being imported into their Dominions. This they

they think amounts to a Demonftration of the Decay of our Trade.

To clear our Hands of Things, as we go, I fhall anfwer this briefly, the Fact is true, but the Inference is falfe.

1*ft*. *The Fact is true*, (in part, tho' not in the whole) the Wealth of *England* having been fo vifibly raifed, by the Improvement of our Woollen Manufacture, (not forgetting our loud and impolitick Boafts of that Wealth too, and how the Woollen Manufacture has been the only Caufe of it). This has fet other Nations at Work as far as they can, *tho' the fartheft has been but little,* to imitate thofe Manufactures; to work up their own Wool, and employ their own Poor; and we have no Reafon to blame or reproach them with it at all; we do the fame.

2*dly,* For the Encouragement of the People to do thus in thofe particular Countries, their Princes have, generally fpeaking, prohibited the *Englifh* Manufactures, efpecially fuch Kinds, as their Subjects can make, from being imported into their Dominions; nor can we blame the faid Princes for this, for we do the fame. Thus far I fay is true.

3. But the Inference is falfe, the Trade, no nor the Manufacture is not decay'd for this; thefe Prohibitions and Imitations amount to no more than this, that the People of thofe Countries do make fome

woollen

woollen Goods there, such as the course Wool of *Saxony, Poland, Bohemia,* &c. will admit; and thus the poor People in those Countries may be said to be clothed with their own Manufacture; but it seems to be little more, than instead of the rough Sheep-Skins, which, 'tis known, the Boors in those Countries wore before: For we find the very coursest of our Kersies, Dozens, Duffells, and *Yorkshire* Cloths, which are the meanest of our Manufacture, are exported even to those northern Ports (where they were used to go) in as great Quantities as ever: As for the fine Medly broad Cloths, and *Spanish* Cloths, which *England* is so particularly noted for, they do not so much as pretend to imitate, or to prohibit them; but the Quantity exported to *Hamburgh,* to *Gottenburgh,* to *Dantzick,* and to all the *Baltick,* is as great as ever, and perhaps greater; and if I were to go thro' all the Ports of *Europe* with the Enquiry, it would be hard to shew where the Decay lyes; but that if one Place sinks, another rises; and if one Kind of Manufacture declines, another advances.

N. B. THESE Prohibitions have been, some of longer standing, such as in *France, Prussia, Sweden,* &c. and some of a shorter Date, as now lately in *Silesia,* in *Austria,* in *Piedmont,* and several Parts of *Germany,* and at last in *Spain;*

Spain ; and we may expect the like in other Parts.

UPON the whole, admitting all these Prohibitions of our Manufactures, and all their being imitated and set up in foreign Parts, *as above*, yet it is not easy to prove, neither can I see Reason to allow, that the Exportation of the woollen Manufacture of *England* is at all lessen'd, and consequently, the Consumption Abroad is not abated, or the Trade in particular decay'd : What Abatement of the Consumption may have happen'd in this, or that particular Part of the World, is not the Case, nor is it worth our Debate ; all Nations are, and ought to be at Liberty to set their own Poor at Work, if they can, and to prohibit what foreign Manufacture they please for their Encouragement : But as the woollen Manufacture of *England* is an Article the most extended in Trade, of any other Thing of its Kind in the World, it cannot be expected, but it may sink in one Place, and rise in another ; flourish here, and decay there, and the demand alter, as the Customs of Countries alter, and yet the Grofs of the Trade may be the same ; As the Sea, they tell us, gains in one Place upon the Land, and the Land encroaches in another Place upon the Sea ; and yet, neither the Sea or the Land abates or encreases in Quantity, only vary in their Situation : And thus it is in our Trade, the Consumption of

the

the Manufacture fpreads in one Place, and draws back in another ; one Nation opens the Door to it, and another fhuts the Door againft it ; but ftill the Quantity goes away, it is exported abroad, bought, fold, and confum'd ; and we do not find any Age pafs, when more of it, either in Quantity or Quality, was ever fent abroad, than is now, or fo much by a great deal : How then is the Trade under a Decay ?

3. The next Branch of the Complaint, is, that the Confumption of our woollen Manufacture is leffen'd at Home.

This indeed, tho' leaft regarded, has the moft Truth and Reafon in it, and merits to be more particularly enquired into: But I might ask the very Complainer himfelf here, fuppofing the Fact to be true, Why do we not mend it, and that without Laws, without teifing the Parliament and our Sovereign, for what they find difficult enough to effect, even by Law ? I fay, Why do not the People of *Great Britain*, by general Cuftom, and by univerfal Confent, encreafe the Confumption of our own Manufactures, by rejecting the Trifles and Toys of Foreigners, why do we not appear drefs'd in the Growth of our own Country, and made fine by the Labour of our own Hands?

All the Kings and Parliaments that have been or fhall be, cannot govern our Fancies: They may make Laws, and fhew you the Reafon of thofe Laws for your Good ; but

two

two Things among us are too ungoverna-
ble, *viz.* our Paffions and our Fafhions ;
the firft is at prefent out of my Way, but
the fecond is directly to my Purpofe.

SHOULD I ask the Ladies, whether they
would drefs by Law, or clothe by Act of
Parliament, they would ask me whether
they were to be Statute Fools, and to be
made Pageants and Pictures of ? Whether
the Sex were to be fet up for our Jeft, and
the Parliament had nothing to do, but
make *Indian* Queens of them ? That they
claim *Englijh* Liberty, as well as the Men,
and as they expect to do what they pleafe,
and fay what they pleafe, fo they will wear
what they pleafe, and drefs how they
pleafe.

IT is true, that this Liberty of the Ladies, their *Paffion* for their *Fajhion*, has
been frequently injurious to the Manufactures of *England;* and is fo ftill in fome Cafes, as I fhall obferve again in its Place ;
but I do not fee fo eafy a Remedy for that,
as for fome other Things of the like Nature. The Ladies have fuffer'd fome little
Reftraint that Way, as in the wearing *Eaft-
India* Silks, inftead of *Englijh;* and Callicoes, and other Things, inftead of worfted
Stuffs, *'and the like;* and we do not fee they
are pleas'd with it.

BUT as I am talking in this Article to
the Complainers, I would have them direct their Complaints where they ought to
be

be directed ; the King and Parliament have
reftrain'd thofe Things by Law, and farther
they really cannot go; we muft turn the
Complaint to the People themfelves, and en-
treat them to encourage the Manufacture of
England by a more general Ufe and Wearing
of it. This alone would encreafe the Confumption, and that alone can encreafe the Manufacture it felf, as we fhall fee in its Place.

AND yet, if even this Part were examin'd
critically, it would appear, that the Complaint is not right plac'd; the Manufacture
is not in its felf declin'd fo much, as the
Confumption is divided into feveral Manufactures, which perhaps were not known
before, but under one Denomination ; fuch
as the Cotton Manufacture in *Lancafhire*
and *Chefhire*, the Linen Manufacture in
Scotland now become our own by the Union; and the Linen Manufacture much encreas'd of late in *England* it felf, and the
fame in *Ireland,* which tho' not our own,
we find it much for our Intereft to encourage ; if by the Confumption of thefe the
Confumption of the Woollen Manufacture
is divided, I cannot fay this can be call'd a
Decay of our Trade, at leaft as the Ufe of
thefe Goods is now brought on, not in the
Room of our Woollen Manufacture, but
in the Room of the Callicoes, the Ufe of
which was lately prohibited: They are not
therefore the Reafon of any prefent Decay of
the Woollen Manufacture; but if there
was

was a Decay in the Confumption of the
Woollen, it was done by the faid Callicoes
before; of all which I fhall fpeak as I
go on.

UPON the whole then it does not appear, that our Manufactures are leffen'd,
or that the Confumption of them is abated
either Abroad or at Home, but rather the
contrary ; and that our Trade in general,
and even our Woollen Manufacture in particular, is greatly encreas'd, and is at this
Time arriv'd to fuch a Magnitude, as it
was never at before. And here it occurs
to notice a particular Thing, which may
be of Ufe to us in its Kind, on feveral Occafions, *viz.* That the Magnitude of the
Manufacture is really at prefent its only
Grievance, being encreafed to fuch a Degree, by the Ignorance and Wealth of the
Manufacturers, that it is too great for its
felf; the Quantity too great for the Confumption; or at leaft too great for the Market, tho' the Market was intirely open, and
uninterrupted by any Rival Manufacture,
or any Prohibition whatfoever. And here I
ask to be fpared a Word or two of the prefent imprudent Encreafe of the Woollen Manufacture of *England*, by the ill Conduct of
the Manufacturers in particular Cafes; and
how unjuftly a Check of that Encreafe is
called a Decay of the Trade.

A s the Veins may be too full of Blood,
fo a Nation may be too full of Trade ; the
fine

fine frefh Rivers, when they run with a
full and gentle Stream, are the Beauty and
Glory of a Country ; they water the Mea-
dows, moiften the Earth, drive our Mills,
fill our Moats and Canals, carry our Veffels, and enrich the whole Nation; but
when fwell'd by fudden and hafty Showers,
they turn rapid in their Courfe, over-
flow their Banks, and rife to an undue
Height; then they turn frightful and dangerous, drown the Country, and fometimes
the People ; carry away Cattle, Stacks of
Corn, Bridges, Buildings, and whatever
ftands in their Way, leaving Mud, and
Sand, and Stones among the Grafs, and rather ftarve the Land, than affift to make
it fruitful, and thus they become a Grievance,
not a Blefling to the Publick ; on the other
Hand, when by long Drought their Sour-
ces are withheld, the Streams fail, the Rivers are dry, the Mills ftand ftill, the Boats
lye a Ground, the Lands are parch'd up, and
the whole Country fuffers.

OUR Manufactures of Wool in this Nation, bear a juft Analogy with this Cafe,
like a flowing Stream, they are in their
profperous Courfe the Wealth and Glory of the Country: While the Trade
flourifhes Abroad and at Home, and the
Confumption makes a moderate current
Demand, the Manufacture goes on at a
fteady, chearful, even Pace, the Wool is confum'd and wrought up, the Poor are employ'd,

ploy'd, the Mafter Manufacturer thrives, the Merchant and the Shop-keepers go on with their ufual Strength, and all the Trade flourifhes.

1. Upon fome fudden Accident in Trade here comes a great unufual Demand for Goods, the Merchants from Abroad have fudden and unufual Commiffions, the Call for Goods this Way or that Way encreafes, this makes the Factors fend large Orders into the Country; and the Price of Goods always rifes according to the Demand: The Country Manufacturer looks out fharp, hires more Looms, gets more Spinners, gives more Wages, and animated by the advanc'd Price, is not content to anfwer his new Orders only, but he continues the Excurfion he had made into the Country for Spinners, &c. runs on to an Extremity in Quantity, as far, or perhaps farther, than his Stock will allow; and in a Word, gluts the Market with the Goods.

2. The Accident of Trade, which from Abroad fill'd the Merchants Commiffions, and the Factor's Orders being over, thofe Demands are alfo over, and the Trade returns to its ufual Channel; but the Manufacturer in the Country, who had run out to an unufual Excefs in his Bufinefs, without Regard to the Circumftances of it, having not ftopt his Hand as his Orders ftopt, falls into the Mire; his Goods lye on Hand, the Poor which he call'd

from

from the Plow and the Dary to fpin and
weave, are caft off again, and not finding
their Way prefently back to their old
Drudgery, lye and ftarve for Want of Work,
and then they cry out Trade is decay'd,
the Manufactures are loft, Foreigners encroach upon us, the Poor are ftarv'd, and
the like.

WHEREAS the Sum of the Matter is, the
Manufacturer went mad, his Stream run
over into a Flood, he run himfelf imprudently out of Breath; and upon a little
Start of the Trade, willing to furnifh the
Orders all himfelf, and loth to let a Neighbour come in with him, run himfelf out,
drag'd the Poor into his Bufinefs, nay perhaps robb'd his poorer Neighbour of his
Workmen, by giving high Wages; and
when the Trade ftops a little, he runs
a-ground; fo the Poor are ftarving, and
ready to mutiny for Want of Work: And
this we call a Decay of Trade, whereas
the contrary is manifeft feveral Ways.

TRADE muft certainly decay, if we will
run it up to fuch a Length, as to make
more Goods than the World can confume:
But it is not to be juftly call'd a Decay
of Trade, 'tis only abating of the Flood;
the Waters were out, and now they
are down again, and reduced to their old
Channel.

LET us examine a little fuch Accidents
as may raife or fink our Manufacture as
above,

above, or as perhaps have done fo at this Time, and fee if it does not hit exactly with this Account.

1*ft*, THE late Accident of a Plague in *France*. Upon that fad Occafion, the Commerce being entirely ftop'd between *France* and *Spain*, and indeed all other Parts of the World, the Manufactures of the City of *Marfeilles* in particular, and the Country adjacent, being wholly interrupted, occafion'd a very great Addition to the Trade of *Great Britain*; particularly for fuch Manufactures as the *French* ufed to fend to *Turkey*, to *Spain*, and to *Italy*; and the Merchants Commiffions from Abroad were vifibly enlarged hither for near two Years, upon that particular Occafion: It was plain they cou'd have no Goods from *France*.

THE like Occafion added to the Encreafe of our Trade, upon the concluding of the Treaty of *Utrecht*, after the Confufions in *Spain* had put a Check to the Trade between *England* and that Country, for feveral Years; as likewife again upon the Accommodation with *Spain*, after the Surrender of *Sicily*, when Trade breaking out like the Sun after an Eclipfe, the Demand for our *Englifh* Manufactures, Bayes, Says, Perpetts, broad Cloaths, Serges, &c. was fuch, that the Manufacturers thought they could never make too many.

THESE Excurfions are not to be caft up in any View of the real Magnitude of the

the Trade, or of the Manufacture, any more than the true Channel of a River is to be judged of, or its Waters measured by the overflowing of a Winter's Rain, as above.

Nor on the contrary is the Stop of those sudden high Demands, by any extraordinary Check of the Call on like Accidents, to be esteemed a Decay of the Trade, any more than the dry Bottom of a large River, when the Stream withheld by a Summer's Drought leaves the Channel empty, can describe the usual Dimensions of that River, or Quantity of its Waters.

Should we ever see here such a fatal Time as that was in *France*, when Heaven sent the Infection among them at *Marseilles*, or as was here in 1665, *God preserve us from it*, what a general Stop would it make to all our Trade? who would send any Commissions hither for *English* Manufactures, when they did not know but every Bale would have a Plague pack'd up with the Goods, as certainly as the Bales of Wool or Hair brought it from *Cyprus* to *Marseilles* ?

Yet this would not justly be call'd a Decay of our Commerce ; it would indeed be a Wound, and a very desperate Blow to it for the Time ; but as it was an Accident to the Trade, so the Cause being removed, the Trade would revive, return to its former Channel, and be the same as before.

If

If now *(to return to the Cafe before us)* the Manufacturers of *Britain*, upon any fuch hafty Demand from Abroad, fhall run rafhly out into Extremes in their Bufinefs, feek out of their ufual Bounds for Spinners and· Weavers, and other working People, and draw them by Thoufands, and Hundreds of Thoufands, as was lately the Cafe, from their other Imployments, fhall they call the Stop of thefe hafty Demands a Decay of Trade? 'tis a Miftake, it is no Decay, it is no more but a Return of the Stream to its ufual ftated Bounds, bringing Trade into its right Channel again, and to run as it did before: And this I take to be the State of our Manufacture at this Time.

It is indeed fomething difficult to make an exact Calculation, and judge between the antient and the prefent Bounds of Trade, and efpecially of the Woollen Manufacture; but I'll make a brief Effay at it.

The Wooll is the principal Fund of the Manufacture, 'tis the Stock upon which it is carry'd on. Now, be the Quantity more or lefs, 'tis the fixt Boundary of the Trade: The Manufacture cannot outrun this Tether; the Maker can go no further than he has Wooll to work on; fometimes indeed one Year may borrow a little of another, but that is generally not fo much as Trade demands more or lefs, but as the Stock of Wooll appears to vary: But when there

there is an apparent Decay or Advance of the Trade in general, then it is to be feen in the Wooll. And thus, I remember, before the Stop was put to the free Exportation of the *Irifh* Woollen Manufacture, the Quantity of the Wooll of *England* was too great for the Manufacture ; and I have heard the Farmers complain of having two or three Years Stock of Wooll before-hand, and that they could not pay their Rent, becaufe they could not fell it off.

THEN it was our great Study to get the Wooll confum'd, as appears by the Act of Parliament for burying in Woollen ; you may fee by the Preamble to that Act, that it was thought to be a publick Good to wafte and confume the Wooll.

SINCE that, we find all the Wooll in *England* too little for the Manufacture ; fo that now we bring in all the Wooll of *Scotland*, which is in fhort an immenfe Quantity, tho' coarfe, and which went formerly moft of it beyond Sea, and yet call for at leaft the Quantity of an Hundred thoufand Horfe Packs from *Ireland* every Year. This is but a very odd Teftimony for the Decay of our Manufacture ; on the other hand, I think it is an unanfwerable Proof of what I have advanced, (*viz.*) that our Woollen Manufacture is very much encreafed : But of this hereafter.

THEY that tell us of the Encreafe or Decay of the Woollen Manufacture, fhould
fix

fix a Standard of the Trade, from a Proportion to which, to denominate this Encreafe or Decay : To tell us it is funk from
what it was juft at fuch or fuch a Time,
as upon a Peace, after a long Interruption
by a War, or after a Plague or the like, is
to fay nothing at all. But let them take
fix or feven Years together, and make an
Eftimate from the Medium, take the Exportation at a Medium, or take the Rate
of Wooll, and the Confumption of the
Quantity at a Medium, and then their
Gueffes (for they can be no more) may at
leaft be probable.

IF formerly we could not confume all
our own Wooll; and now, we not only
confume our own, but all the Wooll of
Scotland, and an Hundred thoufand Packs
a Year from *Ireland;* then either *England*
muft produce lefs Wooll than formerly, or
the Confumption muft be fo much the
greater. I think, that way of Reafoning
is liable to no Exception, except it be the
running it away clandeftinely to *France,*
which is trifling, and I fhall make it appear in its Place, that this Channel is much
fmaller than it was formerly, when our
Wooll lay unfold, as above.

As to the Growth of our Wooll being
alter'd, and that *England* produces lefs
Wooll than formerly, 'tis time enough to
argue upon it, when there is, or can be
one probable Reafon given to fuggeft it,

much

much lefs Evidence to prove it; yet I muſt not wholly paſs it by neither, becauſe, as above, it is the only Exception.

If there is any thing to be judg'd of from Probability, it is on the other Side, *(viz.)* 'tis rather probable the Quantity is encreaſed by the innumerable Number of Acres of Land improved and encloſed within theſe few Years, eſpecially in the North-weſt Parts of *England*, and which breed and feed greater Numbers of Sheep than ever, and thoſe of a larger Breed which are prodigiouſly encreaſed in *England*.

I might run out here very profitably upon this Subject, and give Reaſons from the general Way of Sheep-keeping in *England* at this Time, by which it wou'd eaſily be proved, that the Quantity of Wooll is encreaſed by the Encreaſe of the large Breed of Sheep which are raiſed now, *not* on the *Cotſwold* Hills of *Glouceſterſhire,* the South *Downs, Salisbury* Plains, and ſuch open Counties, as formerly, where the Soil is poor, and the Sheep ſmall, and the Fleeces light, tho' fine, and of a ſhort Staple in Proportion to the Creatures: *But* in the rich encloſed Grounds of *Leiceſter* and *Warwickſhire,* the Fens of *Lincolnſhire* and *Norfolk,* the Iſle of *Ely,* the Marſhes of *Rumney* in *Kent,* the rich Lands on the Bank of *Tees* and on the *Wier* in the Biſhoprick of *Durham,* and thro' all the Counties of *Northampton, Huntington, Hertford,* and
Bucks ;

Bucks; for the Truth of which, I need do no more than appeal to the Knowledge of the honourable Reprefentatives of thofe Countries.

As the Encreafe of thefe Sheep is manifeft, and that one of whofe Fleeces is equal to three of the weftern Counties, 'tis very improbable the Quantity of Wooll fhould be declin'd in *England*; and if the Wooll is not declin'd, then the only tolerable Objection is removed, and my Argument ftands granted, or at leaft fully confirmed, of which this is the Abftract.

When the Growth of our Wooll in *England* was much lefs than it is now, yet there were frequent Difficulties in having it be confumed by the Manufactures.

Now the Growth of Wooll in *England* is encreafed, yet it is not fufficient to fupply the Confumption of it by the Manufactures.

I think the Confequence is natural then, namely, that the Manufactures muft be encreafed.

To bring all this to our prefent Purpofe,

The Manufactures are prodigioufly encreafed, whether prudently, or rafhly, beyond a due Proportion to the Demand, it matters not upon a Stop or Check of that Demand, we complain of a Decay of Trade; the Queftion is, whether that Complaint is juft?

I infift, that it is not, nor does it prove any thing of a Decay of Trade; only, that
the

the Manufacturers having rafhly made immenfe Quantities of Goods more than the Trade of all *Europe* ever did or can call for in a conftant Demand, the Trade is returned to its natural Channel, after an imaginary and cafual Start out of it by the Accidents of foreign Commerce.

IN fhort, upon the Occafions mentioned above, the Manufacturers have made their good Fortune in Trade a Bubble upon themfelves, and having over-run the Market with their Goods, it returns upon them like the late *South Sea*, and every thing goes back from its imaginary to its intrinfick Value.

THE Demand abates the Advancement, the Price finks, the poor Spinners and Workfolk are difmifs'd to ftarve: But the Caufe is not in the Trade, but in the Workmen, not in the Manufacture, but in the Manufacturers; the Quantity of Goods made are too many for the Confumption, and the Market is perhaps glutted for a Year or more to come; and thus and no otherwife the Commerce is abated; that is, there is no real Abatement of the Trade, only it muft have Time given to wafte the over-made Quantity.

FROM the whole we may obferve here how many Ways the launching out a Manufacture to an undue Extent may be prejudicial to a Nation in general; 'tis like a Tradefman that over-trades himfelf, and runs out beyond the Compafs of his Stock; the Confequence

fequence is, that upon the leaſt Accident in Trade, his Credit is ſtagnated and ſhaken, and the Man is undone; and 'tis a juſt Obſervation in the Tradeſmen of this Nation, that there are many more ruined by too much Trade, than for Want of Trade.

IT is very unjuſt and unfair Dealing by the Publick, firſt to glut the Market, and over-run it with Goods, and then complain that the Market is dull: How ſhould the Reſpiration of Trade be preſerved, when 'tis choak'd and ſuffocated with Goods? When *Blackwell* Hall is empty, the Trade breathes; but when we ſee it piled up to the Ceilings; the Yards, the Paſſages and Staircaſes throng'd, Trade ſuffers, it is oppreſs'd with Quantity, and muſt die if not relieved.

LET the Trade of *Great Britain* go on in its uſual Channel, the Magnitude of it is ſufficient of it ſelf; all Exceſſes hurt it; I do not think Trade receives any Advantage from thoſe ſudden Starts and Advances of Price, as hinted above, but what the Manufacturer makes one Way, he loſes another, and the Poor loſe by it both ways.

I remember after the late Plague in *France,* and the Peace in *Spain,* the Run for Goods was ſo great in *England,* and the Price of every thing roſe ſo high, that the poor Women in *Eſſex* could earn one Shilling to one Shilling and Sixpence *per diem* by Spinning:

Spinning : What was the Confequence,
'twas too plain to be conceal'd.

THE poor Farmers could get no Dary-
Maids; the Wenches told them in fo many
Words, they would not go to Service for
Twelve-pence a Week, when they could get
nine Shillings a Week *at their own Hands*, as
they called it ; fo they all run away to *Bock-
ing*, to *Sudbury*, to *Braintree*, and to
Colchefter, and other Manufacturing Towns
of *Effex* and *Suffolk*.

THE very Plowmen did the fame, and
the Ale-houfes in the great Towns were
throng'd with them, young Fellows and
young Wenches together, till the Parifhes
began to take Cognizance of them upon
another Account, too dark to talk of here.

WHILE this Hurry lafted, the Bayes were
call'd for in prodigious Quantities, and the
Price rofe from 12 *d. per* Ell to 16 *d.* befides
the Advance upon the Parcels, an Article
particular to that Bufinefs.

As foon as the Demand flack'd from
Abroad, all thefe loofe People were turn'd
off, the Spinners went a begging, the Weavers rofe in Rebellion, and the Parifhes
were left throng'd with Baftards, which was
all that we might fay was got by that
Bargain.

WHEREAS, had the Merchants been obliged with the Goods as faft as the ordinary Numbers employ'd in the Manufacture
could have wrought them, the Market had
held

held the longer, the Merchants had had their Goods the cheaper, and the Markets Abroad would have been fupplied at laft too.

But, by that unadvifed rafh Hurry, nothing follow'd but Confufion; the Demand ftopt; yet the Makers run on as long as they were able, the Bayes were pawned in every money'd Man's Hand in the Country, and the Price funk to 11 d. *per* Yard at *London;* fo that a confiderable deal of Money was loft by every Piece made, the *Bay - Makers* broke by Dozens, and thus they went on; and now they as well as the Weft Country Men tell us, that the Trade is declin'd.

Now is this to be called a Decay of Trade? no not at all; there is ftill a moderate Demand, and the Trade, were the Glut of Goods taken off, would be where it was: But the Run has ruin'd them ; the Money to be gotten blinded the Manufacturers, they could not keep within the Compafs of their own Grafp, and fo funk in the neceffary Stop of the Trade that follow'd.

To judge then of the Decay of the Trade, we muft bring it back, as I faid, to a Medium of Years, and fee how it was carry'd on, and to what Degree, in fuch a Time, for 10, or 20, or 30 Years ago, and then compare it with its prefent worft Circumftances, and I venture to fay, we fhall not find the Trade decay'd at all, but rather encreafed in all the Manufactures of *England.*

I have

I have dwelt upon the encreafing Exportations of our own, and Importations of the Goods of foreign Growth, in the three laft Chapters, as an Evidence of the Magnitude of our Trade. If our Trade is declining, why do our Importations and Exportations encreafe? And if they do not encreafe, let the Oppofer of this Part tell us the Time when they were greater, or even equal to what they are.

Some have attempted this Part, and indeed 'tis the only way to convince us, that our Trade is declin'd; for if neither our Importations or Exportations are decreafed, which Way will they go to Work to fhew the Decreafe of our Commerce.

I might enquire of thefe phlegmatick Computers, firft, Whether is our Shipping decreas'd or not? I confefs, I have not yet heard it fo much as fuggefted; and tho' it is true, that it is not eafy to determine that Point, yet I think I am upon a Square with the Complainers, when I fay, that when ever they pleafe to enter into the Computation, I fhall be ready to begin an Enquiry on the other fide, which I believe will be convincing; in the mean time, let me refer the Reader to a View of the Weftern Coaft of the Ifland, and let them look narrowly into the Encreafe of Shipping at *Briftol, Liverpool, Whitehaven, Dumfreis, Glafgow,* and all the fmaller Ports on that Side from *Pembroke* Haven to the Firth of *Clyde,*

Clyde, and tell me if there are not a thoufand Sail of Ships more employ'd on that
Side, I mean Merchant Ships, befides Fifhing Boats and fmall Craft, more than were
ever known before. I might go round the
Ifland, and make like Obfervations; but, as
before, I meet with no body that makes any
Objection of that kind.

WE have two Trades, they tell us, which
are evidently declin'd, and the Shipping,
which was ufually employ'd in them, apparently leffen'd; and thefe are firft, the
French Trade, and fecondly, the Fifhing
Trade.

FOR the firft, *'tis true,* the *French* Trade
is leffen'd; but 'tis a Truth fo evidently,
and I might fay fo infinitely, to our Advantage, by our having made almoft all their
Manufactures (of which we took off fuch
exceeding great Quantities) our own; that
no Man can with Juftice call it a Decay or
Declining of our Trade in general, that our
Trade with *France* is leffen'd; on the contrary, 'tis no more than this, all that Part
of our Trade, which we loft by, is leffen'd,
and all that Part, which we gain'd by, is
or might be, if we pleas'd, encreafed and
preferv'd; whoever confiders the Importations of wrought Silks, Brandy, Paper,
Hats, Glafs, and feveral other Manufactures,
for which we paid *France* two Millions a
Year, turn'd all upon their Hands, and all
thofe things fupply'd at Home by the Labour

bour of our own People. For even the
Grofs of the Brandy, formerly *French,* is
now fupply'd by the Diftillers of Malt Spirits at Home, which, as to the common
Confumption, is turned all into the meaneft
of Liquor; but however, 'tis fuch as the
People eagerly clofe with, and by that
the Importation of Brandy is certainly reduced from nine thoufand Ton to lefs than
two thoufand Ton a Year.

ALL the reft of the *French* Goods, which
were formerly imported from thence, fo
much to our Lofs, being now made at Home,
I hope no Man can be fo weak as to call that
a Declining or Decreafe of our Trade; on
the contrary, 'tis a happy Encreafe of it,
for that the Confumption is at leaft the
fame, and our own People have the Profit of the Making; the Confumption is the
fame among the rich, and our own Poor
take the Money inftead of the Poor of
France.

As to the *French* Wine Trade, the Queftion anfwers it felf, the Stream only is turned from *France* to *Portugal,* the Quantity
of Wine confumed is not the lefs; and as it
is farther to fetch, the Shipping is rather
encreas'd by it than abated; the Ships not
being able to make fo many Voyages as they
did before, there muft be the more Bottoms, or the more Tonnage in larger Ships
employ'd, and either of them are an Encreafe
to the Navigation.

As

As to the Fishing Trade being decreased, it is begging the Question in a notorious Manner, and I think needs no Answering. On the contrary we see it lately encreased by a very great and probable Undertaking of the *Greenland* Fishery ; we see also several Proposals on foot for farther encreasing the *Scots* Fishery, and our other Fishing must be necessarily encreased by the Addition of our Dominion in *Newfoundland*, by the late Peace, where our Room for encreasing the Fishing is greatly enlarged. And it cannot be deny'd, but that the *English* Fishing on the Banks also is actually encreased : We must therefore be allow'd to say that Part needs no Reply till the Fact be prov'd.

LET us next enquire what one particular Trade in all our Foreign Business is impair'd, what Goods of Foreign Growth are they which lye by us unsold, and with which our Markets are glutted, or which our Merchants give no more Commissions for, being not able to consume them at Home, or export them to other Places Abroad.

I shall be very brief in the Inquiry.

I begin with the *East India* Company ; their Trade has been crampt by Prohibitions at Home, and by new Invasions from Abroad ; their Silks and Callicoes forbidden to be worn, in Favour of Rival Manufactures of Linen and Silk ; their Commerce invaded by a Rival Company at *Ostend* ; yet

yet we fee laſt their Sale amounted to almoſt eleven Hundred Thouſand Pounds *Sterling,* which allowing it to be half yearly, as really is the Caſe, can very ill be called a ſinking Commerce.

TAKE our Plantation Trade, the Iſland of St. *Chriſtopher's* being our own by the late Peace, we fee improv'd and increas'd to ſuch a Degree, that the Return of Sugar, Ginger, *&c.* is now as great from thence as from *Barbadoes ;* and the Plantations in *Jamaica* are ſo evidently encreas'd, that we are told in a few Years they will raiſe ten Thouſand Hogſheads of Sugar and Cocao more than ever they did before.

IN a Word, whereas formerly we had a Glut of Sugar from our Colonies, and were diſtreſs'd for a Market to diſpoſe of the Overplus, 'tis now evident, that ſince the great encreas'd Conſumption of Coffee and Tea in *Great Britain,* all our Colonies are hardly able to ſupply the Conſumption; and from Thirty Thouſand Hogſheads of Sugar which formerly we imported, 'tis certain we now import from ſeventy to eighty Thouſand Hogſheads in a Year, from all our Colonies, not reckoning the extravagant Bulk of the Hogſheads, which now generally contain from ſeventeen to eighteen hundred Weight of Sugar in each Hogſhead, one with another, ſome of them much more.

IN

IN like Manner, the Plantations in *Virginia* and *Maryland* are encreafed to fuch a Magnitude, that I am told they produce now from eighty to an Hundred Thoufand Hogfheads every Year; a Quantity fo great, compar'd to what has formerly been produced, that if it be all difpofed of, no Man can fay the *Virginia* Trade is not infinitely increafed; befides the great Export of Provifions from *Virginia,* that is to fay, from *Chefeapeak* Bay, which they fend to our Ifland Colonies, more by fome Hundreds of Sloops Loading a Year, than ever they fent before, which is one great Caufe of the *Virginia* Planters falling lately into the Trade of buying Negroes from the Coaft of *Africa,* which they never ufed to do formerly.

As our Ifland Colonies are thus mightily increas'd and improv'd, as it is moft certain they are; their People encreafing, they neceffarily demand a much greater Supply of Provifions from our other Colonies on the Continent of *America,* than they had before; and this encreafes the Trade of thofe Colonies, fuch as of *New-England, New-York, New-Jerfey,* Eaft and Weft; *Penfilvania, Carolina,* as alfo the Trade from the *Canaries, Maderas,* &c. *Cape de Verd* Iflands for Salt, and the Coaft of *Guinea* for *Negroes:* So that here is a manifeft Encreafe of all the Commerce of both the Eaft and Weft *Indies.*

WHERE

Where then fhall we find a Decay? where is there a Stagnation, what Trade languifhes, and where is it that we drive lefs Bufinefs than we did before?

Portugal will not pretend to it ; I might fay the whole World is Witnefs to the manifeft Encreafe of our Trade with the *Portuguefe,* who alone 'tis plain take off more of our Woollen Manufacture, fince the late Encreafe of their Commerce to *Brafil,* than both the Kingdom of *Portugal* and *Spain* ufed to do before: So that our Trade to thofe Parts is extremely improv'd.

'Tis true, there may be fome cafual Abatements of our Exportation to fome particular Parts of the World, and efpecially as Things ftand at this Time, by the War, or by the unfettled Circumftances of the Nations, with refpect to Continuance of Peace or War ; yet nothing can be argued upon that Suppofition, but what all Trades, and all trading Nations are fubject to, and ever will be on the like Occafions.

Let us next view the *Italian* and *Levant* Trades, which are very great Articles, and which bear a confiderable Part in the great Balance of our general Commerce ; the Turky Merchants have indeed complain'd, but what is the Complaint ? If the juft Part be examin'd, it will appear to lye here, *and here only*; not that the Goods they carry Abroad want a Market, but that the Silk they have brought Home, has, from
what-

whatever Neglect we yet know not, abated in its ufual Finenefs and Goodnefs ; and that to fuch a Degree, that the Manufacturers here, that is the Weavers, could no longer make ufe of it, at leaft not in fuch Works, and to fuch Purpofes as they had formerly done ; and fo the Trade may have fuffer'd, not from the Abatement of the Market Abroad or at Home, but from the Merchants not taking Care to import a good Commodity.

THIS can no more be call'd a Decay or Lofs of the *Turkey* Trade, than it would be a Lofs of the Trade now carried on by the South Sea Company to *America* ; if the Returns for their Goods fhould be made in a falfe Coin, or in counterfeit Pieces of Eight in ftead of the true ; The Trade therefore is not funk ; for if the Weavers cannot ufe the *Turkey* Silk, becaufe it is deficient in Quality, they muft ufe other Sorts ; that is to fay, fine *Italian* and *Piedmont* thrown Silks, or *Bengale* raw Silk in the Room of it, and 'tis certain they do fo. And it is worth while to obferve on this Occafion, how far this has been the Cafe, and how the Importation of thofe Silks has encreafed, as the other has prov'd inferior ; fo that the Silk Trade has not been leffen'd at all.

N. B. It was alledg'd in the late Difpute between the *Throwfters* and the Weavers before the Houfe of Commons, that as the *Turkey* Silks were brought

over

over worfe than formerly; fo the *Eaft
India* or *Bengale* Silks came better
than ever, and accordingly were more
in Demand : For it will for ever be
true, that whatever Materials of a Manufacture are furnifh'd from Abroad,
and decay in Goodnefs, they will decay in the Ufe, fink in Price, and at
length fink out of Demand, or they
will make the Manufacture they are
employ'd in fink in its Value, which is
ftill worfe.

Where then fhall we look for a Decay of
our Importations? if to the Navy, that is
already anfwered in the Difcourfe of the
Shipping : If the Number of Ships employ'd
is not abated, as I believe our worft Enemies
will not fuggeft, then our Commerce to the
Eaft Country cannot be abated; by our Eaft
Country Trade, is always underftood our
Trade in Hemp, Flax, Tar, Pitch, Iron,
&c. That is to fay in general, Naval Stores;
Now, 'tis manifeft by the Cuftom-houfe
Books (to which I refer) that thefe are not
abated; but on the contrary, very much
encreafed, notwithftanding our great Importation of Tar, Oyl, Mafts, *&c.* from
our own Colonies.

In what Part of the World then is our
Trade decay'd, and in what Branch of our
Bufinefs does it lye? for thofe People that
infift upon the Decay of our Trade, and
that make fuch loud Complaints about it,
ought

ought to let us know they do not raiſe
groundleſs Complaints, that would be call'd
Clamour and Diſaffection, and would look
like ſomething particularly piquant, which
I am loth to ſuggeſt.

I muſt therefore call upon them for their
Explanations, and to let us ſee the Place
where our Trade is decay'd, and what
Goods they are, the Conſumption of which
is leſſen'd and decay'd either at Home or
Abroad ; with ſuch needful Deſcriptions of
Trade in general, as may convince us there
is no equivalent Encreaſe in other Branches
to make it up, and to balance the Abatement.

THE immediate Reply to this, is what
I have mention'd already, (*viz.*) The mi-
micking our Woollen Manufacture in ſeveral Parts of *Germany*, by which the Demand of thoſe Manufactures from *England*
is abated, and may in Time be laid aſide in
thoſe particular Countries, ſuch as our
Bays, Flannels, Chamlets, Says, and ſeveral other kinds of Goods.

BUT what does this amount to in the
general Article of our great Manufacture?
let particular Caſes be what they will, let
Saxony, Swiſſerland, Piedmont, Auſtria,
and Twenty more Places, if you could
name them, interfere with, ſupplant or prohibit this or that Manufacture, and make
a viſible Decreaſe of the Conſumption here
or there : If the Conſumption is encreas'd
in

in other Parts of the World, be it a Thoufand Miles, or Ten thoufand Miles from *Germany*, the thing is anfwered, the Manufacture is the fame.

THE Queftion lies nearer Home, the Enquiry, like the fearching for a Difeafe, is in the vital Part ; the Search is at the Heart, if the Pulfe of the Trade beats true and ftrong, the Body is found, Wind and Limb ; is in a State of Health, and flourifhing in fpight of all the little Cafualties that may happen in other remote Parts.

THE Queftion in the Manufacture has no difficulty at all in it; and yet it feems that thofe Gentlemen who infift upon the Decay of the Manufacture do it upon the Prefumption, that there is no coming at the Negative ; but I fhall put it upon a Certainty which perhaps they may not forefee. The Queftion is in few Words (as before) Is the Quantity of Wooll wrought up, or is it not ? If all our Wooll is wrought up, nay if it is not fufficient for the Manufacture, then the Manufacture cannot be declined.

IT is within thefe Five and twenty Years, that we found the Wooll of *England* lye on Hand unfold, and the Farmers in the Sheep-feeding Countries, fuch as *Northampton, Leicefter, Lincoln, Warwick, Norfolk,* and many other Places, had generally two or three Years Wooll upon their Hands unfold, and the Price low, and very little Demand for it.

BUT

BUT now, and efpecially fince the feveral Acts prohibiting the *Eaft India* Silks,
Callicoes, Chints, and other Goods of
that Kind, we find the *Englifh* Wooll not
only all ufed up at Home, but alfo the
Irifh and the *Scots* Wooll brought over in
unufual Quantities to help; and yet the Price
holds up, and there is no Glut of Wooll in
the whole Ifland; how then can the Manufacture be declin'd? unlefs you will firft
make it appear, that the Quantity of Wooll
is abated in *England*, which I believe will
not be pretended, and if it were, would
be hard to prove.

I might very profitably employ a whole
Chapter here to prove to you, that the
Quantity of Wooll in *England* is fo far
from being leffen'd and decreafed, that it
is greatly encreafed for many Years paft,
and continues every Year to encreafe: I
could prove it by proving the Encreafe of
the Number of Sheep in *England*; and the
Encreafe of Sheep would be prov'd paft
Contradiction, by the Improvement of Culture, the enclofing vaft Tracts of Land in
almoft all Parts of *England* which lay open
before; and which being now improved
either by the Plowman, or by the Grazier,
ftill occafions greater flocks of Sheep, and
thofe of the beft and largeft Kind, to be
fed than were before.

I could add to it the vaft Improvement
made on the North-weft and Eaftern Coafts
of

of *England*, as alfo on the Coafts of *Wales*, by faving and draining Lands from the Sea, and from the Rivers, by which multitudes of Sheep are fed, as they are in *Rumney* Marfhes mention'd above: The almoft incredible Improvement of Land in the Countries of *Cumberland*, *Durham* and *Northumberland*, by which the Number of Sheep are encreafed on that Side the Country in a Manner, I fay, hardly to be believed.

I might alfo fpeak of the improv'd Methods, even in the breeding and feeding of Sheep, by raifing them upon the plow'd and fallow Lands, upon Salt Marfhes, and other Grounds, fuch as were never known by our Anceftors to feed Sheep before. And, *laftly,* I might infift upon an Article little confidered, but which is really of more Importance as to the Encreafe of Wooll than all the reft, *Namely*, that the Nation is univerfally fallen into a way of breeding larger Sheep than they did before: So that not only the Numbers of Sheep are encreafed by many Thoufands of Acres being employ'd to feed and breed, which never fed a Sheep before; but even the Sheep themfelves are of a different Kind, and two Sheep produce more Wooll than three Sheep, and in fome Places, than four Sheep did before. To bring this into Evidence, we need do no more than appeal to the meaneft of the Country People in *Lincolnfhire*
and

and *Leicestershire*; in the first you will see the feeding and breeding of large Sheep spread from the Country of *Lincoln* only, to which formerly it was confin'd, into all the level Grounds, Marshes and Fens of *Norfolk, Suffolk, Cambridge* and *Huntington*; from the County of *Leicester* the same Breed of Sheep is spread into the Counties of *Warwick, Stafford* and *Northampton*, and even the smaller Breeds of those Counties, which they now call Stubble Sheep, and which feed on the fallow and common Fields, are of a larger kind than ever before.

To look into the North, we see the Improvement in the Countries of *Durham* and *Northumberland*, running all into a large Breed of Sheep; and you may buy as large Mutton at the Markets in the City of *Durham*, as any you can buy at *Leadenhall*; I affirm it, and dare bring it to a Proof on any just Occasion; and we see large *Northumberland* Sheep brought up yearly for Sale in great Droves into all these Southern Parts of *England*, especially into *Essex* and *Suffolk*.

If then there were no Encrease in the Numbers of our Sheep, the contrary of which is true to a Demonstration; yet if we run into a larger Breed, the Wooll may still be encreased as much as if the Numbers were encreased; but as it is apparent that both the Breed is altered, and the Generality

lity of the Sheep-breeders run into another larger Kind, and the Numbers of Sheep by the Encreafe of Culture and Enclofure is encreafed alfo. How then can we pretend the Quantity of Wooll in *England* is declin'd ? The Weight of this Part of the Argument may be fum'd up thus.

I f the Numbers of Sheep are not decreafed, nor the Breed of the Sheep degenerated, then the Quantity of our Wooll cannot be decreafed or abated.

I f the Quantity of Wooll is not abated, and yet it does not lye on hand, and want a Market, then the whole Growth of our Wooll is evidently ufed up and manufactured ; for it would not be bought if it could not be ufed.

A g a i n, take it in the Reverfe.

I f our whole Growth of Wooll is not only bought and ufed up, but that we buy great Quantities of Wooll and Woollen Yarn from *Ireland,* to fuch a Degree, as has been faid, that it amounts to an hundred thoufand Packs a Year :   Then 'tis evident that the whole Growth of our Wooll is not equal to our Manufacture.

I f it is true, that our whole Growth of Wooll is not equal to our Manufacture ; that is to fay, that it is not fufficient for our Supply ; but that greater Quantities than ever are brought in every Year from *Ireland* and *Scotland,* all of which (clandeftine Trade excepted) is ufed up, and manufactured

&tured in this Part of *Great Britain* called *England,* as has been proved: Then the Manufacture of Wooll in *England* cannot be leffen'd or decay'd; but on the contrary, is evidently improv'd and encreas'd.

  N. B. A s to the Exception for clande-ftine Trade; it is mentioned indeed to anticipate any Cavil which might be raifed upon the Omiffion, as if we did not know there was fuch a Trade as owling or running of Wooll carried on among us; but the Quantity fo carried off, tho' too much, with Refpect to the Injury done our Trade, yet is fmall, and indeed not worth naming, in comparifon of the Bulk of Wooll, which the Growth of the whole King-dom produces, and of which we are now fpeaking.

C H A P.

Chap. II.

An Enquiry whether the Exportation of our other Goods, the Growth or Manufacture of England, *or the Home Consumption of them is decreased or declined.*

 HAVE mentioned the Produce of our Colonies, and prov'd that they are evidently encreafed, as well in their Exports to one another, as in the Confumption and Re-exportation of their Produce here in *England*.

I have mention'd the Encreafe of our Woollen Manufacture, and prov'd it to a Demonftration by the Confumption of the Wooll.

It feems only to remain, that we fhould enquire into fome other Trades which are profitably carry'd on among us, and fee whether they are not declin'd in Proportion, and to make way for the Encreafe of the Woollen Manufacture; for if other Branches of Commerce are declin'd in Proportion, the Woollen Manufacture, how-

ever

ever great, may be encreafed, and yet our Trade in general be declin'd too, and at the fame Time.

BUT I perfuade my felf, it will be hard to find any part of the Product of *England* which can be faid to be declin'd and decreafed, either in its Exportation to Countries Abroad, or in its Confumption at Home.

THE Product of *England* has been already at large defcrib'd, the Wooll is fet in the Front as the Chief, and it is fo; but it is not the only Product, nor are the Woollen Manufactures the only things which employ the People of *England,* and fet their Hands to Work; there are feveral Manufactures in *England* which employ a vaft Number of People in which the Wooll is no way concern'd, and upon Examination, we fhall find, (1.) fome of thefe are wholly now a mere modern Improvement, and on which no Hands were fet to Work, no Stock employ'd before.

2. OTHERS, tho' known before, are yet exceedingly improv'd and encreas'd, and confequently employ many Hands which were unemploy'd before, which in fhort is the effential Part of all Improvement in Trade.

I fhall give Examples of fome of thofe Manufactures, which are more remarkable than others, and by which the moft confiderable Number of Poor are employ'd, and

and Materials confum'd; for the reft, it
fhall fuffice only to name them.

1. The *Bone Lace* Manufacture. It is
true, that there was always, perhaps, for
fome Ages paft, a Manufacture of *Bone
Lace* carry'd on in *England*; but the Improvement and Encreafe of it within about
20 to 30 Years paft is fuch, and fo vifible,
that he muft be utterly ignorant of Trade
that is not convinc'd of it. In former
Times, the chief Place for this Manufacture
was about *Buckingham, Stony Stratford,*
and *Newport Pagnaell,* vulgarly *Newport
Pannel;* you have it now fpread, almoft
entirely over the Counties of *Buckingham,
Bedford* and *Oxford,* and far into the Counties of *Berks, Northampton, Cambridge,
Hertford* and *Surrey,* efpecially where any
or all thofe Counties border on the firft:
It is alfo erected in the Weft, and efpecially
in the Counties of *Dorfet* and *Wiltfhire,*
where particularly at *Blandford* they make
Lace of an exceeding high Price, and not
outdone, *Bruffels* Lace excepted, by any
out of *Flanders, France,* or even *Venice* it
felf. In a word, this Manufacture is fo
much encreafed in *England,* that it employs
many Thoufands of our People more than
ever ; and if I may credit the Report of
the Country where 'tis chiefly made, where
one was employ'd by it 30 Years ago, above
100 are employ'd by it now, and thefe of
the moft idle, ufelefs and burthenfome Part
of

of our People (I mean fuch as were fo before) are the principal Hands employ'd, *viz.* the younger Women, and female Children. Thefe were a real Charge upon the diligent laborious Poor, fuch as the Hufband-men, the Farmers, and the Handicrafts of other Trades ; and are now made able to provide for themfelves, and eafe their Parents and Parifhes of a dead Weight, which was in many Cafes infupportable ; but I cannot dwell upon the Particulars, which otherwife would be profitably enquired into. In fhort, 'tis believ'd there are above an Hundred Thoufand Women and Children employ'd, and who get their Bread by this Manufacture, more than did formerly ; for 'tis the Encreafe of it that I am now difcourfing of ; and this Encreafe has an Effect upon the general Commerce of this Kingdom, very much to the Advantage of *England*, for Example.

1. In employing all this great Number of People in a Manufacture which employ'd, as may be reafonably fuppos'd, the like Number of People in another Country, (*viz.*) in *Flanders* ; fo that it may be faid to be taking the Bread out of the Poor of *Flanders*, and putting it into the Mouths of the Poor of our own Country.

2. It is a Turn in the Balance of Trade to the Advantage of *England,* in fupplying us with the fame Quantity of Goods by the Labour of our own Poor, which we, till now,

now, bought abroad, and which buying abroad, was always attended with this as a Confequence, that either we paid for them in Money, or in our own Manufactures; whereas (if the firft) that Money, is now kept at Home; and (if the laft) thofe Manufactures muft be paid for to us in Money, as they certainly are.

2. ANOTHER encreas'd Manufacture is that of wrought Iron and Brafs: I need not refer to the Towns of *Birmingham* and *Sheffield*, and the People of *Hallamfhire*, a Diftrict well known to the Nailers and hard Ware Men of *Barnfely* and *Rotherham*: But I appeal to the Iron Works of the late Sir *Ambrofe Crowley*, and his Son Alderman *Crowley*, at *Newcaftle* upon *Tyne*; and above all, to the fame fort employ'd in *London*, where they certainly make the beft Cutlery Ware at this Time in the World.

IT is not many Years fince the beft Sciffars, the beft Knives, and the beft Razors were made in *France*, and the like of the fine Watches, Tweezars, and other fmall Ware; nothing is more evident in Trade at this Time, than that the beft Knife Blades, Sciffars, Surgeons Inftruments, Watches, Clocks, Jacks and Locks that are in the World, and efpecially Toys and gay Things are made in *England*, and in *London* in particular; and our Cuftom-houfe Books, will make it appear, that we fend daily great

Quan-

Quantities of wrought Iron and Brass into *Holland, France, Italy, Venice,* and to all Parts of *Germany, Poland* and *Muscovy.*

IN a Word, no particular Manufacture can be nam'd, which has encreased like this of the hard Ware, I mean, in *Great Britain*; and 'tis still an encreasing Manufacture: To make Calculations, and Comparisons, seems to be piquant in the Case, and particularly pointed at this or that Nation; but let it point where it will, the Fact is plain; 'tis the like in the grosser Part of the Trades, as our Toys, Scissars, Razors, Knife and Sword Blades outdo the *French*; so our common Bombs, Shells, Grenades, Caldrons, and all sorts of cast Iron, as much outdo the *Germans,* the *Legois,* or the *Dutch.*

IT is the like in wrought Brass; most of the Brass Locks of all the fine Palaces in *France,* if narrowly inspected, will be found to be *English*; the fine Gold Watches in the Pockets of the Grand Seignior, the Czar of *Muscovy,* and the Sophy of *Persia,* or the great Mogul, are generally *English*: We send our Toys to the Court of *France,* and the *English* Knives and Razors have quite outdone the *French.*

BY this Means it comes to pass, as I am well assur'd, that there are above 200000 People employ'd in the Manufacture of Iron and Brass in *England,* more than ever were before: Perhaps this may be of the most

moſt as to Numbers, nor will I take that
Part upon my ſelf, tho', if it be true,
that the late Sir *Ambroſe Crawley* did employ 30000 People in his own particular
Part, the reſt may be more than probable.
But this, upon the whole, will (I doubt
not) be allow'd, (*viz.*) that there is a viſible
Encreaſe of our Trade in Iron and Braſs, as
well as it is a Manufacture, as it is a Mer-
chandice ; for there is a manifeſt Encreaſe
of the Exportation and Home Conſumption, as well as an Encreaſe of Employment
for the People.

    N. B. IN this Article ſhould be included
the Mines of Copper lately improv'd
in *England* and *Wales* ; as alſo the
Battery and *Braſs Mills* and *Founda-*
ries, which are in themſelves very
conſiderable ; and if we may credit the
Repreſentations made to the Parliament a few Years ſince, do employ
many Thouſands of our People more
than were ever employ'd in thoſe
things before.

THESE are Improvements in Manufacture and Trade ; and as they teſtify an Encreaſe of Trade, we can ſee no Room yet
to ſuggeſt that the Trade of *England* in
general is declin'd or decay'd.

    3. THERE are ſome other Articles yet
more conſiderable than theſe, and one of
them is the broad Silk Manufacture ; I cannot paſs it over ; it is an Encreaſe of this
very

very Age. It is a Surprise to the World, as well in its Quantity as in its Value, and in the admirable Perfection which our People are arriv'd to in it, and the little Time they have had to raise it to the Degree which it is arriv'd to.

I t is but a very few Years ago, that the making of broad Silks began in *England*; the *French* and the *Italians* carried the World before them (as to Trade) in that particular Article; what Attempts had been made in *England* were chiefly at *Canterbury* by the *Walloons* and *French* Refugees, and they were so beaten out by the *East India* Silks, that if I am not misinform'd, there were not 20 Looms left at Work in the whole City of *Canterbury*, some say, not half so many.

When the *French* Trade prevail'd, and before the Stop of Commerce between the two Kingdoms began by the late War, the most moderate Calculations valued the broad Silks which were imported from *France* and *Itally* at 1200000 Pounds *Sterling per Annum*; some say, we took off as much as that Value in the *French* Silks only, whereof one Half at least in *Alamodes* and *Lustrings*, the Manufacture of *Lyons*, and the Provinces upon the *Rhosne*.

But be it so or not; for we are not adjusting the Value of Things, in that or any other Part of that Country, but the general Tide or Current of the whole Trade; of which I
might

might venture to fay, it was known to the whole World, that is to the whole trading World, that it run to the Advantage of *France*, with a full Stream directly from *England;* I mean as to the Silk Manufacture, all which Trade is now funk, I fay, funk and loft as to *France* and *Italy*, to the infinite Advantage of *England;* and this not that *England* may be faid to leave off wearing Silk: No, far from it; as our Wealth is encreafed, we do not pretend our Pride or Vanity is abated; our Ladies go as gay, and our Houfes are furnifh'd as rich as ever, and perhaps more fo, and in the fame Kinds and forts of Silks, Luftrings, Mantuas, Velvets, *Padua* Soys, Garden Sattins, the beft and richeft Brocades, and the beft and richeft of all forts of Silks: But the Difference lies here, that whereas we bought them before, now we make them at Home, we fet the *French* Men of *Tours*, of *Lyons, Avignon*, and the Countries about them at Work before, and the *Italians* of *Milan, Mantua, Genoa, Florence* and *Naples*, and paid them all at a vaft Expence of *Englifh* Money, a Profufion of Money, even a Million 200000 *l. Sterling* a Year; whereas now our own Poor gain all that Money; our own Merchants import the Materials, our own Manufacture purchafes the Silk, the Drugs and Dye Stuffs; and the whole Manufacture of broad Silk is an Encreafe upon our Commerce. But I

fhall

fhall fay no more of this here, becaufe I
fhall have Occafion to mention it again,
when I come to fpeak of the *Englifh* People
improving upon the Manufacture and Inventions of other Nations.

4. I proceed therefore to another vifible
Encreafe of Trade, which fpreads daily
among us, and affects not *England* only,
but *Scotland* and *Ireland* alfo, tho' the
Confumption depends wholly upon *England ;* and this is printing or painting of
Linen. The late Acts of prohibiting the
Ufe and wearing of painted Callicoes, either in Cloths, Equipages or Houfe Furni-
niture, was without Queftion aim'd at improving the Confumption of our Woollen
Manufacture, and in Part it had an Effect
that way.

But the Humour of the People running
another way, and being ufed to, and pleafed
with the light, eafie and gay Drefs of the
Callicoes, the Callicoe Printers fell to
Work to imitate thofe Callicoes, by making
the fame Stamps and Impreffions, and with
the fame Beauty of Colours upon the
Linen, and that this fell upon the two particular Branches of Linen, call'd *Scots*
Cloth and *Irifh* Linen : I need not take
any Pains to prove this. The Confequence is
alfo evident, (*viz.*) That the Linen Manufacture both in *Scotland* and in *Ireland* are
confiderably encreas'd upon that Occafion,
and many hundred thoufand Ells of Linen

are

are yearly imported from *Scotland* and *Ireland,* and printed in *England,* more than ever
were before ; fo that this is an Article wholly new in Trade, and indeed the Printing
it felf is wholly new; for it is but a few
Years ago fince no fuch thing as painting
or printing of Linen or Callicoe was known
in *England;* all being fupply'd fo cheap, and
perform'd fo very fine from *India,* that nothing but a Prohibition of the foreign printed
Callicoes could raife it up to a Manufacture
at Home; whereas now it is fo encreafed,
that the Parliament has thought it of Magnitude fufficient to lay a Tax upon it, and a
confiderable Revenue is raifed by it.

I T may be enquired here concerning the
great Numbers of People employ'd in thefe
Improvements, what were they employ'd
in before ? and how do we call it an Improvement, if they are only taken from one
Manufacture into another.

THIS might be fully anfwered, if we had
Room here to enquire critically in the feveral Counties where thofe particular Improvements are made; we fhould there find,
that in almoft all the Improvements and Encreafe of Bufinefs above mention'd, fuch as
the Manufactures of Bone Lace, the Brafs
and Iron Manufactures, the Haberdafhery ;
and in a Word, all the other improv'd
Manufactures, except that of Broad Silk
weaving, the People employ'd were not at
all employ'd in the Woollen Manufactures
before,

before, but were, generally fpeaking, out of Bufinefs, idle and unemploy'd, there being no fuch thing as Woollen Manufactures fettled in the Counties and Towns where thofe Improvements have been made, fuch as *Buckinghamfhire* and *Bedfordfhire*, *Sheffield*, *Birmingham*, and *Newcaftle* upon *Tyne*.

THE broad Silk Trade indeed, being chiefly carried on in the Cities of *London*, might be faid to employ fome of the People formerly employ'd in the Woollen Manufacture in the fame Place, (*viz.*) *Spittle-Fields:* But then it muft be added, that even that Encroachment was only upon the Abatement of fuch Woollen Goods in that Place, which were imprudently launched out into before, upon the foolifh Expectation of a great Encreafe of the Woollen Trade, by the Prohibitions of *Eaft India* Goods; fo that even in this Part the Silk Trade has very little, if at all encroach'd upon the Woollen, tho', if it had, the Exchange had very little alter'd the Cafe.

UPON the Whole, after the narroweft Search, and with the utmoft Impartiality, I cannot fee that we have any Room to fay our Trade is decreas'd, whether we fpeak of our Woollen or other Manufactures; whether of Goods imported or exported; whether of the Home Confumption, or the Con-

Confumption of our Growth Abroad. On the contrary, we have great Reafon to in-fift, that our whole Trade is encreafed to a very great Degree; it remains only in a fum-mary Way, to account for the Encreafe of our Commerce both Abroad and at Home.

PART

PART III.

Of the Improvement of the English *in Trade; upon the Inventions of other Nations, and the Encreafe of our Commerce upon thofe Improvements; in which we have beaten out the faid Inventors from their own Trade; likewife of the feveral Improvements of our own Product, and of our own Invention: By all which our Trade is greatly encreafed.*

T is a Kind of Proverb attending the Character of *Englifh* Men, That they are *better to improve than to invent*, better to advance upon the Defigns and Plans which other People have laid down, than to form Schemes and Defigns of their own; and which is ftill more, the Thing feems to be really true in Fact, and the Obfervation very juft.

WHETHER

WHETHER this Reproach upon them is raifed upon the Suggeftions of Foreign Obfervers, or whether it be our own upon our felves, is not worth while to examine ; it feems we are very willing to grant the Fact.

UPON this Suppofition then my Subject feems to be adapted to the national Temper ; I offer here a Scene of Originals, for the improving Genius of our People to work upon a Stock of Invention for them to improve upon: May they take the Hint, try their Hands, and go to Work upon them with the ufual Succefs.

HENCE moft of our great Advances in Arts, in Trade, in Government, and in almoft all the great Things, we are now Mafters of, and in which we fo much exceed all our Neighbouring Nations, are really founded upon the Inventions of others ; whether thofe firft Inventers were private Men, or Nations of Men, 'tis not material.

EVEN our Woollen Manufacture it felf, with all the admirable Improvements made upon it by the *Englifh,* fince it came into their Hands, is but a building upon other Mens Foundations, and improving on the Inventions of the *Flemings :* The Wooll indeed was *Englifh,* but the Wit was all *Flemifh ;* we had the Materials, but no more underftood the Virtue of them, than the World underftood the Making Gun-powder, tho' they had always the Sulphur and Salts, which are now the

proper

proper Ingredients of that dreadful Com-
pofition.

WE had the Wool, but underftood
neither how to comb it or card it, fpin it
or weave it; nay, we cannot be faid to
know, that it was capable of thofe manual Operations, or what Spinning and Weaving was, any more than if we had not
known what the Wool was : But when, *as
has been obferv'd,* by the Direction of King
Henry VII. the *Englifh* were put upon the
general Notion of Improvement, inform'd
of the Profit of manufacturing it, and but
once directed how to go about it, by the
Flemifh Agents hir'd to inftruct them:
How foon did they outdo their Teachers,
and to what a Pitch of Improvement did
they rife in a few Years ? Till now we fee
the World ambitious of imitating us in
the fame Manner, and to rival our Manufactures, are obliged to hire Inftructers
from hence, and to learn of thofe who were
themfelves but Learners before.

I might enter into almoft all the Improvements of Art in which the *Englifh*
fo much now excel the reft of the World :
How in feveral Manufactures we have
turn'd the Scale of Trade, and fend our
Goods to be fold in thofe very Countries
from whence we deriv'd the Knowledge
and Art of making them.

THUS we were all faid to learn the
Art of building Ships from the *Genoefe*
and

and *French,* and at this Day fo effectually
outbuild them all, that the *Genoefe* often
buy Ships in *England,* and the late King of
France, the great *Lewis* XIV. procured
the Model of our Ships from *England,* by
which to build his Capital Men of War ;
among which that glorious Ship burnt by
Englifh at *La Hogue,* called the *Royal
Sun,* was faid to be built by the Model of
the *Royal Sovereign,* an *Englifh* Man of
War, built in the Time of King *Charles* the
firft, and rebuilt in King *Charles* the fecond's Time, and the Drafts of it were it
feems tranfmitted to *France.*

Fʀᴏᴍ the *Venetians* and *French* we
took the Art of *Glafs-Making,* and of
Cutlery, and feveral others ; till now we
outdo our Teachers, and export Glafs
Wares, Brafs Locks, Fine Keys, Knives,
Sciffars, Razors, Surgeons Inftruments, and
Joyners Tools, to thofe very Places ; and
you may fee tbe Doors of the Royal
Apartments at *Verfailles,* (as is faid above)
furnifh'd with fine Brafs Locks and nice
Hinges from *England,* becaufe *France* can-
not produce the like.

I might give Examples of the like Kind
in many other Cafes, wherein we excel in
the Improvement thofe very People, who
fo much excell'd us in the Invention; of
which the Silk Manufacture is now a furprifing Example, in which we fo much out-
do the *French* themfelves, who were our
Teachers,

Teachers, and of whom we always bought the richeft and fineft broad Silks the whole World could produce, that we now fell broad Silks even into *France* it felf.

To begin with probable Improvements in Colonies and Plantations ; *Columbus* a *Genoefe* by Nation, difcover'd the Coafts of *America,* and his Succeffors the Adventurers upon thofe Difcoveries, took Poffeffion for the King of *Spain :* It is true, they fpread themfelves upon the Continent, reduc'd, or rather deftroy'd the Nations who inhabited the feveral Countries, poffefs'd the immenfe Wealth of the Natives, and being led by the Hand to the Mines of Gold and Silver, and the other rich Produ&t of the Place, they vouchfafed, as we may fay, to ftoop and take it up; but we can charge them with very little of Improvement : The Sin of Diligence cannot be lay'd at their Door, nor have they to this Day, after almoft 200 Years peaceable Poffeffion, brought the moft fruitful and richeft Provinces and Diftri&ts of *America* to be much more produ&tive than they were before ; not a Manufa&ture of any Value ere&ted to employ and improve the People ; not any Advantage confiderable made of the Labour of the many Thoufands of the Natives, who ftill remain among them, and are as willing as able to work for them for a Trifle ; not any Culture carried on, no not in the moft fruitful

Pro-

Provinces, to encreafe the Product equal to the Strength of the Soil.

On the contrary, the *Englifh* tho' planting near 100 Years after them, and taking, as it might be called, the Fag-end of the Difcovery, the northern, cold, and barren Parts, without Silver and Gold, without Mine or Mineral, without any apparent Product; yet how has the improving Genius of the *Englifh* brought Gold out of their Drofs.

I fay Drofs; for fo it was with refpect to the firft Difcoverers; and in their Efteem all our Colonies were but, as we may fay, the Dregs of the *Spaniards* firft Extraction, the Refufe Part of their Conquefts, their meer Leavings, that Part of the Country which they did not think worth fo much as looking into.

What were all our Colonies upon the Continent, but a little narrow Slip of Land upon the Sea Coafts, in the cold, wild, unhofpitable Climates of the North? And what our Ifland Colonies, but a few little defpicable Iflands not worth the *Spaniards* pofleffing, hardly worth their naming, in Comparifon of their vaft Pofleffions on the Continent; nay not worth naming in Comparifon of the vaft Iflands of *Cuba* and *Hifpaniola,* one of which is bigger than all our Iflands put together; and yet *Cuba* and *Hifpaniola,* tho' equally rich and productive, and infinitely full of natural Wealth, are

are left unplanted, as not worth their Pains
to improve.

> *N. B. Barbadoes* is not above 70 Miles
> in Circumference, and *Hifpaniola* is
> above 400 Leagues, *Nevis* not above
> 20 Miles, and *Cuba* above 690 Miles in
> Length.

But let us turn our Eyes now and view
the Effects of the improving *Englifh* Genius,
the Colonies of *New-England* and *Virginia,*
defpis'd by the *Spaniards,* as well before we
difcover'd them, as afterwards; for the fame
Columbus, which difcover'd *New-Spain,* difcover'd all the Northern Coaft, but left it a-
gain as not worth while to plant and poffefs
it. I fay, thefe barren, cold, poor and uncultivated Climates, the Leavings of the *Spa-*
niards, How have we improved upon them
to infinite Advantages?

Not difcouraged by the Severity of the
Cold, by the Surface over-grown with Bri-
ars and Thorns, by the early Oppofition of
the Natives, a Race of People fierce and
falfe, untractable, treacherous, irreconcil-
able, bloody and mercilefs, even to the moft
horrible, and almoft inexpreffible Cruelties,
who would rarely make Peace, and more
rarely keep their Agreements when made.

Often maffacred and butcher'd, and
fometimes quite driven away by the Fury
of the Savages, often ftarv'd out and famifh-
ed, and either the whole Body of Planters
wafted, and perifhing with Cold and Want,
and

and as often being reduc'd to Extremities, forc'd to abandon the Country in the utmoſt Diſtreſs, and return ſtarving home.

BUT never to be diſcouraged, how have they by the meer Force of indefatigable Application, planted, inhabited, cultivated thoſe inhoſpitable Climates, thoſe ſuppos'd barren Countries, thoſe trifling little Spots of Iſlands, not thought worth looking at by the *Spaniards?* How have they brought them to be the richeſt, the moſt improved, and the moſt flouriſhing Colonies in all that Part of the World? So populous, ſo fortify'd, the People ſo rich, the Product ſo great; and which is more than all, ſo adapted to Commerce, ſo univerſally embarked in Trade, that it is at this Time an unreſolved Doubt, whether brings the greateſt Wealth to *Europe,* take the Exportations and Conſumptions of Manufacture there into the Account of the Return, the Sugars, Tobacco, and other rich Productions of the *Britiſh* and *French* Colonies; the Fiſh, the Corn, the Fleſh, the Furrs, *&c.* I ſay, Which are the greateſt in Value, theſe, or the Gold and Silver of *Mexico* and *Peru?*

BUT not to weigh the Particulars, and come to reckon by Ounces and Drams, this is certain, and will be granted, that the Product of our improved Colonies raiſes infinitely more Trade, employs more Hands, and I think, I may ſay by Conſequence, brings in more Wealth to this one particular

lar Nation or People, the *English,* than all
the Mines of *New Spain* do to the *Spaniards.*

AND not to infift only upon the little
Share *Spain* it felf reaps from the Returns of
Gold and Silver, made to and landed in their
Country ; moft of which runs out again in
the very fame Species in particular Channels of Trade, to other Nations: I fay, not
to infift upon this, take the Opulence, the
growing Greatnefs of the *Britifh* Colonies,
the Numbers of their People, and how prodigioufly every Day encreafing ; and above
all, that the Encreafe of Navigation, the
Number of Ships employ'd, nay Ships built,
and Seamen nurs'd up, the Wealth and Addition of Strength we reap from them, which
is not eafy to calculate. I fay, add this to the
Account, and, I doubt not, it will be granted, that the Return of Wealth from *America* to this Nation, is equal to the Return of
Gold and Silver from *New* to *Old Spain.*

LET any Man calculate the Value of our
Returns in Sugar, Ginger, Indigo, Cotton,
Cocoa, Drugs, Spice, and other Goods,
from the Iflands only, with the Furrs or
Peltry ; the Rice, Tobacco, Train and Turpentine Oil, Tar, Mafts, and abundance of
other things: Then let them add the Inter-
change of their other Product, between the
feveral Colonies, one with another; fuch as
the Supply of Corn, Peafe, Rice, Meal,
Beef, Pork, Beer, Horfes, Leather, Fifh,

Lum-

Lumber, &c. of all which, the Quantities are exceeding great; and in which Trade, feveral Hundreds, nay fome fay Thoufands, of Ships and Sloops, are conftantly employed.

In Return for which, a very great Quantity of Rum, Molaffes, Cocoa, Ginger, Sugar, &c. is fent back to the Main-Land Colonies on the Continent; *of which,* all that they cannot confume is fent to *England* for Returns.

If thefe things are caft up together, including the Confumption of the Woollen Manufacture of *Great Britain,* and of all the Hard-ware Manufacture; alfo the Cordage, the Hats, Gloves, and other Leather Manufactures : In a word, the Confumption of all the other *Britifh* Goods fent thither, the Comparifon of Trade will be, out of Queftion, on the *Britifh* Side ; feeing almoft all the Goods exported from *Spain* to their Colonies in *America,* are firft bought from other Countries.

Had the *Spaniards* been an induftrious, improving Nation, like the *Englifh,* the Iflands of *Cuba* and *Hifpaniola* alone, having been planted and improved, as our fmall Ifland of *Barbadoes* is improved, would have produc'd more Sugar, Cotton, Indigo, Cocoa, Piemento, and other valuable things, than all *Europe* could have confumed ; and they would have been able to have fupply'd all their other Colonies with Flefh, fuch as
Beef

Beef and Pork, and with Rice and other things, more than they could confume.

IN lieu of which, thofe fruitful Iflands are now left to lye wafte, untill'd, unplanted, and the great Difcoverers have not made any one Step that deferves the Name of Improvement upon them, except only the fortifying the Port of the *Havana ;* which Neceffity almoft drove them to for the Protection of their Commerce to their other Colonies, and forming the Rendezvouz of their *Galleons,* in their paffing and repaffing between *Europe* and *America.*

WHEREAS, take our Colonies on the *Leward* Iflands only into Confideration, (here indeed we have improv'd to the utmoft) there is hardly an Inch of Ground loft in the Ifland of *Barbadoes* that can produce one Ounce of any thing more than it does; the like perhaps cannot be faid of any one Spot of Ground in the World, which containing in the whole not above 70 Miles in Circumference, employs and maintains above 100000 People, including the Negroe Slaves, enriches the Planters to a furprifing Degree, and fully employs above 200 Sail of Ships and Sloops, always running with Provifions of Fifh, Flefh, Corn, and Cattle, from *North America,* Wine from the *Maderas,* and with Slaves (Negroes) from the Coaft of *Africa,* and with Manufactory and Merchant-Goods from *Great Britain* and *Ireland.*

THE

THE fame, in its Proportion, might be faid of the Ifland of *Jamaica,* where the *Spaniards* were the Difcoverers, that is, in the room of the Inventors, and made little or nothing of it, and we are the Improvers; and what that Improvement is, we all know: That Ifland for its Planting, and its other Advances of Trade, is at this Time the greateft Article in all our *Weft India* Commerce; and if fome nice Calculators may be allowed to judge right, the Product of the Ifland of *Jamaica,* and the Confumption of Goods there from *England,* or which goes that Way, to *New Spain,* makes the Trade of the Ifland fuperior at this Time to the Trade of all our other Iflands; that is to fay, the Iflands of *Barbadoes, Nevis, Antegoa, Mountferat,* and *St. Chriftophers,* put together, and this Trade every Day encreafing too.

NOR is the Improvement of *Jamaica* improperly call'd advancing upon the Invention of others; for the *Spaniards* did for themfelves make feveral Experiments in Trade; they planted originally in *Jamaica* feveral things, which were then meer Inventions in Planting, which the *Englifh* have fince improved upon, and which are not to be produc'd in any of the other *Englifh* Iflands; fuch as the *Cocoa, Piemento, Indigo,* and feveral other things which the *Englifh* have fince brought to a great Perfection by their Improvement.

THEY

THEY likewife laid the Foundation of that fecret Commerce with the *Spanifh* Colonies, which the *Englifh* have improv'd to fuch a Degree, as it is even threatning to the whole Trade of *New Spain ;* for when the *Englifh* conquer'd the Ifland from the *Spaniards,* thofe *Spanifh* Families, which remain'd upon the Ifland, keeping up a Correfpondence with their Friends and former Acquaintances in *Cartagena,* St. *Martha,* and the Coaft of *Caracas,* and all the other Ports of that Country, that Intimacy became the Foundation of an advantageous Correfpondence, fince carry'd on ; and the improving *Englifh* brought forth from it a Trade grown up by Time, and the particular Encouragements of fucceeding Ages, to a prodigious Magnitude.

BUT thefe are things behind us, and may perhaps be call'd, *looking back to what is paft ;* whereas the Eyes of Mankind are rather fix'd upon things before them ; and where we talk of Inventing and Improving, the Enquiry is, what Inventions are now upon the Anvil, for our improving Genius to work upon ? What is there that at prefent offers for the Application of an ingenious People ? And this brings me to the grand Head propofed in this Treatife, *(viz)* Schemes of Improvement in Commerce, which are to be the Subject of this latter Part of the Work.

CAP.

Cap. XI.

Being a Proposal *for rooting out thofe Nefts of* Pyrates *and* Rovers, *the* Turks *or Moors of* Tunis, Tripoli, Algier, *and* Sallee, *who have for fo many Ages infefted the* Mediterranean *Seas, and the Coafts of* Spain *and* Portugal, *to the infinite Lofs and* Difcouragement *of all the* Trading Nations *of* Europe.

With a Scheme for the Improvement of Trade, *by reftoring and eftablifhing the ancient Commerce on the North and North-Weft Coaft of* Africa.

IN fpeaking of *Africa,* as it once was the the Seat of Commerce for the whole World, we muft look back as far as to the flourifhing State of the *Carthaginian* Government ; but it fhall be as fhort as can be defired..

IT is true, as has been obferved by a well informed Writer on this Subject, that the *Romans* (like the *Turks* in our Time) were no Friends to Trade; they carry'd on their War for Glory; like meer Soldiers they fought to conquer, and conquer'd to plunder, not to plant and people the World: So far were they from encouraging or improving the Commerce and Wealth of the Nations they fubdued, that they overthrew and deftroy'd the greateft Trading Cities in the World ; fuch as *Corinth, Syracufe,*

cufe, *Carthage,* and all the Cities of *Ægypt* and *Africa:* Inftead of encouraging Trade and Navigation, they murther'd the Merchants, burnt their Ships, and carry'd away the People, which are the Life and Support of Manufacture and Trade.

On the other hand, the *Carthaginians,* as they had the richeft Soil and a numerous People, (for *Africa* was then infinitely populous) they improved the firft, and employ'd the laft, to the utmoft; their People were as rich as they were numerous; they carry'd on Trade to all the Parts of the World, planted Colonies, built Cities Abroad, and Ships at Home; and wherever they came, whether by Conqueft, or by Confent, they planted the Country, not deftroy'd it, carry'd People to it, not away from it; and, in a word, made them rich, not plunder'd and ftarv'd them.

Carthage and *Corinth* at that Time were the two great Emporiums of the World; *this* carry'd on all the Commerce of the *Weft* and *that* of the *Eaft: Corinth* manag'd the Commerce of *Afia, Perfia,* and *India,* and brought the Wealth of the *Eaft Indies,* the Spices, the Silks, the Callicoes, the Gold, the Diamonds, and in a word, the whole *Indian* and *Perfian* Trade in Caravans; Part from *Ormus* and the Gulph of *Perfia,* to *Baffora* and *Bagdat,* by Water, and thence by Caravans to *Aleppo* and *Scanderoon;* and fo by Sea to the Gulph of *Cenchræa* and *Co-*

rinth,

rinth, another Part to *Trapezond* in *Armenia,* and by the *Euxine* Sea thro' the Straits of *Bosphorus* and the *Hellespont,* and thro' the *Archipelague* to the same Gulph, and so to *Corinth.*

Carthage, on the other hand, planted Colonies, and extended their Possessions upon the Coast of *Spain,* as well within as without the *Straits;* built Cities from *New Carthage,* now call'd *Carthagena* in *Spain,* to the *Groyn,* as well in the *Mediterranean* as in the Ocean, and from *Tangier,* then a populous City of 100000 Inhabitants, to the *Cape de Verde* on the West Side of *Africa,* and from thence into *America* it self; which, there is no room to doubt, was discovered if not peopled from *Africa,* by the indefatigable *Carthaginians;* and had never been lost and forgotten to this Part of the World, if the *Romans,* those Destroyers and Enemies of all Improvement, Commerce, and Navigation, had not so utterly ruin'd *Carthage,* not the City only, but the very Nation, as not to leave them a Name under Heaven; and so of course caus'd all their remotest Settlements to be abandon'd; and in consequence, at last forgotten; *but that by the way,* it requires, and indeed deserves too long a Digression for this Place.

Now, when these two Cities of *Corinth* and *Carthage* fell, (for they were destroy'd by the *Romans* within a Year of one another) Trade receiv'd a mortal Wound; I may say the

the Trade of the whole World did fo ; and as thofe Cities never recovered, fo the Trade, which was fixed among them, decay'd and dy'd, was divided and fcatter'd, and, in effect, loft ; for it never fully recover'd it felf, no not to this Day.

THE Colonies, which the *Carthaginians* planted, funk and dy'd away, and many of them lie in Ruins to this Day; efpecially on that Side of the Ocean from the *Straits Mouth* to *Cape None ;* for as the *Carthaginians* planted Colonies for Trade, the Trade being loft by the Overthrow of the Merchants in the Mother City *Carthage,* the new planted Cities, and the Sea Ports, were ruined of courfe, and perifhed, as a Child ftarves when the Nurfe is taken from it.

IT is true, the City of *Carthage* was rebuilt, and recover'd it felf *in fome Degree,* under the Government of the Weftern Emperors ; and efpecially as thofe Emperors were Chriftians, and were Encouragers of the Induftry and Application of their Subjects ; then, *I fay,* the trading Genius reviv'd very much, efpecially in *Africa,* and the Climate and Soil of that Country being particularly productive of many valuable things, and thofe things adapted to Trade, and encouraging to the Merchant, the *African* Merchants carry'd on a very confiderable Bufinefs ; Navigation alfo being very much their Peculiar, they traded by Sea to all the known

Parts

Parts of the World, but nothing like what they did before.

The principal Branches of their Commerce in thofe Times, as we gather from the Hiftories of the neighbouring Countries, confifted, 1*ft.* in exporting the Growth of their Country, and the Manufacture of their People, juft as it is with us in *Britain:* For the Nature of Commerce is ever and every where the fame. And 2*dly,* in importing again the Product of other Countries, either for their own Confumption, or for Re-exportation to remoter Parts, which had not the fame Product.

Their own Product confifted chiefly in Corn and Cattle, and among the laft, chiefly Horfes, of which they furnifhed great Numbers to mount the *Roman* Cavalry ; for the *Numidian Horfe* were then, as the *Barbs* and *Jennets* (which are the fame) are now, fam'd for their Beauty, Swiftnefs, and fine Shapes, thro' all the *Roman* Empire.

But above all their Product, the moft valuable were their Wax and Copper, in both which they ftill excel the whole World ; alfo their Corn, Fruit, Druggs, and rich Gums, all which remain to them.

For Manufactures, we do not indeed read of their Woollen Manufactures, or at leaft, not much : But the *Carthaginians,* as well as the *Ægyptians* (and both were *Africans*) are fam'd for the Product of fine Linen ; and 'tis to be fuppofed the Soil produc'd

a vea very fine kind of Flax, which, as the Fund of that Manufacture, they improved to great Advantage; but that Part is now loft.

As to their Importations, we are affur'd they fetch'd Tin and Lead from *Great Britain,* Gold and Wine from *Spain,* for old *Spain* ever produc'd much Gold; Silks and fine *Eaſt India Goods* from *Corinth* and *Alexandria ;* what Trade they had with *Gaul (France)* we do not find, but the other was very confiderable, and is fufficient to our Purpofe. Thus ftood their Condition flourifhing in Wealth and Commerce, when the *Romans,* as above, to the eternal Infamy, not Glory, of their very Name, deftroy'd them all.

As by that general Rule, I fay, the Trade of the World receiv'd a mortal Wound; fo when I fay they reviv'd under the *Roman* and *Grecian* Emperors, it was apparent all their Recovery and Encreafe was owing to their Commerce; that alone reftor'd them, and enrich'd them; and they were in *Juſtinian*'s Time the moft valuable Branch of the Weftern Empire, with refpect to the Taxes they paid, and the many Regiments, or rather Legions, they raifed, for recruiting the *Roman* Armies under *Beliſarius* and other Generals ; and this continued long afterwards, even in the moft declining Times of the Weftern Empire.

BUT

But this rifing Wealth of *Africa* was too rich a Bait for the Times ; the Deluge of barbarous Nations, which overthrew the *Roman* Empire, broke in upon them alfo; and the *Vandals,* over-running *Spain,* fpread themfelves into *Africa,* wafted and over-run the fruitful Plains, and deftroy'd and overturned the populous Cities; and in a word, Trade funk a fecond Time, under the unfupportable Burden of War, the *Vandals,* over-running all, ruin'd and pof-fefs'd the Country.

As the *Vandals* came in over the Bellies of the native Inhabitants, fo fome Ages af-ter them the *Saracens, Arabians,* and *Ma-homitans,* came in over the Heads of the *Vandals.*

With thefe, not the old *Africans* only were rooted out; not only Religion, but at laft Trade too, funk quite out of the Coun-try; for, as the Followers of *Mahomet* are, wherever they come, like the *Romans,* the Deftroyers both of Commerce and Cultiva-tion, fo it was here.

Trade and Improvement being thus, I fay, as it were rooted out in *Africa,* the Moors fpread themfelves, by a rapid and ir-refiftible Torrent, over all *Spain* and *Por-tugal,* carrying all before them, and keeping Poffeffion of it almoft the Space of 800 Years; and as for *Africa,* they have by a ftrong Hand kept Poffeffion there ever fince:

To

To bring all this to the cafe in hand, Thefe *Mahometans,* as I have faid of the *Turks,* have very little Inclination to Trade, they have no Guft to it, no Tafte of it, or of the Advantages of it; but dwelling on the Sea-coaft, and being a rapacious, cruel, violent, and tyrannical People, void of all Induftry or Application, neglecting all Culture and Improvement, it made them Thieves and Robbers, as naturally as Idlenefs makes Beggars: They difdain'd all Induftry and Labour; but being bred up to Rapine and Spoil, when they were no longer able to ravage and plunder the fruitful Plains of *Valentia, Granada* and *Andalufia,* they fell to roving upon the Sea; they built Ships, or rather, took Ships from others, and ravag'd the Coafts, landing in the Night, furprifing and carrying away the poor Country People out of their Beds into Slavery.

THIS was their firft Trade, and this naturally made Pyrates of them; for, not being content with landing and plundering the Sea-coaft of *Spain,* they by Degrees being grown powerful and rich, made bold and audacious by their Succefs, they arm'd their Ships, and began to attack firft the *Spaniards* upon the high Seas, and then all the Chriftian Nations of *Europe,* wherever they could find them. And thus this wicked Trade of Roving and Robbing began.

WHAT

WHAT Magnitude they are fince that arriv'd to, what Mifchiefs they have brought upon the trading Part of the World, how powerful they are grown, and how they are erected into States and Governments, nay into Kingdoms, and as they would be called, Empires (for the Kings of *Fez* and *Morocco* call themfelves Emperors) and how they are, to the Difgrace even of all the Chriftian Powers treated with as fuch, is Matter of Hiftory, and I fhall meddle no more with it here, than is abfolutely nery to my prefent purpofe.

THE firft Chriftian Prince that refenting the Infolence of thefe Barbarians, and difdaining to make Peace with them, refolved their Deftruction, was the Emperor *Char.* V. He was mov'd with a generous Compaffion, for the many Thoufands of poor unfortunate Chriftians which were at that Time kept among them in miferable Slavery; and from a noble Principle of fetting the Chriftian World free from the Terror of fuch Barbarians, he undertook fingly, and without the Affiftance of any other Nation, to fall upon them with all his Power.

IN this War had he been join'd by the *French* and *Englifh,* and the *Hans* Towns; (as for the *Dutch,* they were not then a Nation) he might have clear'd the Country, at leaft he might have clear'd the Sea Coafts of the whole Race, and have planted Colonies of Chriftians in all the Ports, for the

the Encouragement of Commerce, and for the Safety of all the European Nations.

BUT *Francis* the firſt King of *France,* his mortal and conſtant Enemy envy'd him the Glory of the greateſt and beſt Enterprife that was ever undertaken in Europe ; a Thouſand Times beyond all the Cruiſadoes and Expeditions to the *Holy-Land,* which coſt *Europe* a Million of Lives, and an immenſe Treaſure, during one Hundred and twenty Years, to no Purpoſe.

A s it was, and tho' the Emperor was aſſiſted by no one Prince in *Chriſtendom,* the Pope excepted, (and his Artillery would not go far in battering Stone Walls) yet he took the Fortreſs of *Goletta,* and afterwards the City, and the whole Kingdom of *Tunis ;* and had he kept the Poſſeſſion, it might have been a happy Fore-Runner of farther Conqueſt ; but miſcarrying in his Attempt againſt *Algier,* by the meer Hand of Heaven, who we may hope reſerved that Conqueſt for the Glory of Princes and Powers yet to come, and a terrible Storm falling upon his Fleet, the farther Attempt was laid aſide, and the Kingdom of *Tunis* returned to its former Poſſeſſors, by which Means their Pyracies are ſtill continued.

MY Propoſal upon this Subject conſiſts of two Parts.

Firſt, THE Neceſſity there ſeems to be upon all the Powers of *Europe,* eſpecially the Marine Powers, to free themſelves from
the

the Infolence of thefe Rovers, that fo their Subjects may be protected in their Perfons and Goods from the Hands of Rapine and Violence, their Coafts fecured from Infults and Defcents, and their Ships from Capture on the Sea.

Secondly, THAT this cannot be done effectually, but by rooting out thofe Nefts of Robbers on the Coaft of *Africa,* and at leaft driving them from the Poffeffion of any of the Towns, Ports and Harbours, fo as that they may have no more Ships to appear upon the Seas.

Thirdly, THE Eafinefs of the Conqueft, if the *Englifh, Dutch, French* and *Spaniards* would but pleafe to join their Forces, and Fleets, and fall upon them in feparate Bodies, and in feveral Places at the fame Time ; the needful Quotas both of Ships and Troops might be alfo adjufted here.

Fourthly, THE Benefit of Commerce, which would immediately follow, by fettling the Government of the Sea Coaft Towns in the Hands and Poffeffion of the feveral united Powers, fo that every one fhould poffefs the leaft in Proportion to the Forces employed in the Conquefts *of it.*

THE three firft of thefe merit well to be fpoken to, and that largely too, but I have not Room for it here, the laft is particularly before me.

IT cannot be denied, that the Coaft of *Africa,* fome few Places excepted, is a
fruit-

fruitful rich Country; and tho' by its Latitude it muſt be exceeding hot, and that (eſpecially on the Eaſtmoſt Parts of it) there are many Deſerts and waſte Places given up to ſalt and Sand, and fit only for the Retreat of the wild Beaſts, ſuch as Lions, Leopards, Tygers, *&c.* the fierceſt and moſt ravenous of thoſe we call Beaſts of Prey; yet even in that Part there are Valeys and Plains interſperſt among the wildeſt Deſerts, and which are fruitful, yield Corn in abundance, and Cattle, with ſeveral Fruits and other Productions, fitted not for the Uſe of the Inhabitants only, but for Merchandize, and in Quantities alſo ſufficient for both.

THE general Product of the Country, and in which the chief Wealth conſiſts, and upon which a Trade with them would be ſettled, if the Country was in the Hands of Chriſtians, is as follows.

Corn	Skins of Beaſts
Salt	Drugs and Gums
Wool	Almonds
Horſes	Pomegranates
Wax	Oſtrich Feathers
Honey	Lions and Leopards
Corall	Proviſions of ſundry
Copper	Kinds.

IF the Quantity of all theſe is ſo conſiderable as we find it to be, even now, under

der the Indolence and Sloth of the moft
barbarous People in the World, how may
we fuppofe all thofe valuable Things to be
encreas'd in their Quantity, by the Induftry
and Application of the diligent Europeans,
efpecially the *French* or *Dutch,* or *Englifh;*
all which Nations joining in the Conqueft,
we might reafonably fuppofe fhould have
their feveral and feparate Allotments of
Territory upon the Coaft, and in the Country adjacent.

WE might alfo reafonably fuppofe, that
the Moors being in the Confequence of
fuch a Conqueft, driven up farther into
the Country (for I have not been propofing
the rooting them out as a Nation, but only
the fupplanting or removing them from a
Situation, which they have juftly forfeited
by their Depredations upon other Nations)
and being obliged to feek their Subfiftence
by honeft Labour and Application, I fay
we may reafonably fuppofe, that even thefe
may be taught to apply to the Cultivation
of the Earth by the meer Neceffity of their
Circumftances, and may be brought to encreafe the Product by their Labour for
all thofe Chriftian Nations.

As the Product of the Country would thus
be encreas'd, and Multitudes of People
would be encouraged by the Advantages of
the Place, to go over and fettle upon it;
the Manufactures and Merchandizes of *Eu-*
rope would by Confequence find a new Confumption,

umption, and the many new Ports and
Harbours, where thofe Chriftian Nations
would fettle, would be fo many new Markets for the Sale of thofe Manufactures,
where they had Little or no Sale or Confumption before: And this indeed is the Sum of all
Improvement in Trade, namely, the finding
out fome Market for the Sale or Vent of
Merchandize, where there was no Sale or
Vent for thofe Goods before; to find out
fome Nation, and introduce fome Fafhions
or Cuftoms among them for the Ufe of our
Goods, where there was no Ufe of fuch
Goods before, to vend our Goods at new
or differing Ports, may be no Encreafe
of Commerce, or to fend them to new and
differing Places, becaufe they may ftill be
fent from thence to the fame People, and
to the fame Nations as the laft Confumers,
who confumed them before.

THUS fending our *Englifh* Manufactures
to *Jamaica,* to be fold there by the
Sloop-Trade; that is, by clandeftine Commerce with the *Spanifh* Smugglers, or to
the *Spaniards* of *Cartagena*, and the Coaft
of *Caracas,* is no new Confumption, tho'
it be a new Market; becaufe it is only
felling to the fame People, who would
otherwife call for the fame Manufacture,
and other Goods from *Old Spain,* and they
from *England;* fo that it is as Water iffuing
out of the fame Fountain, and running into
the

the fame Gulph or Pond, only by new Channels.

THUS likewife the Eaft India Company fending *Englifh* Broad Cloth to the Gulph of *Perfia,* to be fent from thence to *Ifpahan,* to *Georgia,* and other Places in that Country, to be fold to the *Perfians*, and others, as the laft Confumers; is only fupplying the fame People, who were fupplied before, with the fame Goods from *Alleppo* and *Scandaroon*; fo that it is only taking the Trade from the *Turkey* Company, and transferring it to the Eaft India Company, which is no Encreafe of Commerce, the laft Confumers being the fame.

BRING this to the Cafe of the *Barbary* Trade; it is true we have fome Trade there now, and fome Places might on fome Accounts be called the fame Markets: But fuppofe the *Barbarians* to be removed as above from the populous Cities and Provinces of *Algier, Tunis, Tripoli,* &c. and driven up the Country, in order to fupprefs Pyracy and Robbers; and fuppofe thofe Cities, *&c.* peopled with a new Nation, or new Nations made rich by Commerce, and the Country adjacent cultivated and peopled after the Manner of *Europe,* and thofe People living, cloathing, furnifhing their Houfes and Equipages, and feeding after the Manner of Chriftians, and Chriftian Nations: Let it be anfwered, what Kind of Commerce would there be then? And
would

would it be twenty Times what it is now, or would it not? befides delivering *Europe* from the Depredations of powerful Thieves, and their Commerce and Navigation from the Rapine of a mercilefs Crew, who are the Ruin of Thoufands of Families, and in fome Senfe the Reproach of Chriftendom: I need fay no more, the Propofal is great, but far from Impracticable, 'tis worthy being undertaken by the Princes and Powers of *Europe*; and what would bring more Glory to the Chriftian Name, than all their Inteftine Wars, one againft another, the Scandal of *Europe;* and the only Thing that at firft let in the *Turks,* and other Barbarians among them.

CHAP. III.

Being a Propofal for the Improvement and Encreafe of Commerce upon the Weftern Coaft of Africa, *the Coaft of* Guinea, *from* Sierra Leon, *vulgarly called* Seraloon, *to the Coaft and Gulph of* Benin.

HAT great Improvements might be made in Trade, on the north Coaft of *Africa* I have fhewn I think paft Contradiction; the only Objection, *Which as the Cafe ftands, I think is no Objection at all,* is, that it muft be made

made by Conquest, a Thing attended with Difficulty, Hazard, Expence, and a Poffibility of Mifcarriage.

However eafy it is to remove all the Objections of that Kind, it is not my Bufinefs here, nor have I Room for it ; but I mention them here to illuftrate and fet off the happy Circumftance of another Propofal of Improvement on the fame Continent; I mean this of *Guinea.*

Here are no Conquefts to be made, no Enemies to fight with, at leaft none worth naming ; and yet here is a vifible, an apparent, an undifputed Improvement to be made, of which this only is to be faid, That 'tis rather wonderful, that it has never yet been attempted, and gone about with Vigour and Refolution, than doubtful whether it would fucceed, if it were undertaken.

The Climate on the Weft Coaft of *Africa,* at leaft within the Bounds mention'd, is fufficiently known, being from the Latitude of about 13 Deg. to that of 5 Deg. North of the Line: The Soil is good in moft Places, very fruitful, well water'd, notwithftanding the Heat of the Climate, with abundance of fmall Rivers, and in fome Places with very great ones.

The Commerce to this Country is carried on, if a Kind of Stagnation of Bufinefs, or a going backward thro' innumerable Difcouragements may be call'd a carrying it on, by the *Englifh* having Poffeffion

feffion of the Coaft, and having made Settlements in proper Places, with Forts and Caftles, and other Strengths for defending thofe Settlements, as well againft their Chriftian Neighbours by Sea, as their Savage Neighbours on Land.

THE Trade carried on here, whether by the *English*, or other European Nations, confifts in but three capital Articles, viz. *Slaves, Teeth,* and *Gold;* a very gainful and advantageous Commerce, efpecially as it was once carried on, when thefe were all purchas'd at low Rates from the Savages; and even thofe low Rates paid in Trifles, and Toys, fuch as Knives and Siffars, Kettles and Clouts, Glafs Beads, and Cowries, Things of the fmalleft Value, and as we may fay next to nothing; but even this Part of the Trade is abated in its Goodnefs, fince by the Strife and Envy among the Traders, we have had the Folly to inftruct the Savages in the Value of their own Goods, and inform them of the Cheapnefs of our own; endeavouring to fupplant one another, by underfelling and overbidding, by which we have taught the Negroes to fupplant both, by holding up the Price of their own Productions, and running down the Rates of what we carry them for Sale.

THUS that gainful Commerce once fuperior to all the Trades in the World, which carried out the meaneft of all Exportations, and brought home the richeft, is finking
dayly

dayly into a Kind of Rubbifh as to Trade; and we are fometimes faid to buy even the Gold too dear.

But all this while here is not the leaft Ufe made of the Land; the fruitful Soil lies wafte, a vaft extended Country, pleafant Vallies, the Banks of charming Rivers, fpacious Plains, capable of Improvement and Cultivation, to infinite Advantage, lie wafte and untouch'd, over-run with Shrubage and ufelefs Trees; as a Forreft trod under Foot with wild Creatures; and the yet wilder Negroes, who juft plant their Maize, and a few Roots and Herbs, like as we do for our Garden-ftuff, and all the reft is left naked, and thrown up to the Wildernefs.

Now, why is all this wafte? What mean the *Englifh* and the *Hollanders,* and other diligent Nations, to negleƐt fuch Advantages? Why do they not enclofe, fence, and fet apart fuch Lands for Cultivation, as by their Nature and Situation appear to be proper for the moft advantageous ProduƐtions?

Let the fame Climates be examin'd in other Parts of the World, and the Soil in thofe Climates be compared with the Soil in the fame Latitudes on this Coaft; and if it is the fame, or fo near the fame, as no vifible Difference is found in them, why fhould they not produce the fame Harveft, the fame Plants, Fruits, Druggs; or, whatever

ever grows and is produced in one, why
fhould it not be planted, grow, and produce
the fame in another?

LET us reduce this to Practice, and bring
the Latitude of Places together, with the
Productions proper to thofe Places: For
Example,

1. THE Coffee-Berry is the natural Product of the Earth at *Mocha,* on the Eaftern
Bank of the Red Sea, and the South-weft
Point of the *Arabia Fælix*, in the Latitude
of 13 to 14 Deg. there it grows, thrives, and
produces, as it were wild, and with the leaft
Help of Labour imaginable ; what Affiftance
of Art is added to it, is after the Fruit is
ripen'd and gather'd, *viz.* in the curing and
drying the Berry, and preferving them for
a Market ; and that is to be done in the
fame Manner in any Part of the World as
well as there.

The diligent *Dutch* feeing the Eafinefs of
the managing and curing the Berry, and how
that Part had no Dependence, either upon
the Earth, the Air, the Water, or any thing
elfe more there, than in another Place, took
the Hint, and planted the Coffee Tree in
the Ifland of *Java*, near their City of *Batavia,* there it thrives, bears, and ripens every jot as well as at *Mocha;* and now they
begin to leave off the Red Sea, and bring
20 to 30 Tons of Coffee, at a time, from
Batavia, in the Latitude of 5 Deg. S.

NOT

NOT content with this happy Improvement, others of the same Nation have made the like Experiment, in near the same Latitude, in another Quarter of the World, and with the like Success; and now they begin to bring large Quantities of Coffee from *Surinam*, on the North Coast of South *America*, Lat. 6½ Deg.

WE are told likewise, tho' this, however probable, I do not affirm, that the less industrious *Portuguese* are planting it on the Coast of *Brasil*, about the *Rio de St. Francisco* in the Latitude of 12 Deg.

AND besides these, we are assur'd the *French* have planted it with Success at their Colony of *Port Dauphin* on the Island *Madagascar*, in Lat. 23½ Deg. S.

THE *Dutch* indeed planted it without Success at the Cape *de Bon Esperanza*: The Reason is plain, the Place was too cold, and it might as well be planted at our Colonies of *Virginia* and *Carolina*, the Cape lying, as we all know, in Latitude 34 Deg. 20 M. or thereabouts.

BUT if at *Batavia* and *Surinam*, in Latitude 5 to 6 Deg. if at *Mocha*, in Latitude 14 Deg. if at *Port Dauphin*, in Latitude 23½ Deg. why not at *Seraloon* under Cape *de Verd*, in Latitude 13 to 15 Deg.? Why not at Cape *Coast* and at *Accra*, in Latitude 5 to 6 Deg.? And, in a word, Why not upon all the Grain Coast, Tooth Coast, Gold and Slave Coast, where we have a free Possession, feffion, Strength for Protection, and Soil for Production? But I proceed,' I fhall be fhorter in the next Articles, becaufe the Argument is the fame.

2. THE *Sugar Cane.* Our Succefs with the Sugar Canes is well known, it is produced to an infinite Advantage in our Ifland Colonies of *America.* From *St. Chriftophers* in Latitude 17½ Deg. and *Jamaica,* in Latitude 18 Deg. to *Barbadoes,* in Latitude 13 Deg. It is produc'd by the *Portuguefe* in the *Brafils,* in the fame Latitude, South of the Line from the Port of *Phernambuquo,* in the Latitude of 9 Deg. to the Bay *de Todos los Santos,* or Bay of *All Saints,* in the Latitude of 13 Deg. 20 M. and it is produced by the *Spaniards* on the Continent of North *America,* in the Provinces of *Guaxaca, Guatimala,* &c. in the Latitude of 14 Deg. And why not then by us on the Coaft of *Africa,* where we have the Choice of the Country in the very fame Latitude from the *Gold Coaft* in the Latitude **6,** to the Cape *de Verd* in the Latitude 15.

ADD to this the particular Advantages which offer themfelves to the Planter, in fuch an Attempt as this, on the Coaft of *Africa,* which he has not, nor can have, in any of thofe Parts where the Sugar is now planted, efpecially by the *English.* For Example,

1. THE Eafinefs of procuring Negroe Slaves, which would here coft from 30 s. to

50

50 s. or at moſt 3 l. *per* Head; whereas they
are at this Time in *Barbadoes* and *Jamaica*,
worth from 25 l. to 30 l. a Head; at the
Braſils from 30 l. to 40 l. and to the *Spaniards* in the Provinces of *Guaxaca*, *Guatimala*, &c. 50 to 60 l. *Sterling per* Head.

    N. B. The Difficulty of keeping the
Negroes from running away, is not ſo
great as ſome imagine, ſince as they are
brought from diſtant Provinces, tho' it
be upon the ſame Continent, they know
nothing of their own Country; nor
do they underſtand the Language of
the next Negroes, any more than
they do *Engliſh;* and if they ſhould
fly to theſe neighbouring Negroes, they
would but make Slaves of them again,
and ſell them to the Ships; ſo that the
Slaves would not be apt to fly, and if
they did, the Loſs would not be near
ſo great as in *Jamaica*, *&c.*

    2. The Eaſineſs of getting Proviſions,
which they would be ſo far from fetching
from *Ireland* or *New England*, as our Colonies of *Jamaica* and *Barbadoes* do, and at a
very monſtrous rate; that they would be always able to furniſh themſelves as they do
now by the Produce of the Soil; as for Rice,
Indian Corn, or Maize, with Roots, ſuch
as Potatoes, Parſneps, Carrots, Plantans,
and innumerable other Sorts, they grow
freely upon all the Coaſt.

                  3. The

3. The Shortnefs of the Diftance, and the fafe Paffage between *England* and thefe Colonies, is fuch, that the Voyage is often perform'd in 12 or 15 Days; whereas fix to ten Weeks is counted no bad Voyage between *Jamaica* and *London :* The Expence as well as other Inconveniences of which are exceeding great, and the Difference would give the Sugars of *Africa* a great Advantage at Market.

3. I come next to the Planting of *Tea.* Every one that has been the length of *Amoy* or *Chufan* on the Coaft of *China*, knows that the Tea is produced chiefly in the Provinces of *Xantung, Nanquin* and *Canton*, as alfo in the Iflands of *Japon* or *Japan*, moft of it between the Latitudes of 30 Deg. and 24 Deg. North of the Line. With how much greater Advantage then of the Climate, might the fame Plant be produced at *Seraloon* and on the Gold Coaft of *Africa*, the Plants being fetch'd from *China*, as well as the Method of curing it; which, according to Mynheer *Nieuhoft*, is not difficult.

I need fay very little to the Advantages of raifing fuch a profitable Plant fo near Home ; the thing explains it felf; and the Difficulty of making the Experiment, feems to me to be little or nothing. Nay, I am told, that in the Governor's Garden at Cape *Coaft* Caftle, there is, or at leaft was, in the Time of the Government of Sir *Dalby Thomas*, a large Plant of *Tea* planted, and
that

that it grew and thrived to Admiration: I confefs I cannot fee why it fhould not.

I fhall conclude this Head with one yet more confiderable than all the reft; and that is, the great Article of the Spices, fuch as Nutmegs, Cloves, and Cinamon; the two laft are found in the Iflands of *Ternate* and others adjacent in the Latitude of 2 to 4 Deg. the *Nutmegs* indeed are found only at *Banda* and fome fmall Iflands adjoining and almoft under the Line, and fo it may be doubtful, except in the fame Latitude, which is farther South than any of our Settlements in *Africa* go: But the Trial might be made of that too. But as to the Clove, it is found in the Ifland of *Borneo* at *Gilolo*, and feveral other Iflands, from the Latitudes of 2 to 7 Deg. which is exactly the Climate of our Gold Coaft; likewife the Cinamon is found in *Ceylon*, in the Lat of 6 to 7 Deg. and hits punctually with this Coaft; and we can fee no Reafon why the fame Climate on the Shore of *Africa* may not by the Help of Art produce the fame Fruit.

I fum up all with obferving, That there is no reafon to doubt, but all or moft of the Productions, either of the Eaft or Weft *Indies*, might be produced here; fuch as the Cotton, Ginger, Sugar, Cocoa, Piemento, Indigo, and feveral others known at *Jamaica*; as alfo the Cochineal, the Vinelloes, and even the *Peruvian* Bark alfo, if Induftry and

Appli-

Application were fet on work to plant them.

I cannot quit the Improvements which might be made on the Coaft of *Africa*, without mentioning a great Correfpondence carried on among the feveral Nations in the northern Part of that Country, which *even as it is now* caufes a great Commerce over Land, taking Notice withal how wonderfully it might be improv'd : This Trade is faid to be carried on by the Negroe Natives, upon the great River *Nigris* or *Niger*; or as our Seamen call it corruptly, the River *Gambia,* in Conjunction with the Natives of feveral Nations, upon the fame River, Eaft from the Shore; and by all thefe together correfponding with the Moors on the north Coaft of *Africa,* at *Fez,* at *Morocco,* at *Mequinefs,* and other Cities, where they now carry on a Commerce, by vaft Annual Caravans. They tell us, that it is already a very great Trade; but how would our Propofal not only encreafe this Trade it felf, but quite change and alter the very people themfelves, while the North Part of the Country, (being Chriftians,) the Savage Part would be foon civiliz'd, and become fo too, and the People learn to live to be cloth'd, and to be furnifh'd with many Things from *Europe,* which they now want; and by Confequence would with their Manners change the very Nature of their Commerce, and

and fall in upon the Confumption of the European Manufactures.

IT would be needlefs to lay out Schemes of Commerce among the Inhabitants of the Nations within thofe fouthern Lands; Numbers of European People being but once fettled on the Sea Coaft, would foon fpread the Commerce into the inland Nations, and employ and enrich the Inhabitants, by inftructing them in the Arts of living, as well as of Trade; and this brings me to a View of one of the greateft Scenes of Improvement in the World, which is in fhort this, (*viz.*)

THAT there needs little more than to inftruct and inure the barbarous Nations in all our Colonies, Factories, &c. in the Arts of Living; clothing with Decency, not fhamelefs and naked; feeding with Humanity, and not in a Manner brutal; dwelling in Towns and Cities, with Oeconomy and civil Government, and not like Savages.

IT is the moft unaccountable Miftake of its Kind that can be imagin'd, that one fhould fuppofe civilizing Nations do not encreafe Commerce; the Contrary is evident in all our Colonies: Civilizing the *American* Savages, who inhabited the Countries on the Back of the *European* Colonies in *North America,* as well our own, as thofe on the *French* Side at *Quebeck* and *Canada*; what has been the Confequence? Take it in the following Particulars, which tho' few and fmall in the feveral Articles, are yet confiderable

derable in the whole, and abundantly confirm the Propofition.

THE Indians or Natives, before the Europeans came among them, had neither Houfes, Cattle, Clothes, Tools, Weapons, Ammunition, or Houfhold Stuff; their Cattle were the Beafts of the Forreft, their Clothes were the Skins of Beafts, their Weapons Bows, wooden Swords, Clubs, Javelins and Darts, pointed with Teeth and Bones of Fifhes, their Ammunition Arrows and Stones, their Houfes meer Wigwams, Hovels and Huts, their Houfhold-ftuff Earthen Pans hardned in the Sun, their Beds Matts and Skins laid on the Ground; they could ftrike no Fire, but by rubbing two Sticks together; they had neither edg'd Tools or other Tools, for they had neither Iron, Steel, Brafs or Lead; no Grind-ftone or Mill-ftone; their Meat was Flefh dried in the Sun, and their Drink no other than cold Water.

THE fame Indians even thofe remaining wild and favage almoft as before; yet being convinc'd by their Conveniencies, and prompted by Neceffity, ferve themfelves of us with an infinite Number of Things, for the abundant Accommodation of Life; and thofe that are more civilized, do it more; and thefe altogether encreafe our Trade; *for Example*, take their own Goods firft, with which they purchafe ours. They fell the Dear Skins, Bear Skins, Fox, Beaver, and other Furrs; all
which

which together (as is faid above) our Merchants call *Peltry :* Thefe I fay they fell to our People, and a very good Merchandize they are, and make a good and great Return.

WITH thefe they buy our Woollen Manufactures for their Clothing, fuch as Duffels, Blankets, Halfthicks, Kerfies, and fuch courfe Goods; and others alfo of Leather, with which they drefs and keep themfelves warm, in the coldeft Seafon ; alfo they buy Caps, Stockings, Hats, Shoes, Gloves, for the fame hard Weather.

IN order to provide Fuel and Food, they buy *for the laft* Fire-Arms and Ammunition, fuch as Powder and Shot, and *for the firft,* Hatchets and Axes, Knives, Bills, as alfo Spades, Shovels, Pickaxes, and other Tools fitted for their Work: For the building and furnifhing Houfes to dwell in ; they buy all Kinds of edg'd Tools, as alfo Nails, Spikes, Hammers, Saws, Chifels, &c. wrought Iron for Hooks, Hinges, Locks, Bolts, and many other Things: For their Houfhold Stuff likewife they fometimes buy Chairs, Stools, Benches, Beds, Bedfteads, and the like; alfo Pots, Casks, and other Veffels of Earth, Pewter, Brafs and Wood, and in a Word every Thing they want, which either Art or Trade can fupply them with.

ALL thefe make Trade, and as thefe Demands encreafe, the Trade and Commerce of *Europe* muft encreafe; for Encreafe of the

Civi-

Civiliz'd People is an Encreafe of Commerce in the Main, let the Degree of their Demands be more or lefs.

WHAT then have the People of *England* more to do, but to encreafe the Colonies of their own Nation in all the remote Parts, where it is proper and practicable, and to civilize and inftruct the Savages and Natives of thofe Countries, wherever they plant, fo as to bring them by the foftelt and gentleft Methods to fall into the Cuftoms and Ufage of their own Country, and incorporate among our People as one Nation.

I fay nothing of chriftianizing the Savages, 'tis remote from my prefent Purpofe; and I doubt much more remote from our practice, at leaft in moft Places; but I fpeak of an Incorporation of Cuftoms and Ufages, as may in Time bring them to live like Chriftians, whether they may turn Chriftians or no.

To bring this Home to the Coaft and Country of *Africa*, of which I was but juft now fpeaking; let them calculate the Improvements propofed in Bufinefs, in Planting, Fifhing, Shipping, and all the necefary Employments that would attend a publick improv'd Colony; and let them tell me, if the Confequence would not be a Confumption of Manufacture, among a People where there was none before, and in a

Place

Place where we had no Commerce to carry on before.

Nor let any weak-headed Chriſtian ſuggeſt, that this would be to anticipate our Weſt India Trade, ſupplant our other Colonies, and weaken us on one Hand, while it ſtrengthens us on another ; let thoſe who talk ſo, conſider, 1 *ſt,* the great Improvements propoſed, without meddling either with Sugar, Ginger, or any of our Iſland Productions, and how great the Improvement might be firſt made in theſe Things. And, 2 *dly,* Let me add, that as it is evident all our Iſland Colonies are not at this Time ſufficient to ſupply our Markets with Sugar, including the Quantity demanded for Exportation, the Quantity cannot eaſily be too great; nor indeed is there any Danger of it; ſo that thoſe phlegmatick Objections are eaſily to be anſwered, and need take up no Room here : Let us ſee the Improvement begun, and let us ſee the Danger begun, of overcharging our Markets, and hurting the Trade of our Iſlands, and let us hear if the Iſlands complain; it is then Time enough to anſwer thoſe Scruples, at preſent I muſt acknowledge they merit no Conſideration.

On the other Hand, there is a vaſt Ocean of Improvement in View upon the *African* Coaſt, (tho' the ſingle planting of Sugar was omitted) and as there are as well on this Side of the Country, as on the Eaſtern

Shores,

Shores, of which I come next to fpeak, vaftly populous Nations, nay Empires, where
there are Millions of People yet to trade
with, who were never traded with before
the prevailing on thefe Nations to civilize
and govern themfelves, according as inform'd Nature would foon direct them,
would neceffarily introduce Trade, confume
Manufacture, employ Shipping, employ
Hands, and in Time eftablifh fuch a Commerce, as would be more than equal to any
one foreign Exportation we have yet to
boaft of.

CHAP. IV.

Being a PROPOSAL *for an Encreafe and
Improvement of the* Britifh *Commerce on
the Eaft Coaft of* Africa.

THERE is but one confiderable Country in the World that we have any
Knowledge of upon the Surface of the Globe,
to which the Inhabitants of *Europe* have no
Commerce, or with whom they have no
manner of Converfe: And this is the great
Empire or Clafs of Kingdoms call'd *Ethio-
pia* or the *Abyffines*.

THERE

There are but three Ways for us to come at any Part of this Country in a Courſe of Trade or Correſpondence, and at preſent they are all made impracticable.

1. Over Land from *Tripoli* and the Coaſt of *Barcan;* and were the *Tripolins* reduced, according to the Tenour of our firſt Propoſal, for rooting out thoſe Enemies of fair Trade, the Rovers of *Barbary,* this Trade would certainly be ſet on foot by Caravans, as is done in *Aſia,* from *Aleppo* to *Bagdat,* to this Day.

2. Up the *Nile* from *Grand Cairo* into the Lake of *Dombea:* But tho' this is ſaid to be in Uſe at ſome certain Times when the River is not ſwell'd beyond its Bounds and Banks; yet thoſe that have examin'd it more nicely, tell us, that thoſe People are miſtaken, and that the Cataracts or Water-Falls, which are frequent in the River, from within 160 Miles of *Grand Cairo* South, cut off all Poſſibility of a Navigation, or of any Commerce by Water farther that Way.

3. The third Way is by the Coaſt of the *Red Sea;* and this alſo is cut off, by the *Turks,* who have ſeized upon all the Weſtern Shores of the *Gulph* or *Red Sea,* and driving the *Æthiopians* from the Coaſt, have either ſhut all the Nations of the World out from the *Æthiopians,* or have ſhut up the *Æthiopians* from converſing with the reſt of the World,

THE

THE Commerce however is apparently practicable from the Coaſt of that *Gulph,* farther South than the *Turks* have yet poſſeſs'd it; and there are two particular Rivers on that Coaſt, *viz.* *Zeila* and the *Houache,* which I am aſſur'd, as well as I can be of things which we have ſo little Intelligence of, are navigable far in within the Country, and beyond the Coaſt, which the *Turks* are poſſeſs'd of; and that by theſe Rivers, a Commerce may be eſtabliſhed into the very Centre of *Æthiopia,* which is indeed the richeſt and the moſt populous Part of it, and that the Mouths of thoſe Rivers are open for any Nation to ſettle and fortify at; which Settlements would be eaſily defended, by having but two Ships of Force, from 40 to 50 Guns, always there, by whom alſo going and returning, the Trade would be carry'd on round the Cape.

IT may be ſuggeſted, that ſuch a Trade would be within the Circle of the *Eaſt India* Company's Charter; to which it would be effectually anſwer'd, Why then does not the Company open the Trade, and make a Settlement themſelves? If they do not, no excluſive Privilege of Commerce is granted to any Men, or Company of Men, to damn or deſtroy a Trade, but to improve and carry it on; and if they inſiſt on their Charter to have the Right of Trading to *Æthiopia,* but will not trade, their Right is ſo far void of courſe; otherwiſe they may as well
tell

tell us, they have a Charter granted them, to fhut out the Kingdom of *Great Britain* from the *Æthiopian* Trade, which would be abfurd, and contrary to the Nature of the Thing.

I need fay no more to this Part, as to its being practicable; I fhall at any Time mark out the Way, how to put it in Practice, and to open the Commerce, and prove that the *Æthiopeans* have, on many Occafions, fhewed themfelves willing to embrace fuch a Propofal; it remains only, to fhew a little Sketch of the Trade it felf, and the Improvement which it might be to the Commerce of *Great Britain* in particular.

1. CONTRARY to the whole Tenor of our Correfpondence in the *Indies,* this Trade would be exceeding much to the Advantage of *Great Britain,* becaufe they would both receive our Growth and Produce, and make to us Returns in *Specie;* whereas, in all the Trade of *India* and *China,* our Cafe is the reverfe; for there we cannot fell our own Goods at all, and cannot buy theirs, but with ready Money. They will take off none or but few of our Manufactures, nor will they fupply us with theirs, but for hard Silver; to the exhaufting, not of *England* only, but even of all *Europe,* of their ready Money.

2. The People, tho' the Country is hot, go all modeftly and decently cloathed; and 'tis known by thofe who have travell'd among them,

them, that they would buy our *English* fine Cloths in particular, such as are carry'd to *Ægypt* and *Persia,* if they could come at them; and some Essays of that Kind have been made from *Grand Cairo* by Land, tho' not such as are considerable enough to be called a Trade.

UPON the whole, such a Trade would be infinitely advantageous; seeing, the Return for whatever of our Manufactures could be sold there, would be in Gold, in Ivory, Sulphur, Civet, Salt-Peter, Emralds, and such like valuable Goods: There are other Productions, which we have seen from thence also, as Deer Skins in exceeding great Quantities; Hides of black Cattle; Leopards and Lions Skins, and others of those Kinds; also fine Copper, and some very rich Gums and Drugs, of which I cannot give the Names, except Frankincense, Gum-Arab. and *Aloes Socotrina.* I have been told of many others, but without Certainty enough to affirm it.

IN Exchange for these, we should without Fail introduce our broad Cloths, fine Scarlet Shalloons, Sayes, Serges, and such other thin Stuffs as are usually worn in hot Climates; besides a great Quantity of hard Ware Manufactures, wrought Iron and Brass, edged Tools, Weapons, Fire-Arms, Ammunition, Lead, Pewter, Tin, fine Linen, and perhaps Silks also; for we are well assur'd they have no more Trade
with

with *India* or any other Parts of the World than they have with *England*.

THUS you have three great Articles for the Improvement of the *British* Commerce on the Coaſt of *Africa* only, all practicable, and all capable of raiſing an immenſe Conſumption of our Woollen Manufactures, where there was little or no Conſumption for them before: One of which Articles, *viz.* that of *Guinea*, is actually in our own Power, and ſo little to be ſaid againſt the Experiment, that nothing of its Kind is more wonderful, than that it has never yet been propos'd to the World, and the Attempt not made.

CHAP. V.

Being a PROPOSAL *for turning the whole Trade for Naval Stores, Timber, Deals,* &c. *from the Eaſt Country, and from* Norway *and* Sweden, *to our own Colonies, and yet without putting the Government of* England *to the dead Charge of* Bounty-Money *on that* Importation.

A Fourth Improvement of Commerce lyes alſo within our own Reach, and ſome dull and weak, unperforming Steps have been made, which looked as if we knew
the

the Advantage of it ; but I fay, in fo phlegmatick a Manner, as if, like *Solomon*'s Slug-
gard, we *would not pluck our Hands out of
our Bofom to put them to our Mouths.*
This is the transferring our Demand of Naval Stores, Timber, Deals, Mafts, *&c.* from
Norway, Sweden, and the Eaſt Country,
to our own Colonies in *America ;* Countries, without Exception, as able effeƈtually
to fupply us with Hemp, Flax, Tar,
Turpentine, all Kinds of Fir, Timber,
Deals, Pipe and Hogſhead Staves, and perhaps, in Time, with Iron alfo, as all the
Nations mention'd above, and with proper
Encouragements, would foon produce them
all as cheap.

Several Attempts have, as I have
noted above, been made at this, as if we
own'd the Profpeƈt of Advantage, but knew
not how to bring it to bear; all that has
hitherto been offer'd for the Encouragement
of this Commerce, and to make it praƈtica-
ble, has been that of a Bounty, to be paid in
England, upon the Importation, fo to encourage the Merchant: But, with Submiſſion,
this is not fufficient to make a Trade of it,
and is but upon one Species of the Goods
neither; whereas, the Encouragement muſt
be univerfal, if you expeƈt the Trade ſhall
be fo.

Before I proceed upon this important
Article, which feems to have great Difficulties in it; which Difficulties yet I profefs

to remove, I muſt lay down one Foundation ; which neverthelefs, tho' I think 'tis undoubted, yet we do take upon the Credit of the Inhabitants of *New England,* and the other Colonies on the North of *America ;* if they deceive us, they only therein deceive themſelves, and we are where we were.

THE fundamental is this, *viz.* That they are able to furniſh a fufficient Quantity of Hemp, Flax, Tar, Turpentine, Fir, Timber, Deal Boards, Maſts, Yards, Pipes, and Hogſhead-Staves, *&c.* fully to ſupply the whole Demand of *Great Britain* and *Ireland,* ſo as that we ſhould ſuffer no Scarcity, cr want of thoſe Goods, tho' we ſhould abſolutely prohibit their Importation from any other Place.

BY being able to furniſh, I am to be underſtood thus ; for I muſt not ſpeak more for them, than they ſpeak for themſelves ; and it is meet we ſhould be very exact in thoſe Things we call firſt Principles : I ſay, I am to be underſtood not that they have Hands enough at preſent to fell and cut out the Quantities of Timber, *&c.* draw and extract the Tar and Turpentine, ſplit out the Staves, *&c.* for that, I believe, at firſt, would be a Difficulty, tho' it would ſoon be maſter'd ; but that the Country, and the Woods, have a fufficient Quantity of all theſe ; that they are not to be planted, or waited for till grown ; but that they have

have a boundlefs Extent of Woods, as well on the Hills as on the Plains, unexhaufted, and indeed, unexhauftible; which are fufficient for all our Demands, and much more.

LIKEWISE, I do not fay, or infift, that they do now produce or plant a fufficient Quantity of Hemp and Flax to fupply our Demand; but that they have Land enough, fufficient in Strength of Soil, and fufficient in Quantity, and which by cutting down the Woods, would daily encreafe : This I think is undoubted.

N. B. THE Countries where this Supply of Timber and Naval-Stores would be produced, is, in a Word, the whole *English* Part of the Continent of *North-America*, viz. *New-England*, *New-York*, *Eaft* and *Weft Jerfey*, *Penfylvania*, and all the Country, whether poffefs'd or no, upon the great River of *Delaware*, as far as that River is navigable, which may be for ought we know 100 Miles beyond *Philadelphia*.

ALL the Colonies of *Virginia* and *Maryland*, to the bottom of the Bay of *Chefeapeake*, all the Colonies of *North* and *South Carolina*, and all the Rivers thereof; in which laft Colony alone, they tell us, there is as much Fir-Timber growing, as in all the Kingdom of *Norway*.

LIKE-

Likewise it is to be added, that *mutatis mutandis,* the Coin, and Value of Payment confider'd, they will be able to furnifh all thefe Things as cheap as the Eaft Country and *Norway* Trade does now furnifh them.

These Things granted, the Propofal is brought into a narrow Compafs ; all the Difference then between *England* (the Market) and our Colonies, the Producers of thefe Goods, lies in the Price of the Freight, occafion'd by the Diftance of Place, and Length of the Voyage ; how to bring this to a Par, is the whole of the Enquiry : And this is to be done by the feveral Methods following.

N. B. Bounties and Payments of dead Money to the Importer for Encouragement, I reject, as being a meer Charge upon the Nation, tho' not upon the particular Buyer of the Goods, and is not by any Means to be called a leffening the Difparity, only it removes the Burthen from private Hands to the Publick, which is not fufficient ; and fhould it extend to all the Importations, would be a Burden too heavy to bear, even for the whole Nation.

The only Weight I would lay on the Publick, and even that but for a while, is to take off the Duties entirely from all thofe Species of Goods, (not to repeat 'em) and
prohibit

prohibit the Importation from other Places; and not this laft Part neither, till the Colonies were fully entered into the Trade.

THEN for the Freight; we are to fuppofe, that the Freight of all thefe Articles, from the Eaft and North Seas, ftands now at a Medium of forty to fifty Shillings *per* Ton, call it more or lefs ; and fuppofe the Freight of the fame Goods from the Colonies fhould then ftand at a Medium of fix to eight *lib. per* Ton ; fo that the Freight would be three Times as much one way as the other ; 'tis true, this is a very confiderable Article ; and efpecially confidering them to be all bulky Goods alfo.

BUT two Articles will immediately contribute towards, if not be a full Equivalent to this Excefs of Freight.

Firft, TAKING off the Duty upon Importation here, which being very high, fuppofe it, for Argument Sake, to be 20 *per Cent.* may fairly be calculated at one half of the difference, and muft be found by the Importer in the Price of his Goods at Market.

Secondly, LAYING an Impoft, fuppofe it to be about ten *per Cent.* upon all the Importations of *English* Goods into thofe Colonies, and this I infift will be equal to the other half: The Money fo raifed to be paid to the Commanders of the Ships, in fuch Proportions as fhall be adjufted by the

Publick

Publick, and upon fo much Tonage only, as is Loaden upon them of fuch particular Goods.

THE Colonies will never complain of fuch a Duty, becaufe 'tis in a manner paid to themfelves, and is but taking the Money out of one Pocket, and putting it into the other ; the Growth of their Country will be exported; (indeed the wafte Growth, for they burnt it all before) their own People will be employ'd, and will be prodigioufly encreafed, and thefe two are of the laft Importance to them ; nay, they are of fuch Importance to them, that give them but an Affurance of thefe, they may give you Affurance, that in a few Years they will be the greateft, and moft profperous Colonies in the World.

I acknowledge, I defpife (with the utmoft Contempt of their Ignorance) the Suggeftions of thofe Times, when this glorious Scheme of *New-England*'s Profperity was laid afide, (about two and forty Years ago) from a pretended Jealoufy of thofe Colonies growing too powerful, and making themfelves independent ; infinuating, becaufe they were independent in a religious Profeffion, they wanted to be fo in Government; whereas firft, the very Thought, befides a worfe Principle it began in, *viz.* of Party Malice, was to the laft Degree weak and foolifh ; fince 'tis evident, the Profperity, and indeed, the very Being and Subfiftence of *New-England* in Matters of Trade,

Trade, confifts in, and depends wholly upon their Union with, and Subjection to
Great Britain, as the Growth of their
Country, which is the only Article that
fupports their Commerce, is taken off by
the *Britifh* Colonies only : Nor can any
other Nation in Europe take it off but the
Englifh ; and the fame of the reft: For
Example,

THE *Dutch* have no Iflands at all, but
one (remote and fmall) called *Curacao*, able
to do nothing worth the naming. The
French indeed have *Martinico*, a flourifhing
Ifland Colony ; but the Ifland is large, and
produces moft of its own Provifions ; and
if it did not, they have a Colony upon the
Main, *viz. Canada*, which fupplies the
French at all their Iflands with Provifion,
fuch as Meal for Bread, Flefh, Fifh, Peas,
and all other Provifion that they can want ;
and the *French* would never ftarve their
own Colony of *Canada*, to feed *New-England.* But to make it unanfwerable, if
the *French* would do their utmoft, they
are not able to confume or take off, no
not one twentieth Part of the Growth of
our Colonies, who maintain, as fome affirm, 1000 Sail of Ships and Sloops, conftantly running with thofe Things from
the Main of *North America* to the Iflands,
fuch as St. *Chriftophers, Antegoa, Nevis,
Mountferrat, Barbadoes* and *Jamaica ;*
the two laft of which confume a prodigious
Quantity.

THESE

THESE Provifions are the meer Growth of the Country, fuch as Flour or Meal in Barrels, Peas, Malt, Rice and Tobacco ; Beef and Pork, pickled and barrelled; Sheep and Horfes alive ; Beer in Casks and in Bottles ; white Fifh falted and dry'd, and Salmon barrel'd; befides Lumber for building and repairing, as well Houfes as Ships, and Ships and Sloops ready built and finifh'd.

THESE all are the Product of the Country, and the Labour of the People in the Colonies of *New England, New York,* the two *Jerfies, Penfilvania, Virginia* and *Carolina ;* without this Export, thofe Colonies would perifh. It is true, the Iflands would ftarve for want of the Provifions too, at leaft at firft: But on the Continent, if the Iflands did not take off their Product, their Lands which they have been at a vaft Expence to cure, and clear, and plant, would lie ufelefs and uncultivated ; the Swine which the Woods feed for them by thoufands, would overrun them with their Multitude, and be worfe to them in Time, than the Bears and the Wolves ; their Plantations would produce more of every Thing than their Mouths could devour, or than they could find Markets to vend them at ; their Timber would ftand indeed where it was, for no Body would fell it to have it, and they
might

might fet their Woods on Fire as they did formerly, to clear the Land of them.

IN a Word, this being their Cafe, their Intereft ties them to *England,* tho' their Duty fhould not, and to feparate from *England,* would be to be undone.

THEN carry the fame Argument on to the propofed Commerce, for Timber, Naval Stores, *&c.* this would ftill the fafter, (if that were poffible) bind them to their Dependence on *England,* for no Nation in Europe could give them the fame Encouragement : I cannot enlarge upon this Article here, it is evident to all that underftand Trade : If Courtiers and Statefmen are ignorant, let them enquire where they may be inform'd.

I return to the Propofal; having thus ftated the Equivalent, by which the Government may be reimburft what they fhall be out of Pocket for the Experiment ; it remains only to give a brief Account of the Advantages of fuch a Commerce ; take them in a few fhort Heads, for I cannot enlarge them as I ought, for want of Room.

1. INSTEAD of the Trade for Deals and Timber, Tar, Mafts, *&c.* which we carry on now with *Norway,* almoft all for ready Money, and which carries out more Silver in Specie, nay, in our very Coin, Crowns and half Crowns, than the *Eaft India* Company it felf, however little Notice has been taken of it : I fay, inftead of this

difad-

difadvantageous Trade, we fhould then receive all the fame Goods in Exchange for
our own Manufactures, and they would be
purchafed of, and produc'd by the Labour of our own People, the induftrious
Planters, Subjects to the Government of his
Majefty of *Great Britain.*

2. I N S T E A D of having at leaft two
Thirds of thefe Goods brought over in
foreign Bottoms, *Danes* and *Swedes,* and
the Ships navigated by foreign Seamen, to
whom we pay dead Freight in the like ready
Money, and which they carry away in Specie, as above; it would be wholly brought
to us in our own Ships, *New England*
built, and navigated wholly by our own
Seamen.

3. I N S T E A D of a very few *Englifh* Ships
which now ufe the *Norway* Trade, this
new Commerce would at leaft employ a
thoufand Sail of Ships every Year, and all
the Year, and moft of them Ships of Burthen : So that befides the Benefit of building, repairing, and fitting out fo many
Ships, it would be a new Nurfery of Seamen to us, having always 15 to 20000
Seamen employ'd in it.

4. T H E Colonies would be encreafed in
People beyond expreffing ; and confequently, not only the Confumption of Provifions
would be encreafed there, which is, as before, the grand Fund of their Profperity ;
but the Confumption of Manufactures,
and

and all European Exportations to them, would be in Proportion encreafed, which is the grand Subject of my Work. By the Calculations which I have feen, it is fuppofed, not lefs than 100,000 Men would be employ'd in the Woods, cutting and felling Timber, Deals, Mafts, Yards, &c. in the managing and planting of Hemp and Flax ; in the extracting and drawing off the Tar ; and in preparing all the Articles mentioned, to be fetch'd from thence, on Account of this Trade ; and this, befides Women and Children, who could not do much in that Part ; and befides, the building Ships among them, an Article fo confiderable, as well deferves to be handled by it felf.

5. It would effectually furnifh thofe Colonies with Returns for *England*, which they are now greatly diftreffed for, in order to pay the Ballance of their Trade with *England* ; the Quantity of our Manufactures which they take off, infinitely exceeds what they have of their own Growth to fend us in Return, whereas in Cafe of fuch a Trade for the Produce of their Country, they would be at about a PAR with us, and we fhould always be able to call for as much Goods from them, as would pay our felves.

6. By this Means they would receive Silver in great Quantities from *Jamaica*, and the other Iflands, for all that Trade would

would be clear Gain to them, and that Silver alfo would *ftay with them*, which now it cannot do, all being fnatch'd up for Returns to *England* in Specie, tho' it be at 12 *s.* to 14 *s. per* Ounce : So that in confequence of this Commerce , there would be a Circulation of current Money in the Colonies on the Continent, a Thing they have of late been Strangers to.

It would take up a Volume by it felf, to lay open all the glorious Schemes of Improvement in Trade, which would be the Confequence of fuch a Bufinefs, and particularly the Encreafe of our Manufacture here, by the Demand of Goods from thence, when the Numbers of People in thofe Colonies fhould be thus encreas'd ; let any one calculate (that is able to judge of thefe Things) by what it is already, what it muft neceffarily be on an Encreafe of People: Let them caft up the Exportations to the five Colonies on the Continent ; let them confider thofe Exportations to be as they really are, one entire Improvement, derived from meer nothing, or next to nothing in the laft fourfcore Years, for then it was all an Embrio, and fome of them were not in Being as to Trade *(viz.)* *New York* and the *Jerfies* conquered but in 1666 from the *Dutch, Penfylvania* not above 50 Years in Growth, *Carolina* lefs.

Let them tell us, or but guefs at for us, what a glorious Trade to *England* it would

would be to have thofe Colonies encreafed
with a Million of People, to be cloth'd,
furnifh'd, and fupply'd with all their needful Things, Food excepted, only from us;
and ty'd down for ever to us by that immor-
tal, indiffoluble Bond of Trade, *their Intereft*.

LET them confider, that all thofe People
muft fetch from *Great Britain* only, their
Cloths, Woollen, Linnen, Cotton, and Silk;
all their Haberdafhery; all their Manufac-
tures of hard Ware, wrought Iron, Brafs,
Chains, Edg'd Tools, Jack-work, Nails, Bolts,
Screws, &c. all their heavy Ware, fuch as
caft Iron and Brafs, Guns, Mortars, Shot,
Shells, Pots, Caldrons, Bells, Battery, &c.
all their Clock-Work, Watch-Work, even fo
much as their Toys and Trinkets; all their
Houfe Furniture, Kitchen Furniture, Glafs
Ware, Upholftery Ware, Tin Ware; in a
Word, every thing we produce, and every
thing we make, and every thing we import:
'Twould be endlefs to repeat it.

How prepofterous muft thofe Notions be,
and how oddly muft they think, if they can
be faid to think at all, who fuggeft Mifchief
from the Encreafe of our Colonies! Do any
other Nations act thus? Do the *Spaniards*
think their Empires of *Mexico* and *Peru*,
Chili and St. *Martha*, too many and too
great, tho' a hundred Times as large as thofe
I am naming; and tho' they drein even
Spain itfelf of People? Are the *French* jealous

lous of the Number of their People in the vaſt Countries of *Canada* and *Louiſania?* Do they not ſtudy, by all Means poſſible, to en-creaſe them, and to extend theirPlantations?

Have not we People enough to ſpare? Do we not encreaſe till we are ready to eat up one another, (I mean in Trade)? and can we not ſpare enough of the unprofitable Part of our People, thoſe who are rather ſaid to ſtarve among us than to live? Who, if they were well ſettled there, would be Induſtrious, Thrive, and grow Rich; and 'tis by the Induſtrious thatTrade is ſupport-ed, and Wealth encreaſed.

Let us no more amuſe ourſelves, and raiſe the Vapours with our Phlegmatick Thoughts about every little *German* En-croachment on our Manufactures, and the Prohibitions of a few petty Princes in the North. Here we can raiſe a Conſumption of our Manufactures, ſuperior to all the Ob-ſtruction they can give us: Here our Ma-nufactures will never be prohibited; here the Demand will be for ever encreaſing with the People; 'tis like a Mill built by the Lord of the Manor, it grinds for all his Tenants, and is kept going by his own Stream; ſo that on one hand it can never want Work, and on the other hand can never want Water.

I have not Room to ſay more, tho' I ſcarce know when to leave it off. I conclude with telling you in a few Words, that here is the greateſt Opening for an Improvement

of

of our Trade, and the eafieft to put in Practife, that ever was propofed, or perhaps can be propofed to this Nation; and till we go about it, we ought never to complain of the Decay of our Trade, or of the want of a Vent for our Manufactures.

THESE feveral Articles of the Improve- ment of our Commerce, have run out to fuch an unavoidable Length, that I fhall not be able to add fome others, which were in my Defign, and which are equally advan- tageous in Proportion to their Circumftan- ces; but I muft touch lightly upon them, and refer them to farther Occafion.

As the Encreafe of Commerce and People in our Colonies, is, in Confequence of our Property in them, an Encreafe and Improve- ment of our Trade in *England*, and in par- ticular an Encreafe of the Confumption of our Manufactures; fo it is a natural Infe- rence, and evident to Demonftration, that an Encreafe of Colonies muft have the fame Effect.

I therefore lay it down as a Fundamental, that additional Colonies, where the People may plant and fettle to their Advantage, is a vifible Improvement to our Trade.

EMPLOYMENT of our People, or as we call them, our Poor, is the grand Support of our very being as a Nation without it; the Poor would eat us up, the Parifh Rates would *in fhort* devour not the Produce of our Land only, but the Land itfelf; and the

Church-

Church-Wardens would call upon you for 20 *s.* in the Pound for your Beggars.

THIS employing of the Poor is the Effect of our Manufactures; the Magnitude of which is, for that very Reason, already defcribed; but as our Manufactures employ the Poor, fo Trade carries off the Manufactures, or elfe they would foon over-run the Confumption, and come to a full Stop: The Manufactures fupport the Poor, Foreign Commerce fupports the Manufactures, and planting Colonies fupports the Commerce.

HERE you difpofe of your encreafing Numbers of Poor; they go there poor, and come back rich; there they plant, trade, thrive, and encreafe; even your tranfported Felons, fent to *Virginia* inftead of *Tyburn;* Thoufands of them, if we are not mifinform'd, have, by turning their Hands to Induftry and Improvement, and, which is beft of all, to Honefty, become rich fubftantial Planters and Merchants, fettled large Families, and been famous in the Country; nay, we have feen many of them made Magiftrates, Officers of Militia, Captains of the good Ships, and Mafters of good Eftates.

THIS Way therefore, I fay, we difpofe of the growing Numbers of our Poor to an inexpreffible Advantage, as well a publick as a private Advantage: It is a private Advantage, as 'tis really a Benefit to the Poor that go, (for pray take me, as I ought to be taken) When I fay go, I am to be underftood that

I

I mean go freely and voluntarily. I am not moving you to tranfport the Poor, that would be fending them away becaufe they are poor; but thofe who being deftitute of Employment here, are willing to feek it A- broad, would have a vifible Advantage, and would foon give Encouragement to others to follow them, and Thoufands of fuch Fa- milies would raife themfelves there by their Induftry, and grow rich; for where Wages is high, and Provifions low, as is the Cafe there, the Labourer muft be idle, or extra- vagant, or thriving, and grow rich; and the Confequence of the diligent labouring Man there, is always this, that from a meer Labourer he becomes a Planter, and fettles his Family upon the Land he gains, and fo grows rich of Courfe.

THE Advantage to the Publick I have fpoken of, tho' but briefly. I only add here, That befides the Encreafe of Com- merce and People, it neceffarily makes an Encreafe of Seamen, a Point juft now upon the Anvil of the State, and which they find hard enough for the hammering of all the po- litical Smiths of the Nation; all this growing Commerce, to and from our Colonies, muft be carry'd on by Sea; all the Commerce they can have there, one Colony with another, muft be the fame: The firft by large Ships of Force, the laft by Sloops, Ketches, and fmall Ships. The Encreafe of the People en- creafes the Trade, the Encreafe of the Trade en-

encreafes the Number of Ships, and the Encreafe of Ships calls for an Encreafe of Seamen : Thus your Strength, as well as Wealth,
grows with your Colonies, the Climax is
really pleafant to look upon.

More Colonies then is, without Queftion,
extending the Commerce; it is enlarging
the Field of Action; it calls in more Hands
to affift in the Publick Profperity; it employs profitably the unprofitable Numbers
of your Poor, and lays a Foundation of an
extended Trade, and thereby of a ftill larger
Exportation from Home.

Suppose I fhould propofe a Place in the
World, where, if the *Englifh* could plant at
thisTime any Numbers of their People, even
the pooreft and meaneft, fuppofing them only to be induftrious, and willing to live;
for I am not talking of Drones, and *Solomon*'s Sluggards, that will ftarve rather than
work; or, as I have faid above, will not
pull their Hand out of their Bofom to put
it to their Mouth. Such will ftarve every
where, and may as well ftay at Home as go
Abroad : Such will not fow, and how fhould
they reap ? will not plant, and how fhould
they eat ?

But fuppofe, I fay, a Spot of Ground,
where a Body of *Englifh* People being planted, the Country, by its own native Production of Corn and Cattle, would immediately fubfift them; and the being placed in
a Situation to live and trade, they fhould
want

want no other Support from hence, but their firſt carrying over, and the Subſiſtence of the firſt Year, till a Harveſt ſupply'd them : Suppoſe them what Number you pleaſe, from one Thouſand to an Hundred Thouſand, or ſuppoſe them encreaſed from the one Number to the other : Grant me but that they wear Cloths, build, furniſh Houſes as they encreaſe, and that they gain enough to provide neceſſary Things for themſelves ; Is not the Supply of theſe, all Gain to us ? Is not all they take an Encreaſe of the Conſumption of our Manufactures and Produce ? Is not every Ship employ'd between us and them, ſo far an Encreaſe of Navigation ? and ſo of all the reſt : An Encreaſe of Colonies encreaſes People, People encreaſe the Conſumption of Manufactures, Manufactures Trade, Trade Navigation, Navigation Seamen, and altogether encreaſe the Wealth, Strength, and Proſperity of *England.*

BUT where in the World ſhould we plant ? what Country preſents for new Colonies, at leaſt that is not poſſeſs'd or claim'd by ſome other Nation ? and where can we find a Place, where, with the Settlement of the People, a Trade will follow ? and from whence they can, beſides ſubſiſting plentifully in that Place, find Returns to *Europe,* to purchaſe from us the Manufactures they want ? My Anſwer is, that if I do not find out ſuch Places, I have been ſaying nothing all this while : That there is Room enough

ſtill

ſtill left on the Surface of the Globe, not taken up nor claim'd, or pretended to by *Spaniards, Portugueſe, Dutch,* or *French, Dane* or *Swede, Pope* or *Devil*; Places where 100000 People may immediately plant and build, find Food, and ſubſiſt plentifully; the Soil fruitful, the Climate comfortable, the Air healthy, unmoleſted by Savages and Canibals, as in *North America;* unravaged by Lions and Tygers, Elephants and Monſters, as in *Africa*; fill'd with Cattle uſeful and eatable, tame and tractable, abounding with Fiſh, Fowl, Fleſh, wanting nothing but to be inhabited by Chriſtians, and ally'd to the reſt of the Chriſtian World by Commerce and Navigation.

But I am too near the End of this Work to enter upon ſo large a Subject: It muſt be treated of by itſelf.

F I N I S.

A
PLAN

OF THE

English COMMERCE,

BEING A

COMPLEAT PROSPECT

OF THE

TRADE of this NATION, as well the
HOME TRADE as the FOREIGN.

Humbly offered to the Confideration of the KING *and*
PARLIAMENT.

The SECOND EDITION.

To which is added,

An APPENDIX,

CONTAINING

A VIEW of the INCREASE of COMMERCE,
not only of *ENGLAND*, but of all the Trading
NATIONS of EUROPE, fince the PEACE with *SPAIN.*

The whole containing

Several PROPOSALS, entirely NEW, for *Extending*
and *Improving* our TRADE, and *Promoting* the CON-
SUMPTION of our *Manufactures*, in Countries where-
with we have *Hitherto* had no *Commerce.*

LONDON:

Printed for CHARLES RIVINGTON, at the *Bible* and
Crown in St. *Paul's Church-Yard.* 1730

APPENDIX;

CONTAINING

A View of the prefent apparent Encreafe of Commerce in all the Trading Parts of *Europe*; but efpecially in *England*, as it is influenced by the late Peace with *Spain*.

Chap. I.

Of the Encreafe of Commerce *in Foreign Parts.*

INCE the Conclufion of this Work, feveral Incidents falling in the Way for a farther Improvement and Increafe of the *Britifh* Commerce, I found a fhort Appendix abfolutely neceffary for compleating as far as poffible our Views of a profperous and growing Trade.

It is true, Trade is in itfelf a natural Progreffive; its Encreafe is always difcovering itfelf, as new Improvements and Difcoveries prefent themfelves: Sometimes Bufinefs changes Hands, as Countries and trading Sea-Ports change Mafters: Many Times Conquefts turn one Nation out, and
another

another in; and as the Trade goes always with the prefent Poffeffor, fo it is an Acquifition to the People poffeffing, as it was before to thofe that were difpoffefs'd.

BUT when a Nation, whofe particular Genius is formed for Improvement, gets Poffeffion of any new Country, and whofe Circumftances qualify them in a more than ordinary Manner to carry on fuch Improvements in an advantageous Manner, 'tis no Wonder if on fuch Occafions we find new Lights given us into Bufinefs and Commerce, to encreafe them in an extraordinary Manner.

IT is my Opinion, that Trade is at this Time in a progreffive Motion ; encreafing and growing in all the Trading Parts of the World, *Mufcovy* excepted, as well as in *England*; of the vifible Encreafe of it in our Country, I have fpoken at large in this Work, and perhaps fome may think, have dwelt too long upon that Subjeƈt ; tho' I think not indeed, the Parts of it being fo various, and the Confequence of fuch Importance to us, for whofe Reading the whole Work is defign'd.

IF this fhould be true, that the Trade of all the World is improving and encreafing, it fhould be very ftrange that *England*, who apparently trade in a very great Degree with all thofe Nations, fhould not feel the Encreafe in its own Exportations.

BUT I will not fuggeft any thing fo unlikely in our Cafe ; on the contrary, I infift, that

that the Trade of *England*, in, and with all the Trading Nations of the World, is manifeftly greater than ever it was before, the Trade with *France* only excepted ; and that I think was wholly our own Fault, owing to our own Divifions, and Party-ftrife; of which there is no need to fay any more in this Place.

I might appeal to the Knowledge of all the Merclrandizing Part of the World for the Truth of this Affertion ; but I choofe to fpeak to our own Knowledge and Experience, in Terms that fhall be evident to ourfelves, and not fend the *Englifh* Reader out of his Way, to talk to Foreigners, in Things perhaps alfo foreign to their Underftanding.

THAT the Trade of other Nations is encreafed, and encreafing, take in a few brief Heads, in which they that know any thing of Trade, will be convinced without any difficulty.

The *Dutch* are encreas'd, and every Day encreafing in their *Eaft-India* Commerce ; not that they acquire any new Poffeffions, but they every where enlarge and encreafe their old Colonies and Factories ; efpecially by Cultivation, and additional Productions.

I SHALL give but one Example, but it is beyond all Contradiction, namely, that they have brought the Ifland of *Java*, on which their new Capital City of *Batavia* is erected, to produce Coffee ; a Drug, which, till now,

now, was never found in any Part of the World, but at *Mocha* in *Arabia* only.

THIS Coffee they produce now, I fay, in *Batavia*, and that in fuch a Quantity, that we found their laft Ships brought between 7 and 800 Bales.

WE are told alfo, that they have made fome Effays for the Production of Tea; that nice and valuable Plant, which hitherto has been found only in *China* and *Japan.* It is true, we have not yet any great Evidence of their Succefs in this Vegetable, but that it is expected is true, nor is the Event improbable.

IF any Nation in the World might be faid to have filled up a whole Scheme of Commerce where-ever they came, it was the *Hollanders*; we thought them incapable of adding any thing to their paft Meafures in Trade, unlefs they had gained new Poffeffions, which we do not find they aim at: If then we find them encreafing, who were fo compleatly great before, we may expect it with more certainty where the Nations have Elbow-room in Trade, and are frequently enlarging their Poffeffions alfo ; and we do find it is fo, as by many Examples (*viz.*)

THE *Mufcovites*, all owing to the Genius and vaft Defigns of the late *Czar Peter*, not at all to the Stupidity and Weaknefs of the laft ruling Youth, have extended their Conquefts into *Livonia, Ingria,* and *Finland* upon the *Baltick*, on one hand ; and into

Georgia,

Georgia, and the Frontiers of *Perſia,* on the other : With theſe Conqueſts what un-bounded Additions of Commerce have they made ; they bring the Raw-Silk of *Guylan,* erroneouſly by us called *Turky* Silk, croſs the *Caſpian* Sea to *Aſtracan,* and from thence upon the great River *Wolga,* above 2000 Miles by Boat to *Jaroſlaw,* and from thence by new and almoſt unknown Ca-nals to *Petersburg,* from whence we find it brought by Sea again to *Dantzick, Lubeck* and *Hamburg.*

FROM their new Conqueſts in *Finland* and in *Ingria,* and the Country on the Lake *Onega,* we find them bringing Iron, and ſome Copper, as a new and increaſing Trade alſo, of which we have had ſeveral Quantities ; the Iron, I mean, from *Wyburg* in the Gulph of *Finland,* and all the reſt of their Trade which was formerly carried on at *Archangel,* and is now tranſpoſed to *Petersburg* is infinitely increaſed, though juſt now declining again by an Accident of ill Conduct.

FROM the *Muſcovites* let us view the *Danes* ; I paſs the *Swedes,* becauſe they be-ing lately a reduced Nation, and under in-ſupportable Difficulties, have not been in Circumſtances to think much of Improve-ment. But to ſpeak of the *Danes* ; we find them puſhing their Fortune in Trade in a ſurprizing Manner, by forming a new *Eaſt-India* Company with a Capital Stock,

by

by making Settlements, and planting Colonies in *Greenland,* and by making a new Regulation of their Home Commerce, to take it out of the Hands of the *Hamburghers,* and eftablifh it in themfelves, allowing no Foreign Goods to be fold in their own Dominions, but fuch as fhould be imported in their own Ports, and by their own Subjeêts, as at *Copenhagen,* at *Altena,* and the like.

We are told alfo juft now, that the *Swedes,* however difcouraged and reduced (as above) are yet erecting a Company for the *Eaft-India* Trade, and fitting out Ships at *Stockholm,* to fend to the Coaft of *Malabar,* and the Bay of *Bengal.*

From thefe Northern Nations let us confider other Countries ; the Emperor of *Germany,* driven by Neceffity to abandon the *Eaft-India* Trade, opened in fo extraordinary a Manner at *Oftend,* turns the Hands and Stocks of the Company to the Fifhery, as well the Whale-Fifhing, as the Herring-Fifhery.

In his Hereditary Dominions in the *Adriatick,* he encourages the Merchants to ereĉt a new Commerce at *Triefte* and *Fiume,* on the Coaft of *Croatia,* and ufes the utmoft Application to carry on that Commerce by Land and by Water, in a Communication with *Vienna.*

In *Italy,* his Imperial Majefty, with a Genius inclined to encourage Trade, has made *Meffina* a free Port, and does all he can

to

to increase the Trade of that City and of *Naples*, and, as I am told, not without Succefs.

Even the *Spanifh* and *Italian* Nations, far from being efteemed as induftrious and improving, yet are not to be left out, efpecially the firft, who, be it by what Methods of Trade it will, for we know not the particulars, yet it is evident by the Meafure of their Commerce in *Europe,* have greatly enlarged their Exportations to *America* , and by confequence their Trade there muft be enlarged very much.

I find no body queftions the Fact ; the greateft Difficulty is, to find out the Reafon and Occafion of it : Some tell us, that the late Trade which the *French* carried on in the *South-Sea*, has, by enuring the People to a more profufe and expenfive Way of Living, caufed a greater Confumption of *European* Goods, and I will not deny but it may be probable to be fo.

But others, and with more Probability, tell us, that during the Time of that Trade mentioned above to be carried on by the *French* in the *South-Seas*, the ftrict Prohibition always ufed in *Spain*, by which no Perfons could be allowed to go to *New Spain* on Broad any of the Galleons, without a Permiffion or Licentio from the Confulade at *Seville*, or a particular Mandate from the King and his privy Signet. I fay, that Reftraint was neglected, and (efpecially

in

in *French* Ships) great Numbers of People of all the Popifh Nations went over and fettled there, for the fake not only of the rich and gainful Commerce, but alfo on account of the good Living there ; for the *Spaniards* in *America* live in the moft voluptuous and extravagant manner imaginable (confidering them as naturally a temperate People) with the utmoft Profufion in Equipage and Grandeur, and this might be well fuppofed to allure abundance of People, efpecially *French*, *Irifh*, *Portuguefe*, who all flocked over at that Time, the Door being open, and all People that were *Catholicks* being admitted freely to fettle and trade there.

THIS Freedom of paffing in the *French* Ships has, according to the Opinion of thofe People, and with Probability enough, very much increafed the Numbers of Inhabitants in the *Spanifh* Colonies ; not barely by the *French* going over in thofe called the *South-Sea* Ships, which ufually went from St. *Maloes* and *Rochelle*, though very many went over in thofe Ships. But it was obferved that much greater Numbers paffed in other Ships, Sloops and fmaller Veffels, from the *French* Iflands of *Martinico*, *Guadalupe*, and even from *Canada*, *Miffifipi*, and all the other *French* Colonies to *La Vera Cruz*, *Cartagena*, *Porto Bello*, &c. fo that the Numbers of

Inha-

Inhabitants in the *Spanish West-Indies* are exceedingly increased.

Nor is this without Evidence in part ; for that we are assured by several of our own People, who have been in *New Spain*, as well at *Mexico*, as at *Panama*, *Lima*, and other Places, that there are at this Time a great many *French* and *Irish*; for the *Spaniards* always allowed the *Irish* to settle there as a favourite Nation.

Also the *Portuguese* have spread themselves of late very much among the *Spaniards* at *Buenos Ayres*, which joyns to the *Portuguese* Settlement at the *Brazil*, and from whence they can travel by the great River *La Plata*, from the *Paraguay* to the City of *Plata*, and to all the Cities of *Peru*.

By this leaving the Country (as we may say) open to the Accession of Strangers, there is no Doubt but the *Spanish West-Indies* may be grown much better inhabited than formerly, and the Cities more populous, I mean of *Europeans* and Merchants ; and this may be a Reason why, as I observed before, the Exportations from *Old Spain* to *America* are every Year larger than other, and have for some Time been greater than they were for many Years before.

As this Increase of People in *New Spain* has been the Occasion of the encreasing the Exportation of *European* Goods (as without
out

out Queſtion it has) it lets us into another juſt Obſervation; namely, how much in the wrong the *Spaniards* have all along been, to limit and reſtrain their People in *Old Spain* from going over to plant and ſettle in that Country.

IT is true, it may be objected that the *Spaniſh* Colonies in *America* have already drained *Old Spain* ſo much of its Inhabitants, that they want People at Home even to till the Land. But it is anſwered, that then they might have given Liberty to Strangers to have gone over, who, though they might have continued Strangers for the firſt Age, yet in two Generations would as certainly have commenced True-born *Spaniards,* and as really been ſo, as they could have been made in any Part of *Old Spain.*

IN a word, as the Addition of Inhabitants in the *Spaniſh Weſt-Indies,* if it were 100,000 *Europeans,* would be a vaſt Advantage to the King of *Spain's* Dominions in *Europe,* by the Increaſe of his Revenues; ſo it would be to all *Europe* in the Increaſe of their Trade; and eſpecially to *England,* who have ſo great a Share in loading the Galleons: And if this little Increaſe of the People, which has happened to them by the Accident mentioned above, if it may be called an Increaſe, has occaſioned ſuch a new Demand of *European* Goods, as that it is felt hither in the Trade; what may not that Trade come to in Time, when the

Spaniards,

Spaniards, grown wife by their Experience, fhall find Means, as they may eafily do, to People all their Colonies in *America* in a better Manner? But that is not our Bufinefs here.

THE *Portugueze* come to be confider'd next in Trade; a Nation with whom our particular Intereft in Trade is fuch, as that no Nation in *Europe,* nay, fome fay, not all the *European* Nations put together, Trade with them fo much as the *Englifh.* How are the *Portugueze* advanced in their Commerce within about 30 or 40 Years paft?

IT is true, the *Portugueze* had for many Ages been a declining Nation: As to their foreign Affairs, they had loft their great Acquifitions in the *Indies* to the *Dutch,* and their Forts and Caftles on the Gold Coaft of *Africa* to the fame growing Enemies, and their more northernly Settlements upon the fame Continent to the *Moors*; fo that in a word, their Trade was every where decay'd; and as they were prefcribed to narrow Circumftances in their Poffeffions, fo their Trade became narrow in Proportion.

BUT now; as if they were rouz'd from their Difcouragement, and as if they had new Life put into them by their Succefs, they have met with fuch unexpected Advantages in the *Brazils* (having found out an inexhauftible Treafure in the Gold Mines as they are call'd) that their Colonies in that Country are infinitely extended, and their Trade with it ; multitudes of People have tranfplanted themfelves to the *Brazils,* and continue to do fo every Year from *Portugal,* for they give leave to all that will, to go over and to fettle there ; and, in a word, as the People are encreas'd, fo is the Trade, and ftill encreafes daily ; which may be feen by the large Fleets which go and come every Year from *Europe,* that is to fay, from *Lisbon* and *Oporto,* to *Fernambuco, Maranahon,* the Bay *de Todos Los Santos* or *All Saints,* and the *Rio Janiero :* I fay, it is feen and indeed felt by us in *England* and *Ireland* , efpecially by the Wealth we bring, which indeed fills all the World with Gold, as the Trade of *New Spain* does with Silver.

Thefe Fleets carry out fuch an immenfe Quantity of *European* Goods, I mean fuch an encreas'd Quantity, efpecially *Englifh* and *Italian,* that is to fay, *Englifh* Woollen Manufactures, and *Italian* Wrought Silks, that it was obferv'd by a good Calculator, in the Year 1710, that we exported more Goods that Year to *Portugal,* than both *Portugal* and *Spain* together ufually call'd for in a Year : As to the Share which *England* has in this happy encreafing Trade, let it be judg'd of by this, that even at this Time, and while this Appendix is in the Prefs, in an Account from *Lisbon* they
write,

write, that there were then in their Harbour (*that is to fay*, the River *Tagus* or *Tajo*) 6 *French* Ships, 4 *Dutch*, 3 *Flemings* (call'd by them Imperial) 1 *Genoefe*, 1 *Hamburgher*, 2 *Swedes*, and 50 *Englifh ;* fo that the *Englifh* had three times as many Ships there, as all the other *European* Nations put together ; with this Addition to it alfo, that generally the *Englifh* ufe that Trade with larger Ships than the *French* or *Dutch.*

THE Treafure thefe Fleets alfo bring back into *Europe* is immenfely great, and that in Gold too, which is very particular, by which the *Portugueze* are grown exceeding rich ; and not only *England* and *Ireland,* but even all *Europe,* is fill'd with their coin'd *Moydores,* and they are at this Time more plentiful in *Ireland* than *Englifh* Guineas.

THE *Portugueze* alfo have ftrangely improv'd and encreas'd their Dominion, and likewife their Trade on the *Eaftern* Coaft of *Africa* (viz.) that of *Zanguebar,* and the Coaft of *Melinda,* where they fay they have an hundred thoufand Subjects, befides the City, which is very great, and where they have 50 Churches and Religious Houfes, all of modern *European* Architecture ; all which People are fo civiliz'd by the *Portugueze,* and brought fo under the Chriftian Government, that they are brought to clothe and cover themfelves, and that too after the
European

European Manner, tho' they live almoft under the very Line, or in the Latitude of 5 to 11 Degrees, and, till the *Portugueze* came among them, went all naked.

If they have 100,000 People, and perhaps 30,000 in the City (befides the *Europeans* themfelves, who they reckon to be 15,000 Inhabitants in the City): I fay, if thefe go all decently clothed, and went naked before, the Trade for their Clothing, which muft come all from *Europe,* and indeed moftly from *England* originally, muft neceffarily be greatly encreas'd.

The like, in Proportion, have the fame Nation improv'd their Trade on the Weftern Coaft of *Africa,* and, as we may fay, oppofite to that of *Zanguebar,* I mean in *Angola,* where they keep in Poffeffion a vaft Country, and where they have perfuaded the Nations to wear Clothes, which Clothes they fupply from *Europe* ; all which tend to a manifeft Encreafe of the Trade and Manufacture of thefe Parts of the World, from whence thofe Things come.

And this leads us naturally to fee from whence all this vaft Encreafe of Commerce originally proceeds ; and truly the Caufe is one and the fame thro' all the feveral Parts of the World, namely, the Encreafe of People. As it is out of doubt, that the Numbers of People are really encreas'd in all Parts of Chriftendom ; that is to fay, in the Chriftian Nations of *Europe :* So Numbers encreafing,

encreafing, the Trade muft alfo by confequence encreafe ; a fmall Defcription will
ftate the Cafe to the meaneft Underftanding.

IF the People in any Nation are encreas'd, the Confumption of Provifions that
feed them muft encreafe ; thefe Provifions
muft either be produc'd by the Land in the
Country where they dwell, or be brought
from fome other and diftant Country which
muft fupply them.

IF the firft, and they are produc'd at
home (as it may be call'd) then more Land
muft be taken in, and broken up (that is,
cultivated) for the Produce of more Provifions than were call'd for before, be it Corn
to be fow'd, or Cattle to be fed; and more
Hands muft be employ'd for the Cultivation
of the faid Land ; and thofe Hands, whether Servants or Slaves, muft be clothed
and fed ; and all this is Trade.

IF thefe Provifions are not produc'd at
home, but are fetch'd from other Parts,
then that Encreafe of Corn-Land and Feed-
ing-Grounds muft happen in that Country
from whence thofe Provifions were brought,
with the Addition of Carriages, Horfes,
and Servants for a Draught if by Land, or
Ships, Sloops, Boats, Barges, &c. if by Sea ;
and all this is an Encreafe of Trade.

As the encreas'd Numbers of People in
the Country fuppos'd to be fpoken of muft
be fed, fo they muft be clothed ; and as the
firft caufes more Land to be employ'd for
raifing

raifing Corn and Cattle to feed them, fo the laft caufes more Woollen and Linen Manufacture to be called for to cover and clothe them.

This new Demand for Manufacture fets all the Wheels a going, and all the Hands at work, by whom thofe Manufactures are made, to make a greater Quantity than formerly, and fend them to Market; and this is Trade.

Now to bring it down to the prefent Cafe, the *Portugueze* perhaps have no great Increafe of People among them by Generation, though they are a prolifick Nation too ; but if they bring 1co,oco People to wear Clothes, who went naked before, it is the fame Thing exactly to the Increafe of Trade, as if they had fo many new born : Let us trace it again to other Nations, and efpecially to our own.

That the Numbers of People are increafed not only in *England*, but in all our Colonies and Dominions, is moft undoubtedly true; and that the Trade is increafed in Proportion to the People is a neceffary Confequence, and as true as the other ; this coming within the Compafs of our own Knowledge, and capable of Demonftration by our own Experience, will confirm what is faid above, That the prefent Increafe of Commerce is owing to the evident Increafe of People in all Parts of the known World, or to the Increafe of civilized

lized People ; that is to fay, bringing the barbarous Nations, who living in hot Climates defpifed Clothing, and knowing no Crime, underftood nothing of Shame or Offence in it ; I fay, bringing thefe to clothe with Decency, according to the Cuftom of civilized Nations ; this, which is all one, with an Increafe by Generation, that is to fay as to Trade, has in many Cafes made a vifible Addition to the Commerce : We fhall fee more Examples of it prefently.

FIRST, to begin with our own Country, we find an apparent Increafe of our Trade to all our Colonies, on the Continent of *America* ; and we find that Increafe of Trade always bearing a Proportion to the Increafe of the Inhabitants in thofe Colonies, and on the other hand, where any of our faid Colonies have not a manifeft Increafe of People, there the Increafe of Trade is not perceived.

IT is true, that Luxury and Profufion of Living, may make an Addition of Trade. I fhall fpeak of that by it felf, for it muft be owned, it bears a great Share, efpecially among us ; but we have alfo an apparent Reafon for the prefent Increafe of our Commerce, from the happy Conjuncture of Affairs at this Time, of which I come now to fpeak in courfe.

CHAP.

Chap. II.

Of the Influence which the late Peace with Spain *has already had, and may probably have further, upon the Commerce of* England *in particular, on Suppofition of its continuing but a few Years.*

BELIEVE no Man that is acquainted with the Courfe of Trade in *England,* but muft be fenfible that we have for feveral Years paft felt the Wounds which have been made in it, by our feveral Quarrels with *Spain,* and by the Convulfions which the *Spanifh* Trade fuffered in thofe feveral Times of War, which with fmall Intervals have lafted now above twenty-five Years.

THE firft War with *Spain* was fatal to *England,* in the Liberty given, or at leaft connived at, by the King of *Spain* to the *French,* to trade directly to all their Ports in *America,* even from *Accapulco* in the *South-Seas,* to *Panama,* and to *Lima* it felf.

HERE they ravaged the whole Coaft in Trade, filled the *Spaniards* with their flight half-fpun Manufactures ; rifling them of their ready Money not by Hundreds and Thoufands, but by Millions at a Time, even whole Ships Loading of Silver, the greateft

part

part of which would have been ours, or at leaft might have been expected to have come this Way. The *Spaniards* faw it well enough, and looked at it with Regret as the firft Teftimony of the *French* Yoke, which they were fallen under, and could not prevent.

Nor were they without very fenfible Wounds which that Anticipation of their Commerce made in their Home Trade ; for while the Money went away directly to *France,* the *Englifh* apparently flacken'd their Hands in Trade with *Old Spain* ; they did not give Commiffions out with fuch Chearfulnefs for the Goods that were the Growth of the Country, as they would certainly have done, and ufually did; for Example, whereas we have had 300 Sail of Ships gone to *Seville* for Oranges in a Seafon, the few we then had, were brought by Way of *Portugal,* and we made fhift with a lefs Confumption.

Their Limons of *Malaga* we fupply'd as well as we could from *Lisbon, Oporto,* and other Ports of the King of *Portugal's* Dominions, and made fhift with them, tho' not fo good ; and the like, in other Kinds of Goods; for Example.

Their *Sherries* were ordinarily fhip'd at *Cadiz* and *Port S. Mary's,* and S.*Lucar.* Now we enquired not for them ; but they feem'd a fort of Wine that we could do very well without, nor, which the *Spaniards* are very fenfible of, have we ever come into the
drinking

drinking of *Sherry* (to the Degree as we formerly did) to this Day, and perhaps never shall

THE like Decay they found at *Malaga* ; the white *Port* and white *Lisbon* Wines supplying us for a Time, tolerably well ; tho' it is true, when the Trade came to be opened again, the Mountain *Malaga's* recovered themselves in Trade, by the meer Goodness and Value of the Wine it self, which their other Wines could not do.

AT the same Time our Trade with them for Oil ran in another Channel ; for whereas we usually took off a great Quantity of Oil from *Cadiz* and *Seville,* *Majorca* and other Ports, we now turn'd our Eye to *Portugal* , and bought the *Lisbon* and *Oporto* Oils in larger Quantities, and the like from *Gallipoli* and other Ports in *Italy*; so that we soon let the *Spaniards* understand that we could be sufficiently supply'd without them, to their great Loss, and to their no little Mortification.

IT is true, we did buy their Fruit, such as Raisins from *Malaga* and *Alicant, Denia, Xevia* and other Places, because our People would not be without them; but even of these, we abated the Quantity exceedingly, supplying our Markets by help of the Coast of *Barbary*; and had whole Fraights of Almonds, Raisins and Figs, come in from *Algiers* and *Tunis,* and from the *Moors* Ports about *Melilla,* and, in short, all along the

the Coaft; fo that the *Spaniards* felt a dif-
mal Decay of their Home Trade, and plainly enough faw the Caufe; and it was more
particularly manifeft in this, that they ad-
drefs'd their King to offer the *Englifh* an
open Trade with the *Canary Iflands*, as if
they were neutral Places, which our Government, at the Inftance of the Merchants,'
alfo accepted of, very much to the Advantage of the *Spaniards* in particular.

THIS being the State of the Cafe, and
the *Spanifh* Trade fuffering thefe Depredations, as well by the *French* in the *South-
Seas*, as by the common Accidents of the
War in *Old Spain*; it is not to be doubted, but *England* alfo fuffered a Diminution
or Decay in her Exportations; for the *Spaniards*, as I have faid, being throng'd with
European Goods by the *French*, 'tis moft
natural to fay, as well as think, that they
got their Commiffions by the Galleons
the more heavily, and nothing was more
frequent than to have their Letters exprefs
their Uneafinefs, that the ordinary Channel
of the Trade was turned, and that they
were filled with Goods from *France* more
in one Year, than they could confume in
three or four.

UNDER this Diforder of the Commerce,
Things funk for four or five Years, and the
Galleons might be faid to make their Re-
turn every Year not to *Cadiz*, but to Sa nt
Malo, which, as it impoverifhed the *Spa-
niards*

niards on one hand, fo it enrich'd the *French* on the other, and enabled the King of *France* to carry on the War, notwith-ftanding his furprizing Loffes, in fuch a Manner, as almoft wearied out the Allies, and was a main Help by which he fupport-ed King *Philip* on the *Spanifh* Throne. For let Princes flatter themfelves with what they pleafe of the Glory of their Arms, Trade fupplies the Nerves and Sinews of War, and it is by Trade that all their Glory and Triumph are maintained, as was very remarkable in the Cafe now before us.

AFTER this War was happily finifhed by the Treaty of *Utrecht*, the beloved Allies, the *French* and *Spaniards*, had like to have fallen out about this darling Branch of Trade; the *French*, who had found the Way into the *South-Seas*, could not think of for-getting it again; and the *Spaniards*, who had felt the Lofs of that Permiffion, refolved to put an End to it. But though *Lewis* XIV. was a Prince that knew, as well as moft Kings that ever reigned, how to make him-felf be obey'd, yet he found it very diffi-cult to do it here; for the Thirft of a gainful Commerce was not to be quenched, till at laft, not able to refift the Juftice of his Grandfon's Complaint, nor his Grandfon the Importunity of his Subjects, he gave up the Traders as Interlopers, and left them to the *Spaniards* to drive them away by Force which at laft was effectually done, though

though not till three or four Years after the Treaty of *Utrecht.*

ALL this while we in *England* felt the Decay of the *Spanish* Trade; for while the *French* rather loaded than supply'd the Markets in *New Spain,* and Exports from *Old Spain* stopt in Proportion by the mere Course of Things, the Exports from *England* to *Old Spain* lessened by the same natural Consequence.

> *N. B.* THO' there was a Prohibition of Commerce in *Old Spain* with *England, for Form Sake* (as is usual in Time of War) yet the *Spaniards,* who are not able to carry on their Trade either with *America* or at home, without a Supply of *English* Woollen Manufactures and other *English* Goods, always found Ways to come at those Goods, either by Way of *Portugal,* or from *Italy,* or by other Means, such as diligent Merchants seldom fail to find out in like Exigencies of Trade. But when the Reason and Occasion for that Supply ceased, they then ceased to apply themselves to those Ways of getting the Goods, so the Trade ceased of Course.

THUS stood the State of Commerce in *England,* I mean as to the particular Trade with *Spain* for several Years: There were indeed

deed fome fhort Intervals, in which Peace
put a Stop to thofe Violences, and Trade
began to revive in Proportion to thofe fmall
Abatements : But, as I have faid that the
French went on with the *South-Sea* Trade,
though contraband, till they were beaten out
by Force, and till their Ships and Goods
were deftroyed ; yet that took up fo many
Years, that it was hardly brought to Perfection, when the two Nations fell into ill
Terms again, and War broke out between
the *Spaniards* and us, though without any
Declaration, by the fatal Action at *Paffaro* ;
and though that War was fhort, and feem'd
to end by the *Spaniards* being beaten out of
Sicily ; the Peace alfo feemed as fhort-lived
as the War, and the Wounds which were ill
healed, rankled and broke out again, and fo
feveral times alternately, which is too recent
in the Heads of every one, that looks at
all into Publick Affairs, to need any farther
Repetition.

THIS Account of the Decay of our Trade
with *Spain*, is given in fuch a particular
manner to demonftrate, as I doubt not it
will to the Satisfaction of the Reader, the
Propofition which follows, namely, the
Increafe of the fame Commerce, as it now
ftands by the late Tranfaction at *Seville*,
which is manifeftly a Treaty of Commerce
as well as of Peace.

'TIS a certain and natural Confequence
of a good Underftanding between trading
Nations,

Nations, and it has been obſerved that no Peace is durable, or at leaſt has been ſo for any long Courſe of Years, where a Treaty of Commerce has not alſo attended your Treaty of Friendſhip ; not but that it may be otherwiſe where the Nations are not much concerned in Trade, or at leaſt not in Trade with one another ; but that it very ſeldom happens to be ſo, is, I think, undeniable.

THERE are ſcarce any two Nations in the World, whoſe Trade with one another is ſo mutual and ſo great, and above all, whoſe Trade is ſo particularly beneficial on both Sides as the *Engliſh* and *Spaniards ;* the Trade between *England* and *Holland* is the only Exception, and, to avoid any Digreſſions which may not be to the Purpoſe, we will grant that Part and go on.

THE Trade with *Spain* is mutually advantageous, both Sides are exceeding great Gainers, both Sides have unanſwerable Reaſons to deſire the Trade, and to be careful to preſerve it ; we never found a Treaty of Peace and Friendſhip ſo much as begun between the *Engliſh* and the *Spaniards*, but a Treaty of Commerce went along with it Hand in Hand ; and both Nations (ſpeaking of the *Vox Populi*) always rejoyced in it ; the Reaſons are plain, and are the ſame in kind on both Sides.

1. THE

1. The *Spaniards* are Gainers, by having the Growth and Produce of their Country taken off by the *English*; namely, their Wine, Oil, Fruit, Wooll, *&c.* and which no other Nation can dispose of, and therefore the *Spaniards* rejoyce at a Peace.

2. The *English* are Gainers, by having a vast quantity of their most valuable Woollen Manufacture taken off every Year by the *Spaniards*, for their *New Spain* Trade in particular, and having a Return (in the most valuable of all Returns) Silver and Gold, and therefore the *English* rejoyce at the Peace.

And let our Politicians advance what they please to the contrary, this is to me an unanswerable Reason, why the present Peace with *Spain* is like to be durable; namely, that both Sides are Gainers by it; and that both Sides have been lately made sensible (by their Experience) of the Damage received by the past Breaches, and I may add, will be now made sensible of a rising Increase by the present Peace to a greater Degree than ever: *But that by the Way.*

It follows, to consider according to my first Proposition, the Influence which this new Friendship with *Spain* may reasonably be expected to have upon the Commerce of *England*, so as to make it increase.

1. As

1. As to our Trade with *Spain* it felf, by what has been faid already, we may reafonably be fuppofed to grant, that all the Decays of our *Spanish* Trade fhall be reftor'd ; for that Trade being brought to run in its ancient and natural Channel, will certainly recover its ancient Magnitude, and rife up at leaft to all the Heights which it was at before.

But we have many Reafons to expect, that our general Trade with *Spain* will rife to a greater Height, upon the Profpect of an Increafe of People not only in *New Spain*, but in other Parts of the World, than ever it was before. For if the Subjects of the King of *Spain* increafe, as we are now affured they do, fo likewife will their Trade; and if the Trade of the *Spaniards* increafes either in *New* or *Old Spain*, we are fure to have the beft Share of it, as we have always a greater Share in their Trade than any other Nation of *Europe*.

The King of *Spain* has no need to extend his Poffeffions in *America*, they are large enough already, but he wants to have the Dominions which he already poffeffes there better inhabited ; if his People would increafe, they would foon make a better Figure in Trade, than ever they did yet.

Now we are affured, that his People are increafed, and do daily increafe (in *New Spain* efpecially) and not to debate that Part any farther, but take it for granted, the

Com-

Commerce between the *English* and them will increase accordingly.

But this is not all the Dependance of our Trade to *America* for its Increase; but as the Peace with *Spain* opens a free Communication of Trade with all the Ports of *America* in our own Poffeffion, fo it will caufe that Trade to increafe, which, though it is all our own, has fuffered a very grievous and fenfible Decay by the Interruptions of the War. The *Spaniards*, how contemptible foever on other Accounts, have ftrangely embarrafs'd our Trade from the *English* Colonies on the Continent of *America* to the Iflands, fuch as *Barbadoes, Jamaica, St. Chriftopher's, &c.* How many of our Sloops loaden with Provifions have fallen into their Hands? and what terrible Loffes has that Trade fuffered? and as for the Colonies themfelves, the Colony of *New England, New York* and *Penfylvania*, have felt it feverely, and *Carolina* has been almoft ruin'd by it.

All this Trade will now revive, and the Navigation from one Colony to another being uninterrupted and free, muft greatly increafe, becaufe the Number of People, and the Trade by meer Confequence, in all thofe Colonies are vaftly increafed, fince the Conclufion of the Treaty of *Utrecht*.

We may from thence turn our Eyes to the Fifhing-Trade of *America*, I mean fo much of it as is carried on by the *English*

at

at *Newfoundland,* the Coaſt of *Accadia,* and the North Part of *New England* The Increaſe of our Trade there, and in that particular, ſince the Peace with *France,* is really prodigious, and we take three times, ſome ſay five times the quantity of Fiſh which we formerly did, and employ in conſequence a Proportion of Ships and **Men,** greater and more than we did before.

BUT if the Peace with *Spain* appears to be fix'd and ſettled, we ſhall not only take and cure more Fiſh, but we ſhall find a more ſpeedy and eaſy Market for them, when cur'd, and that is an Increaſe which will give Life to all the reſt, and will encourage ſtill more Ships. In ſhort, the whole Trade of the World being increaſing as has been largely inſiſted on, there wanted nothing but Peace to make it ſafe and durable, that all the trading part of the World might be able to traffick one with another, to correſpond and negotiate with Freedom and Satisfaction. Now if this is brought to paſs by the Peace with *Spain* juſt ſettled, then we are ſure that its Influence muſt cauſe Trade to flouriſh.

I THINK I need ſpend no Time to prove, that if Trade in general increaſes, our Trade in particular will feel the Effects of it more ſenſibly than the Trade of any other Nation; for it is manifeſt, that the *Engliſh* Manufactures are ſo blended with the general Commerce of *Europe,* and bear ſo great a Part

in

in the ordinary Imports of every trading Nation, that it is the Freedom of Trade only that we call for: This once obtain'd, we know well enough how, and by what Means, to make our way into the World with our Goods, even by their own intrinfick Value.

In a word, 'tis the Freedom of Navigation that we want, to have the Seas kept open, the Ports all unlock'd, and a free Admiffion of all our Ships into all the Places of Trade where Ships can come, and this is what I expect from the Peace with *Spain.*

And having mention'd here the intrinfick Value of our Manufactures, it opens a large Field to expatiate in upon the Subject of the *Englifh* Manufactures, which in their real Goodnefs and Value do fo evidently excel all thofe of the like kind in any other Country whatfoever; but it is with infinite Satisfaction that I am to add that this Part, howfoever needful, is already perform'd in the former Part of this Work, wherein our Manufactures are enlarg'd upon, and the intrinfick Goodnefs prov'd beyond Contradiction to be greater than that of any other Country; nor does it need other Evidence than what may be drawn from the frequent Attempts of rival Nations to imitate and mimick our Performance; where we may perceive the utmoft of their Pretences are only to come up (or as near as they can) to the Goodnefs and Value of the *Englifh* Manufacture,

facture, no where pretending to excel or exceed.

This I take to be a standing Testimony to the Goodness of our Manufacture; for other Evidences, for there are still many more, I refer the Reader as above to what is already said, and with sufficient Authority, in the Body of this Book.

Nor is this Goodness of our Manufacture improperly mention'd here, for it is the principal and most substantial Support of our present Discourse; 'tis for this reason that a Peace will be of more Importance to our Trade than to the Trade of other Nations, because a free Intercourse of Trade is the chief Thing we want, and on which the Prosperity of our Commerce depends; that obtain'd, the rest turns upon the intrinsick Value of our Exportations as well our Produce as our Manufacture.

Two Things support this Argument, for I wou'd not boast without Ground. 1. We have several Productions to send abroad, which no other Nations yield, and several Manufactures to send abroad which no other Nation make, and these without enlarging and running on into particulars for proof are as follows.

1. For our Produce of the Earth we have *Block-Tin* the Produce of one only County, namely, that of *Cornwall*; for *Devonshire* at present yields very little if any; yet the Quantity of this valuable Metal, so

near

near to Silver in its Kind, is fuch, that it is fufficient to fupply all the reft of *Europe* and all *America*; nor is that little, which is faid to be found in *Bohemia*, to be nam'd with it, being of no Importance in Trade nor any way comparable to it in Value.

2. Our *Lead*, a Metal of a meaner Quality indeed, but infinitely beyond the other in its general Ufefulnefs, and which in Quantity is found very rarely any where, but in this Ifland, where its Production is fo great that it may be faid to fupply all the trading World.

3. Several mineral Drugs and other Products of the Earth are found here or made here, exclufive of moft Nations, and exported from hence, being not to any confiderable Value to be found any where elfe, fuch as *Black-Lead*, *Copperas*, *Alum*, *Lapis-Callaminaris*, *Epfom-Salt*, Coals for Fewel *and the like*.

As for the Effects of our People's Labour, which we call Manufacture, I need not repeat them, they are generally fingular to our Nation, and will therefore come abroad with Advantage; no other Nation being able to furnifh the like or any way equal to them; fo that like the Productions, they force their Way into the World by their own Merit. All which confirm what is faid above (*viz.*) that our Trade wants nothing but an eftablifh'd Peace in *Europe* to improve and increafe it; if our Goods will thus command
a Market,

a Market, 'tis plain, they want nothing but to have free Accefs to the Market, and that is Peace.

WERE this Point duly confidered by the *Englifh*, we ought to be really the moft pacifick Nation in the World, not only endeavouring to live in Peace with all Nations of the World, but bufy to have all the other Nations of the World be at Peace with one another ; then our Trade would meet with no Interruption among them, and they would always be ready to promote an univerfal Freedom of Commerce.

THE Sum of the whole Matter is, that it is evident, our Manufacture being defired and call'd for by all Nations of the known World, it is our Intereft to maintain the general Tranquillity of the World, becaufe by that Means we fhall have the greater Trade.

To the Growth of our Trade we might add, the Increafe of our Navigation, in which the *Englifh* are more particularly concern'd. The Kingdom of *Great Britain* has one vaft Difadvantage by War, more than any Nation under Heaven can fay but themfelves; namely, that by the Multitude of their Shipping they are liable to more Captures than any other Nation ; fo that let them differ with whom they will, and the meaner the worfe, they are fure to be the greateft Lofers at Sea, the Reafon is plain, *viz.* that their Ships fpread the whole Ocean, even, as we may fay, in every

corner

corner of the Globe, *where Winds can blow or where the Waters roll,* no Sea, no navigable River, no Gulph, no Bay, but is full of *Englifh* Shipping; fo that the Privateer Veffels of their Enemies can hardly ftep Abroad, but they fall in with the *Englifh* Ships immediately; and this encourages thofe Nations to fit out fuch Privateers, and in fo great Numbers, whenever they have a War with the *Englifh.*

THIS was fadly prov'd in the Beginning of the late *French* War, when, upon the firft breaking out of that War, the *French* cover'd the Sea with their Privateers, and chopt upon our Ships in every Creek and Corner of the Sea, in fuch a terrible and furprizing Manner, that they took three thoufand Sail from us before (as we ufually fay) we knew where we was, before we could come into any fettled Method for our Convoys, or could ftation our Men of War, fo as to take care of the Trade.

ON the other hand, our Enemies (except only in a *Dutch* War) have no Number of Ships at Sea, fufficient to encourage our People to fit out any Cruizers; nor did we ever make any Hand of Privateering, in all the late War againft *France*; for it was hard to find a *French* Ship (that War) worth taking, in fometimes a whole Summer Cruize.

THE like has been our Cafe in Proportion, in thefe laft Mifunderftandings with the *Spaniards,* for we can hardly call it a

War ;

War; the *Spaniards* took our Ships in the *West-Indies*, in the *Levant*, in the *Straits* Mouth, in the Bay of *Biscay*; and we have made loud Complaint about our great Losses by their Privateers, almost every where ; whereas we might fit out Privateers as many as we pleased, but could hardly ever meet with any one of their Ships except a Man of War or two coming from the Coast and Bay of *Biscay* to *Cadiz.*

This being our Case, 'tis no Wonder that we should rejoice at the Peace, and even that the *Spaniards* themselves should do so also. The War being over, Navigation goes on uninterrupted, the Seas are open, the small Ships go as safe on their Voyages, as the great : Trade mends its Pace, and circulates freer than before, because Navigation is no more interrupted : The longest Voyages are as well secured as the shortest, and the Merchants have nothing to ensure but the Damages of the Sea.

Now, *vice versa*, turn the Tables, and let us carry it on; as we lose more by a War, so we gain more by a Peace, I mean in Trade ; for still I must keep close to the Point in Question; as we have more Ships to lose in a War, so we have more Ships to make good Voyages, and to make quick Returns, when not interrupted by a War; and so we gain more in Proportion than any Nation in the World.

THEY

THEY that have moſt to loſe, have generally the greateſt Opportunities to gain; they run more Adventures; they make more gainful Voyages, when not oppoſed or interrupted; in ſhort, every Article of the Trade is on their Side, they come to more Markets, bring home more frequent and happy Returns.

LET the World then ſay what they pleaſe, we muſt grant of courſe that Peace alone is the Health of Trade, and we expect no proſperous Days to our Commerce but under the Shelter of *Peace.*

IT is obſerved of our Colonies, that every *Engliſhman* going from *England* (ſay it ſhould be to *New England, New York, Penſylvania, Virginia, Carolina,* or any of our Colonies upon the Continent) and ſettling there with his Family and Servants to Plant and Trade, is of ten-fold more value in real Subſtance to the publick Treaſure of *England,* and of ten-fold more weight in the Ballance of Trade to the Nation, when he comes there (*viz.*) into *America,* than he was before in *Old England,* and the like of *Scotland* and *Ireland.*

FIRST his Labour, ſuppoſe him a Carpenter or Bricklayer, or any other Handycraftſman or Artificer, is of five times the Value that it was before; take *England* one Place with another throughout. Secondly, his Proviſions are in their Conſumption of more than five times the Benefit to the Publick

lick to be confumed, tho' not of five times the Price to be bought. And, Thirdly, his Clothes, Furniture, and all Things which he wears and ufes, as they come from *England*, are at leaft of four times the Value that they are here; fo that he is every way a Benefit to the Common-wealth, prodigioufly more than he was before.

If this be fo, then that War which interrupted the Profperity of thefe Colonies is infinitely more injurious to us, even in *England*, than it would be by the fame Lofs, and the fame Interruption of Commerce here in *England:* We are therefore tenfold the Sufferers in the Stop of our Commerce to our own Colonies, than any other Nation can be by the Stop of their Commerce in *Europe*; no Nation having any fuch Intercourfe of their Navigation and Correfpondence and Commerce, among themfelves, as our Colonies have.

This is another Reafon why we fhall be very great Gainers in our Trade by the Advantages of a Peace; for Nature dictates that *by how much* we are greater Lofers in Trade by a War, than any other Nation (be it in any particular Branch of the Trade or in the whole) *by fo much* we are greater Gainers than any of thofe on the Return of the Peace.

Some indeed have had a Notion, that we grew rich by the late War, they mean by the laft War with *France*; I am fure they

they cannot fuggeft it of the War with *Spain.*

EVERY one that has made the leaft Obfervation of Things during that War, might eafily anfwer that Notion to himfelf; the Cafe was this : Experience, and the Length of the former War had taught us, how to ftation our Men of War, to multiply the Number of light Cruizers, and to manage our Merchant Fleets, fo to go, and keep together, that they did not fall fo eafy a Prey to the *French* as at firft; even our *Colliers* were fo well guarded by placing Men of War to be continually Cruifing from one Station to another, all the Way from *Harwich* or the *Nore* to *Newcaftle,* that the Colliers run fafe and almoft fingle, as in Times of Peace; and not a Privateer could fhew himfelf upon the Coaft, but he was immediately fought with and chafed off or taken, fo that nothing could be done, unlefs by a Squadron of Men of War, and that we had always Intelligence of : The like Management was kept up in the Chops of the Channel; where a ftrong Squadron of large Men of War was always kept plying off and on from *Plymouth* to Cape *Ufhant,* allowing an Offing of about twenty Leagues from the latter, which was a Space quite out of the way of our homeward bound Trade; and the like upon the Coaft of *Galicia* and of *Portugal,* from the *Corunna* to Cape *St. Vincent,* or the *Southern Cape.*

By

By thefe Provifions, the Mouth of the Channel was fecured in fuch a manner, that our Trade receiv'd very little Damage for five or fix Year together, except what was done by large Squadrons of the Enemy, and that was very rarely offer'd, but that they were met with, fought with, and fometimes made to pay for their Forwardnefs.

ADD to this, that the *French* Naval Force was broken by thofe two fatal Blows to their Fleet (*viz.*) at *La Hogue,* and at *Vigo* ; I might add a third at *Thoulon*; in all which put together, the Marine Strength of *France* might be truly faid to be dead and buried, and they never appeared at Sea to make any great Figure afterwards.

BUT to bring this down to the Cafe in hand; fuppofing then, that in Virtue of this good Conduct, we got Money during the reft of the War, the Argument is all on our Side. There is a manifeft Difference between getting Money *during a War*, and getting Money *by the War* ; if in confequence of that good Management we traded freely, and with more fafety, and got Money, as I will not deny but might be the Cafe, it was juft what I am now faying ; namely, that we got Money by the Peace ; for *fo far* as that Interval of Safety and Quiet to our Trade refembled a Peace, and came the nearer to the Thing it felf, *fo far* our diligent Merchants made their Advantage of it, pufh'd into Trade, and made

con-

conſiderable Gain ; a true Emblem of what they would have done to a much greater Degree in a Time of eſtabliſhed Peace.

Bu t this was far from getting Money by the War, and amounted to no more than this ; namely, that they did not loſe ſo much by the War, as they had done before: What they got was by Trade, not by the War; all which confirms what I have already advanced (*viz.*) that Trade lives by Peace, and that the Tranquillity of the Nation is the Soul of their Commerce, which concludes this *Appendix*, and eſtabliſhes the Faſt now alledged; namely, That Peace being now ſettled, the Trade of *Europe* will every where advance and increaſe, and eſpecially the Trade of *England*.

F I. N. I. S. *bonus*